THE EMPEROR'S EMBRACE

Also by Jeffrey Moussaieff Masson

Dogs Never Lie About Love:
Reflections on the Emotional World of Dogs

The Wild Child: The Unsolved Mystery of Kaspar Hauser

When Elephants Weep: The Emotional Lives of Animals
(with Susan McCarthy)

My Father's Guru: A Journey through
Spirituality and Disillusion

Final Analysis: The Making and Unmaking
of a Psychoanalyst

Against Therapy: Emotional Tyranny and the
Myth of Psychological Healing

A Dark Science: Women, Sexuality, and Psychiatry in the
Nineteenth Century

The Assault on Truth: Freud's Suppression of the
Seduction Theory

The Oceanic Feeling: The Origins of Religious
Sentiment in Ancient India

The Complete Letters of Sigmund Freud to
Wilhelm Fliess 1887-1904 (Editor)

The Peacock's Egg: Love Poems from Ancient India
(Editor, translations by W. S. Merwin)

The Dhvanyaloka of Anandavardhana with the Locana of Abhinavagupta
(Translator, with D. H. H. Ingalls and M. V. Patwardhan)

Love's Enchanted World: The Avimaraka
(with D. D. Kosambi)

The Rasadhyaya of the Natyasastra (Translator and editor,
with M. V. Patwardhan; two volumes)

Santarasa and Abhinvagupta's Philosophy of Aesthetics

The Emperor's Embrace

REFLECTIONS
on
ANIMAL FAMILIES
and
FATHERHOOD

Jeffrey Moussaieff Masson

POCKET BOOKS

New York   London   Toronto   Sydney   Tokyo   Singapore

POCKET BOOKS, a division of Simon & Schuster Inc.
1230 Avenue of the Americas, New York, NY 10020

ISBN: 0-671-02083-8

First Pocket Books hardcover printing October 1999

10 9 8 7 6 5 4 3 2 1

POCKET and colophon are registered trademarks of
Simon & Schuster Inc.

Interior illustrations by Daniel Roode

Printed in the U.S.A.

For Leila and Ilan

Contents

Acknowledgments

I could not have written this book without my children, Simone and Ilan, or without their mothers, Terri and Leila. Terri is still, twenty-five years later, a wonderful mother to Simone, and Simone and her friend Stephanie are among the sharpest critical thinkers I know. It has been wonderful to spend a year in Boston near them. I never thought I could experience twice the joy that a small being can bring to your life. But as a second-time dad, I know it is possible. Thank you, Simone and Ilan, for being the joy of my life, and thank you, Terri and Leila, for making it possible. I cannot forget my own mother and father. My mother, Diana, is now eighty and still charming and full of the zest for life that she always had. My father, Jacques, died two years ago at eighty-five, and I still dream about him on a regular basis. I miss him terribly. I only wish that I knew then what I know now and could have enjoyed my childhood years with him more fully. Leila, my dearest companion, has read every word of this book in manuscript. Her medical and pediatric knowledge has been an enormous help, her intuition has been invaluable, and her example as an all-loving mother has been essential. My friend Daniel Ellsberg, when he met Leila for the first time, took me aside and said he thought she might come from a different planet, so pure did she appear. I have been with her now for almost five years, and I am inclined to agree. I am the luckiest man alive to be sharing child, home, and love with her.

The idea for the book came from Sally Wofford-Girand, who has many brilliant ideas, and my Italian agent, Vicki Satlow. They had faith in me when I did not. Elaine Markson, my agent in New York, has held my hand for most of my writing career. I only wish I could have benefitted from her wisdom and levelheadedness in my psychoanalytic days. My editor, Nancy Miller, had already edited four of my books, and I knew her skills, but it was still nothing short of miraculous to watch her help me turn this budding idea into a book. Thank you, Nancy, from the bottom of my heart for your faith in me and your friendship over more than fifteen years. I also want to thank the whole team at my new favorite publisher, Pocket Books: Emily Bestler, Pam Duevel, Robin Kessler, Laura Ross, and the new and wonderful publisher, Judith Curr. A special thanks to Erik Wasson for the book's title.

I began writing *The Emperor's Embrace* in the Wagnerian town of Bayreuth, in Germany. We were staying with the Zeidler family, and nothing could have provided a better antidote to the grandiosity of that town. The warmth of their family was so palpable, their love for one another so catching, that I could not wait to sit down and think about family and fatherhood. In Berlin, Professor Dietmar Todt from the department of behavioral biology at the Freie Universität was welcoming and cordial. Dr. Halger Kulmeyer, the librarian at the school of veterinary medicine at the university, was astonishing in his ability to find anything on the Net and get it into my hands five minutes later. This is the second book he has helped me with, and I am most appreciative.

At the inception of this book, I was encouraged by Michael Lamb, who has written so much about human fathers in a broad perspective; by Susan Allport, who has written a wonderful book of her own, *Natural Parenting;* and by Melvin Konner, whose many books and articles taught me about what humans did when they were not overconstrained by culture. Donna Haraway took me for a wonderful walk in the woods of Northern California and imparted wisdom that was just beyond my grasp. My friend Neil Malamuth talked to me about evolutionary psychology, and although he did not convince me, it was a valuable introduction. My friend Dick Trexler tried to talk to me about infanticide in humans, but I am tone-deaf. My friend Nancy Schepper-Hughes gave me her marvelous book about Brazilian mothers that held my interest for days. Rafael Marquez sent me many articles about fascinating frog fathers.

I want to thank my hero in the world of animal behavior, Donald Griffin, who at eighty-three is still inventing new ways to examine the minds of animals, and whose absolute scientific integrity has been a beacon of light to many younger colleagues. It was his three books about animal consciousness that introduced me to a new field, cognitive ethology, which he invented. I feel deeply honored that we have been able to spend some time together while I lived in Boston for one year. I took advantage of the proximity of Harvard to have two memorable lunches with another of my heroes, Stephen J. Gould. I was lucky also to be able to discuss ideas with Richard Wrangham, chairman of biological anthropology at Harvard, who is a charming skeptic and a brilliant researcher. He was kind enough to read the entire manuscript and save me from embarrassing blunders. Irven DeVore, the former chairman of the department of anthropology at Harvard, received me with great courtesy.

When it comes to inspiration, nobody can replace Elizabeth Marshall Thomas. I only wish I had her gifts, both of observation and of writing. Failing that, I can at least acknowledge how her best-selling books have opened new possibilities in publishing about the inner life of animals.

In a similar category is the lesser known but no less talented Hope Ryden, whose beautiful book about beavers deserves more recognition as one of the great classics of animal writing.

Lynn Rogers, a wildlife research biologist with the North Central Forest Experiment Station in Ely, Minnesota, knows more about black bears than anyone in the past hundred years. He is as generous as he is knowledgeable, and I am honored to have been able to speak with him on several occasions.

Richard Alexander, one of the great names of evolutionary biology, had several phone conversations with me and was kind enough to send me his books and articles, which taught me a great deal about a field that is still difficult for me to understand. Two of his illustrious students, Paul Sherman at Cornell and Jim Hoagland, were kind and patient with me on the phone. I admire their work enormously, even when I find myself resisting their conclusions. I am grateful to Sarah Blaffer Hrdy for sending me to David Gubernick at the University of California field station in Carmel Valley. He graciously received me and my family and spent the afternoon showing us around his California mice fields. He sent me all his papers and was eager to teach me about his work. At my age, I seem to have a harder and harder time understanding new information. I think this became clear to the great ichthyologist George Barlow at the University of California at Berkeley. I appreciate his spending time with me, in spite of his antipathy for some of my views about the rights of animals. He is a brilliant man and just watching him disagree with me taught me much. Peter Tyack from the Woods Hole Oceanographic Institute was enthusiastic and helpful about cetaceans. I wish I could have written more about them, but, alas, they are not active fathers. It is still puzzling to me why not.

Marc Bekoff, one of the world's leading experts on canids, has been a true intellectual friend for several years now. Of all the reputable scientists I have met in this new field, his positions about animals are closest to my own views. A man whose seminal articles completely altered an entire field, the legendary Robert Trivers was unexpectedly friendly and helpful to me, a complete neophyte. I am most grateful. Con Slobodchikoff is a scholar after my own heart. Our views coincide almost completely. The same is true of Robert Sussman, who talked to me, skeptically, about infanticide and human universals. John King, who did seminal work on prairie dogs in the 1950s, was a gracious correspondent. The beautiful article he wrote for *Scientific American* changed the way many people think about this playful animal. Peter Tyack knows all there is to know about cetaceans and was happy to share his knowledge. George Burckhardt told me much about the history of ethology. I pestered a number of scholars for articles: Jared Diamond, Stephen Emlen, Randy Thornhill, Gordon Orians, Marc Hauser, Gerald Kooyman. I was always rewarded. James Levine from the Fatherhood Initiative, who has himself written a series of books about fathers, got me a wonderful video of the emperor penguin and chicks. A special debt of gratitude is owed Martin Daly and Margo Wilson at McMaster University, who sent me a series of fascinating articles they have written over the last twenty years. One of the first articles in this field that I ever read was a brilliant one by Martin Daly about why human males do not lactate, and it hooked me for good.

Ashley Montague, at ninety-five, still as sharp as anyone I know, was eager to read the final text of this book. I only hope that he still gets to do so. His book on touching has been an inspiration to many people, me among them.

I had to collect almost a thousand articles to write this book. I could not have done so had it not been for my good friend Elisa Moreno, now a medical student in Australia. I cannot count the number of times she tracked down obscure articles for me in Berkeley. Thank you, Elisa. Thanks, too, to my old friends Bowen Hinton, Alan Keiler, and Marianne Loring.

Luigi Boitani, a wolf expert from Italy, talked to me about wolves and dogs, as did Thomas Daniels. Kathy Dettwyler taught me a great deal about breast-feeding. Nancy Kivette sat opposite me for a week early in the process and forced me to start writing. I needed that.

My sister, Linda, has loved all animals since she was two years old (and I was five). We were raised vegetarians, and I still remember how my parents returned from a trip to France and decided to eat meat. I was confused and did not know what to do. Linda did: She never wavered for a minute in her view that she did not put forks into friends. She is still a vegetarian fifty-three years later. I am glad I always had her example.

THE EMPEROR'S EMBRACE

Introduction

There is a popular belief that in almost all primates, indeed, in almost all mammals, the males are at best uninvolved fathers, contributing nothing to their offspring but their sperm; at worst, they supposedly kill their young. It is not surprising, then, that there is no book written for a general audience about the role of fatherhood in the lives of animals. This, I believe, is the first such book.

How did I come to this topic? My interest in animals dates back to my years as professor of the languages and literatures of ancient India at the University of Toronto. As a Sanskrit scholar, I was aware that animals played a major role in Sanskrit literature: There were ancient stories like the *Pancatantra* (which influenced European fables), with wise turtles; Buddhist legends of compassionate tigers; Hindu narratives about faithful mongooses; Jain accounts of remorseful elephants; folk tales of nostalgic deer.

1

Wherever one turned, the literature was alive with imaginative accounts of the relations between animals and humans. The great epic of India, the *Ramayana,* is about a devoted monkey, Hanuman, who could fly and speak Sanskrit and who helped Prince Rama to defeat an animal-like magician who ruled Sri Lanka. The world of the *Ramayana* is teeming with animals, and their depiction (as of the great-hearted buzzard Jatayu) has influenced Indian attitudes toward these animals down to the present. I was aware that many of these myths may have been purely imaginary, but I was also convinced they answered some deep need for a bond between humans and other animals. I also considered that while these stories projected human qualities onto animals, perhaps animals truly did have lessons to teach us as well. Could the emotional realities underlying these descriptions hold true not only for humans but for animals, too? Zoomorphism might parallel anthropomorphism.

I put these thoughts on hold, however, while I turned my attention to the mysteries of the human mind. In mid-career, I decided to become a psychoanalyst. What intrigued me was the complexity of human emotions. I thought nothing would be more interesting than to study in depth such feeling states as nostalgia, disappointment, sadness, joy, gratitude, sympathy—both clinically (as they occur in the lives of people who go to see a therapist) and in the literature. After eight years of training as a Freudian psychoanalyst, I came away with the heretical conviction that when it comes to human emotions such as love, or even sadness, there are no experts, and that we are all as knowledgeable or as ignorant as anyone else. This career led to a series of books, including a study of Freud and child sexual abuse *(The Assault on Truth),* an account of my analytic training and the flaws inherent in it *(Final Analysis),* as well as a perenially unpopular account of the hollowness at the very heart of psychotherapy *(Against Therapy).*

But I was still fascinated by the range of emotions. What

emotions were not just universal in the sense that all humans everywhere were capable of them, but also transcended our own species and could be found equally represented among animals? In attempting to answer these questions, I wrote two books, *When Elephants Weep* (with Susan McCarthy) and *Dogs Never Lie About Love.* I was convinced that animals felt many of the same emotions we do, and felt them just as powerfully; indeed, I was persuaded that some animals, such as dogs, may feel some emotions more purely than do humans, and that when it came to certain feelings, dogs were superior to humans. (This, by the way, is the reason I often use "who" for animals instead of the usual "which" or "that.")

In 1996 I married Leila Siller, a German pediatrician, in San Francisco. Our one-year-old son, Ilan, was the ring bearer. I was a father for the second time, after an interval of more than twenty years. My first child, Simone, born in Toronto in 1974, was in her twenties. As I cradled tiny Ilan in my arms, his eyes would lock onto mine, then a smile would light up his face with unmistakable delight, or I would see him look puzzled and worried. I now had cause to wonder about emotions in a whole new light. How and when did they originate? Now, at almost three, Ilan exhibits all of the major emotions. I have seen him look highly embarrassed when praised, scream with delight while running on the beach, bend over and carefully examine a hurt ant with obvious compassion on his face, tell me emphatically whom he likes and does not like—in short, express his emotions without restraint in words and deeds and facial gestures. He is a bundle of raw and unmediated emotions, as pure as they are in my dogs. Was this true for other animal children as well? In order to answer this question, I needed to learn a great deal more about animal families and their children's earliest upbringing. I found that the topic of mothers and motherhood was amply represented, whereas there was far less written about fatherhood in the animal world. Was this because there was so little to know, or had this topic been neglected for other reasons? I set about finding an answer.

At the same time, of course, I had good reason to think about fatherhood in a direct and personal way. I was reliving fatherhood. But now I had the benefit of my psychoanalytic training (which at the very least had raised certain important questions about emotions, even if the answers it provided did not satisfy me), my training as a historian of ideas, and my immersion in the literature about animals and their feelings. I read everything I could find (and it turned out to be an enormous literature, though scientific and academic) about the topic of paternity in animals. It was much more difficult than I anticipated, and I had to go much further afield than I first intended. I combed the literature in primatology, ichthyology, ornithology, herpetology, evolutionary biology, sociobiology, and paleontology, looking for information and examples about animal fathers. I collected more than fifteen hundred books that bear on the topic and gathered almost that many articles. At times I felt I had gotten in over my head. After all, I was not a trained field biologist, ethologist, physical anthropologist, or zoologist. I was merely an interested and very curious layman. But, gradually, certain themes began to emerge as the most important ones that I wanted to convey.

At first I wanted to call this book *The Truth about Fathers.* This is because I felt that humans could learn something about the essence of fatherhood by studying how other animals fathered. By the same token, I thought of calling the book *Natural Fathers.* But I realized that the truth about human fathers, at least, is that since earliest times many have used the excuse "it's only natural" to justify their bad behavior, in fact behaving in the way they thought animals behaved, by abandoning, hurting, ignoring, and even murdering their children. Some animal fathers do all these things (though none murder their own young that I know of, except perhaps the bear). Many do not. The behaviors of the more benevolent animal fathers—penguins, wolves, sea horses, marmosets, beavers—are far less known and almost never invoked for the lessons we can learn from them.

How real are the parallels between animals and humans? Certainly the question is anything but trivial. We like to believe that animals behave the way they do because of their genes. Then we ask: Are we, too, prisoners of our genes? Are we creatures destined to behave in certain ways because we have been programmed to do so? Does our conscious choice, our will, count for little? To what extent are we merely a bundle of instincts? This is a topic that could obviously occupy whole books, and has already done so. It is inevitably linked to the idea that there is such a thing as "natural" behavior, ways nature intended us to behave. There are two problems here. One is that we rarely know how much behavior in animals is under tight genetic control, as biologists like to say—that is, inherited—and how much is learned, or acquired. Second, for humans the problem is that, as Margaret Mead pointed out long ago, every society believes its way of doing things is inevitable and natural. Of course there are behavior patterns, actions, even feelings and states of mind that appear more "instinctive" than others. A mother rat, raised in total isolation, will nonetheless build a nest and groom her young; a spider spins a web; a beaver constructs a dam; and the honeybee sculpts a honeycomb. Turtles return to the beach where they were born; the female wasp provides grubs as food for the larvae that will hatch from her eggs. The rat does not need to see her own mother build a nest, the spider spins immediately, the beaver and the honeybee all act from *instinct*. Their behavior appears to be fixed, unalterable, unlearned, unmodified by direct experience. But once we use certain powerful words, like "innate," "biologically determined," "stereotypic," all words used commonly by ethologists, we think we have done with the matter, that no further inquiry or thought is required. Their use can stifle the search for subtleties. These terms are often used to distinguish animal behavior from human behavior, which is considered, by contrast, to be flexible, learned, modifiable by experience, acquired.

But even a songbird is more than the sum of its instincts, as everyone knows who studies the development of song. When young male chaffinch birds are raised without being allowed to hear the song of an adult male, they do not develop the full adult song. For the full song to develop, young birds must hear, at an early stage, the song of an experienced adult. They store this somewhere, and somehow do not reproduce it until much later.

We may belong to a different species than the chaffinch, but we too require examples from older, more experienced adults, we too may store something away and only retrieve it years later, we too are flexible, perhaps more so than any other animal. We can see this very clearly when it comes to fathering. Fatherhood is plastic in humans, ranging all the way from completely absent to entirely present. There are fathers who are with their children twenty-four hours a day, every day for years, and there are fathers who see their children for a few minutes a day, or a few minutes a month, or a few minutes a year, or never at all. Again, only in humans do we find this vast range. There is more individuality in animals than we like to believe—not every lion father is alike, and this applies to gorillas and monkeys and giraffes and just about any animal we can think of. But only to a point. You will not find the same enormous variety of behaviors among animal fathers as you do in humans. Still, we are not all that far removed from our animal ancestry, and specifically, we can recognize that there are certain behavior patterns we were evolved to perform.

One of the most famous poems ever written about a father

and child is Goethe's "Erlkoenig" (The Elf King), which he
wrote in 1782. In some mysterious way this poem captures the
fears and the greatest tragedy that can befall any father. But it
also captures the love and the heartache that can get no deeper.
In the poem, a frightened and heartsick father is riding at full
speed, late at night, through the dark countryside, his sick child
in his arms. The father asks his son why he is so afraid. The child
says that the Elf King has appeared before him and is asking him
to come away with him. It is only the mist, says the father. No,
says the boy, can't you hear him whispering promises to me? Stay
quiet, my child, it is only the wind rustling the dry leaves, says
the father. But don't you see them waiting for me in the dark? It
is only the willows at night, says the father. But Father, the Elf
King has put his hands on me, he is hurting me. The last stanza
of the poem reads:

> *The father shudders, and rides swiftly on,*
> *he holds in his arms the groaning child,*
> *he reaches the courtyard weary and frightened;*
> *in his arms the child was dead.*

Why introduce a book about fatherhood with the story of a
father's panicked love for his dying son? We often think we are
the only species who worries about dying, especially when it is
only a remote possibility, and find it difficult to believe that animals become sad, as we do, when contemplating their own nonex-
istence. We find it doubly difficult to imagine an animal feeling
pain at the *thought* that his or her child (you will forgive my not
using the more appropriate "offspring" in this case) could die.

While we have no direct access to the minds of animals, what
we cannot deny is that animals, especially animal parents, do
all they can to secure the safety of their young. Biology has
attempted to tell us a great deal about why a father should love

a baby, and those reasons, presumably based on Darwin, talk about genetic representation in the future, and how males have been beguiled by clever females. Or they tell us men love children who resemble them. It is not so much that I disbelieve this but that I think it misses deeper causes that we all know about but oddly refuse to ascribe to animals: I loved my children when they were babies for reasons that are difficult to put into words. Neither of them resembled me, and this actually gave me great pleasure: "Look how much themselves they are!" Their helplessness certainly made me feel protective. Protectiveness fairly oozed out of me, and I know that I would gladly have laid down my life to save theirs. Was this pity, compassion, love for my partner, who had produced these marvelous beings out of her own body, or something unknown and perhaps unknowable? It is difficult to say. But when I look at animal fathers protecting their children, risking their lives for them, I see no reason to believe that they don't feel something akin to what I feel. While they write no poem as moving as that by Goethe, who is to say that they could not feel all of those same emotions, and that such poems are inscribed in their own hearts as surely as they are inscribed in the hearts of those of us humans who also cannot rival Goethe in expressing what we feel, but feel it no less deeply?

As for whom the baby loves, whatever hesitation one has in accepting whole cloth the "bonding" hypothesis (that parents, like many animals, need to bond with their children in the first hours after birth or they will never have as close a tie), there seems to me no doubt that children are ready to love the person they first spend time with. I can think of fewer more persuasive accounts than one that comes out of nineteenth-century France. Jean-Baptiste-Felix Descuret wrote a famous medical text in 1841, called *La Médecine des Passions,* describing a "disease" that received extensive medical attention in the 1820s and 1830s and would remain a subject of scientific debate through the 1870s.

That disease was nostalgia, an affliction that French doctors regarded as potentially fatal. The case is as follows:

Eugène L***, born in Paris, was sent to a wet nurse in the Amiens area and brought back to his family when he was two years old. The strength of his limbs, the firmness of his flesh, his coloring, the vivacity and gaiety of his character, everything indicated that he had been well cared for and that he was a vigorous child. During the fifteen days that his nurse remained at his side, Eugène continued to enjoy the most robust health; but as soon as she left he became pale, sad and morose. He was unresponsive to the caresses of his parents and refused all the food that had pleased him the most just a few days before.

Struck by this sudden change, Eugène's mother and father summoned Hippolyte Petit who, recognizing the first symptoms of nostalgia, recommended frequent walks and all the childish distractions that abound in Paris. These techniques, ordinarily so effective in such cases, failed completely, and the unhappy little boy, who was becoming weaker all the time, remained for whole hours sadly immobile, his eyes turned toward the door through which he had seen departing the woman who had acted as his mother. Called again by the family, the practitioner declared that the only way to save the child was to have his nurse return immediately and take the boy away with her again. When she arrived, Eugène erupted with cries of joy; the melancholy imprinted on his face was soon replaced by the radiation of ecstasy and, to use one of his father's expressions, *from that moment he began to revive.* Brought to Picardy the following week, he stayed there about a year, enjoying the best of health. During his second return to Paris, Dr. Petit progressively separated the nurse from the child, first for a few hours, then for a whole day, then for a week, until he was used to being without her. This tactic was crowned with complete success.[1]

Miraculously, medical science did the right thing for this child: allowed him to be with the woman he loved. The child loved the woman because he had spent two years with her, and was at her breast for that entire time. Of course he would love her. The question is, would he ever completely recover from this first lost love? Today we no longer send our children to wet nurses, but we sometimes do the emotional equivalent and then are surprised that the children feel less warmth toward us than we would like. Fathers who want close relations with their children later in life should learn the lesson imparted here: The first years count perhaps beyond their chronological importance.

The Animal/Human Comparison

As a species, we humans have a remarkable capacity to learn from other species. It is one that we may share with very few other animals. Except for dogs, I know of no animal that observes us and strives to be like us. But at another, scientific level, it is only right that we should seek to compare ourselves with other species, as long as we do so out of a desire to expand ourselves rather than to diminish the animal we are studying. After all, we are animals. *Gray's Anatomy* applies to every human on our planet. But much of it applies to other animals as well. The neck of a mouse, a giraffe, and a human may look very different, but all three species have seven cervical vertebrae. People are always amazed to learn that we share more than 98 percent of our genetic heritage with chimpanzees. In fact, genetically speaking, there is a greater difference between a gorilla and a chimpanzee than there is between a human and a chimp. But we also share a great deal of our genetic endowment with animals that do not resemble us at all. We share about 75 percent of our genes with wolves. The point is, we *are* animals, different to some extent from other animals, but not completely different after all.

In one of his notebooks, Darwin wrote: "Having proved mens & brutes bodies of one type: almost superfluous to consider minds." In this shorthand manner, Darwin suggests that since animals and humans are so physically similar, our minds must be similar as well, that we share bodies *and* minds with other animals. And while we do not resemble wolves genetically as much as we resemble chimpanzees, from the point of view of our behavior, we are much more like wolves than like chimps—in the way we parent, for example. We are similar in many other social ways as well. I think this is the reason that we domesticated the wolf into the dog (we should remember that a dog, as far as genetics are concerned, is basically a wolf—another species of wolf, but a wolf just the same) but we have never domesticated any of the great apes.

There is another way in which we are perhaps closer to wolves than to practically any other species. With the exception of the cat, no other animal has chosen to live with us on intimate terms. It is possible that we selected the wolf, but it is also possible that the wolf selected us. And the reason may be this: To some extent, we are a self-domesticating species. We are the only species to have neotenized ourselves, to have attempted (successfully or not) to domesticate ourselves. What I mean is that we have gradually become more like our own juveniles, or at least that seems to be our goal. It is one I agree with. Neoteny refers to the love of juvenile characteristics. It is what makes us find small children delightful, worthy of care and protection. I think wolves appreciate this quality in humans, because it is one that we possess to a greater extent than perhaps any other animal.

Juveniles, in all animals, are more playful than adults. They are less dangerous, tamer, slower, weaker than adults. This is true of human children, too. And it seems to be true across evolution as well. Cro-Magnon man was bigger, stronger, altogether less gentle than the male *Homo sapiens.* It seems we are slowly evolving (even if it is not genetic) away from an earlier model. We seem not to want to be killing machines. Moreover, we admire neoteny when we see it in another species. We may be the only species that reacts to the babies of another species exactly as do its own parents: with a deep desire to protect and take care of the helpless creature in front of us. We are certainly the only species that brings another species into our den to feed it and have it live with us. But the very fact that we ascribe this ability to wolves, as we see in our legends of wolf children, demonstrates once again the similarity that we believe exists between the two species.

There is a great deal of truth in the notion that we, as a species, evolved to do certain things. In this book I attempt to take a fresh look at some of those things from a father's point of view—what I call "natural" behavior because it harks back to our ancestral environment, but also because we find it naturally occurring in a large number of other animals. Inevitably, I have chosen those examples that are most compelling to me. Chimpanzees do not make wonderful fathers, and while the reasons for that might be interesting, the description of the absence of fatherhood would not. So there is no chapter here on the missing father in ape society. But there is one on the wonderful wolf father, and one on lions, bears, and certain monkeys, dangerous dads all, because their stories I felt were worth telling. This is not a scientific textbook. On the other hand, I have not made anything up. What I am bringing to the reader is material I have found buried away in obscure articles and books that made me sit up and pay attention. I hope it will do the same for you.

ONE: The Emperor's Embrace

Could it be that there is a politics of knowledge when it comes to animal behavior? We hear about infanticidal lions but rarely of heroic penguin fathers. Benito Mussolini, the Italian fascist dictator, once said: "It is better to live one day as a lion than a hundred years as a sheep." This remarkable statement manages to combine macho bravura with sheer ignorance (the male lion spends most of the day asleep). In any event, why should the life of a sheep be seen as any less inherently valuable than the life of a lion? To whom is the life of a vegetarian species less interesting than the life of a carnivore? Sheep would no doubt see it otherwise. So too would people who actually study wild sheep. In bighorn sheep, the leader of the herd is simply the oldest ewe, not the most dominant but the one with the most offspring, and even the biggest ram will follow her lead when in the flock. Perhaps this female leadership was another reason for Mussolini to scorn sheep. Dictators might mock penguins, too, but penguins have a great deal to teach us when it comes to parenthood.

Until very recent times, men have played little role throughout pregnancy and the birth of their children. This has often been justified on purely biological grounds. No male animal concerns himself with these issues, we were told; they are of purely female concern. But these comments were made in ignorance.

For anyone interested in the true range of fatherly contributions to pregnancy and birth, few animals can hold such fascination as the emperor penguin. The discovery of penguin behavior is a story remarkable in its own right, and one that is still evolving, since we know far less about the life of penguins in the sea, which is where they spend most of their time, than we do of their life on land. Actually, "land" is used metaphorically here. In fact, emperor penguins never step on shore, even to breed; when not at sea, they live in rookeries on sea ice.

The emperor penguin, *Aptenodytes forsteri* (Aptenodytes means "wingless diver"), was named after the two German naturalists, G. and J. R. Forster, father and son, who accompanied James Cook on his second voyage around the world in 1772-75. The bird they actually saw was the king penguin, but G. R. Gray, who first described the emperor penguin in 1844 in the *Annual Magazine of Natural History,* using specimens brought back by James Clark Ross's 1839-43 expedition, thought their sketches were of the emperor penguin. The first emperor penguin specimen was caught by Thaddeus von Bellingshausen in 1820.

It is an interesting coincidence that the Antarctic was later discovered only because explorers were looking for the breeding colony of this amazing bird, whose hold on the world's imagination has never slackened. Robert Falcon Scott set out to the Antarctic seas in 1901 on board the S.S. *Discovery* to find the eggs of the emperor penguin. He did so because scientists at the time were convinced that the penguin was the most primitive bird on earth (actually not true), and that in order to understand the origin of feathers, an embryo was needed. (There was a powerful but mistaken notion that "ontogeny recapitulates phylogeny"— that is, the embryo recapitulates the evolutionary history of the species—so that examining the embryo of the penguin egg would reveal the development of birds in general.) Little did Scott know that the egg would hold an even more remarkable story—that of nearly unimaginable paternal heroism.

Edward A. Wilson was the zoologist on board, an artist and a surgeon. In 1911 this intrepid investigator set out in late June from Scott's base at Cape Evans for a thirty-six-day round trip. He took with him two brave explorers, Henry Robertson ("Birdie") Bowers and Apsley Cherry-Garrard, who later wrote an account of the passage that has been called the greatest travel book of all time, *The Worst Journey in the World.* Wilson and Bowers never made it back to England. After their winter expedition, they joined Scott on the summer race for the South Pole and died with him of exposure and starvation on that tragic journey—but not before Wilson published a significant, long article on his findings, one difficult to find but well worth the effort. In what follows I paraphrase parts of that account.

The trip was made on foot, Wilson reported, hauling sledges in the darkness of the polar winter night, in some of the worst storms ever recorded, and at temperatures that reached 77 degrees below zero Fahrenheit. The men who made it traveled in the Ross Sea area, across the sixty-five miles from Cape Evans to Cape Crozier and back. The account of their attempts to find the emperor penguin rookery is terrifying. When they finally found it, they camped as near the rookery as possible for three weeks, experiencing a ten-day blizzard, which kept them confined to their completely sodden sleeping bags for seven days under the dark eye of Mount Terror, the windiest spot on earth. When they emerged from their tents, they were on an outlying cone of the mountain about thirteen thousand feet above the sea. Below them lay the emperor penguin rookery on the bay ice; and the Ross Sea, completely frozen over, was a plain of firm white ice to the horizon. The emperors were unsettled, for they knew another terrific storm was brewing. The sky was black and threatening, the barometer began to fall, and before long snowflakes were drifting onto the mountain's upper heights. Wilson realized that these warnings were easily readable to the emperor penguins, and although the ice had not yet started moving the penguins had; he could see a long line of them filing out from the bay to where a pack of some one or two hundred had already collected about two miles out at the edge of the ice.

When Wilson and his team awoke the next day, the gale and smother of snow and drift prevented any of them from leaving camp at all. This continued without intermission all day and night. The following morning, the weather cleared sufficiently to allow the team to reach the edge of the cliff overlooking the rookery. The Ross Sea was open water for nearly thirty miles; a long line of white pack ice was just visible on the horizon from where they stood, some eight to nine hundred feet above the sea. Large sheets of ice were still going out and drifting to the north, and the migration of the emperors was in full swing. Wilson and his colleagues had been in a whiteout, and now they were suddenly confronted for the first time in history with the overwhelming vision of a large colony of penguins.

When one thinks of the immense difficulties of this early encounter with emperor penguins, it is truly a miracle that we learned anything at all about this fascinating animal. Cherry-Garrard, at the end of the second volume of his two-volume "travel" book, speaks of "the darkness, accompanied it may be almost continually by howling blizzards which prevent you seeing your hand before your face," and then finishes his great work with these ringing words: "There are many reasons which send men to the Poles, and the Intellectual Force uses them all. But the desire for knowledge for its own sake is the one which really counts . . . If you march your Winter Journeys you will have your reward, so long as all you want is a penguin's egg."

The three men took some eggs, got lost on the cliff, were nearly killed several times by falling into crevasses, and broke all the eggs but two. That night there was a hurricane and their tent blew away.[2] But the almost unimaginable difficulties and bravery of Wilson and his sailors were for naught. Human arrogance had interfered with objectivity. The embryos Wilson sought so assiduously would not bring the desired knowledge, but a far more momentous secret was encased within the egg—the secret of its father's embrace. The truly remarkable thing about the emperor penguin was not that it was a primitive creature but something that Wilson had missed entirely; what needed to be told was that the emperor was a highly evolved bird with extraordinary paternal behavior. The story he missed was that male penguins are uniquely committed fathers, staying with their eggs through the all but unbearable winter, fasting, balancing the precious egg on their feet, barely moving, hardly sleeping until their mate returned from her time at sea. Perhaps had Wilson been content to simply observe, he might have noticed it, though he would probably not have believed his own eyes. He was simply unprepared for such a heroic feat from a bird, and even less from a father bird.

Penguin Behavior

Most of our myths about animals involve some kind of cruelty, some particularly selfish act, something "beastly." These myths rarely correspond to reality. One such myth about penguins is that when they gather by the open sea they push one resisting penguin into the water and then peer down to watch the result. Then, supposedly, should a leopard seal, with its great speed in the water, devour the hapless bird, his "friends" stay on shore; but if he bobs back up to the surface and begins playing happily in the water, they join him.[3] It is true that the leopard seal, which reaches more than ten feet in length and weighs more than a thousand pounds, is a voracious predator and, along with the orca, is practically the only enemy of emperor penguins, who are powerful enough to protect themselves against other less ferocious predators. There is in fact safety in numbers, and a single penguin in the water has a far greater chance of being taken by a predator than does a whole gathering of penguins. But what really happens when emperors reach the sea involves no pushing; eventually one jumps in, and since penguins seem unable to resist following a lead, the rest dive into the freezing waters as well.

One reason that so many of us are fascinated by penguins is that they resemble us. They walk upright, the way we do, and, like us, they are notoriously curious creatures. Penguins in the wild walk right up to people, touch them, and look as if they were preparing to study them. Diane Ackerman points out that "there is, ordinarily, a no-man's-land between us and wild animals. They fear us and shy away. But penguins are among the very few animals on earth that cross that divide. They seem to regard us as penguins, too, perhaps of a freakish species. After all, we stand upright, travel in groups, talk all the time, sort of waddle." Bernard Stonehouse, the world's leading authority on penguins, believes that they think a human is a penguin who is "different, less predictable, occasionally violent, but tolerable company when he sits still and minds his own business."

Because penguins live only south of the equator, they have no experience of land predators from northern icy climes like the polar bear. The fact that they have no natural enemies on land helps explain their seeming fearlessness. In this way they are like the birds and mammals of the Galápagos Islands, who were, before humans came, without fear. Penguins are also more or less without aggression. They have enormous power in their pectoral muscles, but they use it only for movement, whether in the water or on land, and have never developed it for fighting or even defensive purposes.

Penguins do resemble humans, and no doubt this accounts for our fondness for cartoon images of penguins dressed up at crowded parties, but as fathers, penguins are our superiors. It is the balancing act undertaken by the male emperor penguin, the incubation of that single precious sphere throughout the blackest and coldest winter possible, that captivates our imagination. There is something about the image of male penguins nestling together in the middle of winter on the Antarctic fast ice that makes it lodge in our minds. This is one of the least hospitable spots on earth, with temperatures plunging to minus 80 degrees Fahrenheit and winds howling at more than one hundred miles an hour, where "daylight" consists of less than four hours a day and where the other twenty hours are pitch dark. The penguins huddle there, withstanding terrifying blizzards, many miles from the nearest source of food, cradling their eggs on their feet without eating anything at all for up to four and a half months, while their mates are far away, nourishing themselves at sea. For beginning in March, as the Antarctic days become shorter and with the perpetual night of winter looming, these large birds travel sixty miles from open water to a traditional rookery site (the exact same site is used year after year by the same animals) at the base of the great seaward wall of one of the major ice shelves.

Yes, this is a heroic image, and seems almost impossible. Yet what is so appealing about it is that every detail is true. Unlike mammals, male birds can experience pregnancy as an intimate matter, with the father in many species helping to sit (brood) the egg. After all, a male can brood an egg as well as a female can. But in no other species does it reach this extreme.

Emperor Penguin Society

Let us bear in mind what large birds emperor penguins are. They can be three feet tall, and weigh up to ninety pounds, the size of a large dog. When the males brood they fast, and can lose up to half of their body weight. What do they do all day while they fast and incubate the eggs? They do nothing. Or, more precisely, they do very little. In that cold, in those winds, any activity is exhausting and ill-conceived. The important thing is to conserve energy.

Emperor penguins have evolved an exquisitely polite society. Nobody bothers anyone else. And yet they are not isolated. On the contrary, the extreme conditions of the weather make it imperative that they join together or freeze separately. The number of males assembled in the rookeries is sometimes enormous, up to ten thousand birds. They form what the French call a *tortue* (a turtle—in English it is sometimes called a scrum), which is a throng of very densely packed penguins. There is generally only a single *tortue,* containing all the penguins in the colony. When the storms come, which is most of the time, they move in close to one another, shoulder to shoulder, and form a circle. The middle of the *tortue* is unusually warm and one would think that every penguin fights to be at the epicenter of warmth. But emperor etiquette requires that no penguin seek to advance himself at the expense of another, and in that way every emperor will benefit. It is all very democratic. For in fact what looks like an immobile mass is really a very slowly revolving spiral. The constantly shifting formation is such that every penguin, all the while balancing that single precious egg on his feet, eventually winds up in the middle of the turtle, only to find himself later at the periphery. There are no complaints, just compliance with a remarkable life-saving adaptation to freezing temperatures. Only one-sixth of the body surface of the emperor is exposed when he is in turtle formation, and the birds are also capable of lowering their body metabolism while huddling to save energy.

How do penguins find their mates? Little was known until the close observations of Jean Prévost's French expeditions into Antarctica in the 1950s, which he recounted in his 1961 book (see Suggested Reading). It has not yet been determined whether the birds who form a pair have already paired the previous year. But they do form pairs for the duration of the breeding cycle. They come from the open sea in single file, one behind the other. When they arrive at their destination, they begin the search for a partner. All birds, of whatever sex (which is very difficult for humans to determine), behave identically as soon as they arrive: They rub the sides of their heads with the tops of their wings, first on the right, then on the left. They only do this when they first arrive. It is not entirely clear what function this serves, but it probably has something to do with clearing the ears, since sound will play such a large part in the ensuing couplings. Maybe, too, it serves an obscure function in the mating ritual. King and emperor penguins have vivid auricular patches, golden orange or yellow orange, that are used for courtship. If, in an experiment, one of these patches in a male is painted black, no female penguin will deign to look at the poor male who has been thus disfigured. Perhaps, as in birds in general, these colors say something about parasites (though there are almost none at these temperatures) or physical health in general. Or maybe female penguins just admire color in the all-white environment of the Antarctic.

In any case, one bird, male or female, approaches the other and slowly lowers his or her head with a loud sigh. This is followed by a short song, while the courting penguin keeps its beak pointing vertically down. The other penguin's head is lifted and the bird listens intently. They face each other and are completely still for thirty to forty seconds. Suddenly one of the birds will slowly incline his or her head and begin to sing again, which causes the other to follow suit. That is it: Either they separate and continue the same ritual with another penguin, or they follow one another, a deal having been struck. If they walk off together, they puff up their necks and do an exaggerated swagger. Finding a partner can take anywhere from a couple of hours to a couple of days.

We have to remember that these penguins, preparing to mate, are fasting, since they are far away from the ocean and therefore there is nothing for them to eat. Emperors breeding in the Bay of Whales in the Ross Sea have been found with recognizable pebbles in the stomach that could only have come from sites more than 340 miles away, and the rookery itself can be as much as 100 miles from the sea. It is so cold that the penguins will spend many hours of the day and night (which are practically identical in terms of light) gathered in the large groups, the *tortues.* Often the pair will become separated during the movement of the turtle, but they invariably find each other again, often without any vocalization. Scientists found this out only when they were able to mark individual penguins, for otherwise humans find it difficult to tell them apart. The birds themselves clearly do not have any such problem.

The emperors usually wait for good weather to copulate, any time between April 10 and June 6. They separate themselves somewhat from the rest of the colony and face each other, remaining still for a time. Then the male bends his head, contracts his abdomen, and shows the female the spot on his belly where he has a flap of skin that serves as a kind of pouch for the egg and the baby chick. Unlike the pouch of a marsupial, this is a pouch only in a loose manner of speaking. In reality, it is a fold of loose abdominal skin, a bare (the lack of feathers facilitates the flow of heat) brooding patch, which wraps over the egg to form a warm brood cavity. This stimulates the female to do the same. Their heads touch, and the male bends his head down to touch the female's pouch. Both begin to tremble visibly. Then the female lies face down on the ice, partially spreads her wings and opens her legs. The male climbs onto her back and they mate for ten to thirty seconds.

They stay together afterward constantly, leaning against one another when they are standing up, or if they lie down, the female will glide her head under that of her mate. About a month later, between May 1 and June 12, the female lays a single greenish-white egg. French researchers noted that the annual dates on which the colony's first egg was laid varied by only eight days in sixteen years of observation. Weighing almost a pound, and measuring up to 131 millimeters long and 86 millimeters wide, this is one of the largest eggs of any bird. The male stays by the female's side, his eyes fixed on her pouch. As soon as he sees the egg, he sings, a variation of what has been called the "ecstatic" display by early observers (a male penguin uses this call with his head raised and wings extended to indicate that he has a nest but no partner), and she too takes up the melody. She catches the egg with her wings before it touches the ice and places it on her feet. Both penguins then sing in unison, staring at the egg for up to an hour. The female then slowly walks around the male, who gently touches the egg on her feet with his beak, making soft groans, his whole body trembling. He shows the female his pouch. Gently she puts the egg down on the ice and just as gently he rolls it with his beak between his large, black, powerfully clawed feathered feet, and then, with great difficulty, hoists the egg onto the surface of his feet. He rests back on his heels so that his feet make the least contact with the ice. The transfer of the egg is a delicate operation. If it falls on the ice and rolls away, it can freeze in minutes or it might even be stolen. If it is snatched away by a female penguin who failed to find a mate, its chances of survival are slight because the intruder will eventually abandon the egg, since she has no mate to relieve her.

With the egg transfer successfully completed, the happy couple both sing. The male parades about in front of the female, showing her his pouch with the egg inside. This thick fold, densely feathered on the outside and bare inside, now completely covers the egg and keeps it at about 95 degrees Fahrenheit, even when the temperature falls to 95 degrees below zero. The female begins to back away, each time a little farther. He tries to follow her, but it is hard, since he is balancing the egg. Suddenly she is gone, moving purposefully toward the open sea. She is joined by the other females in the colony, who, by the end of May or June, have all left for the ocean. The females have fasted for nearly a month and a half, and have lost anywhere between 17 to 30 percent of their total weight. They are in urgent need of food.

The female must renew her strength and vitality so that she can return with food for her chick. Going to the sea, she takes the shortest route to reach a polynya (open water surrounded by ice). Penguins appear to be able to navigate by the reflection of the clouds on the water, using what has been called a "water sky."

The male penguin, who has also been fasting, is now left with the egg balanced on his feet. The first egg was laid on the first of May; a chick will emerge in August. Since the seasons are reversed south of the equator, full winter has arrived, with many violent blizzards and the lowest temperatures of the year. Emperor penguins are well adapted to the almost unimaginable cold of these twenty-hour Antarctic nights: Their plumage is waterproof, windproof, flexible, and renewed annually. They may not need tents, but as soon as the bad weather starts, generally in June, the males need some protection from the bitter cold, and nearly all of them find it by forming their *tortues*. What early French explorers like J. Cendron in the 1950s and, later, others noticed during the long (two to three months[4]) incubation period is an almost preternatural calm among the males. This is no doubt necessitated by the long fast that is ahead of them.

Many of them have already fasted, like the females, for two months or more, and must now face another two months of fasting. Moving about with an egg balanced on one's feet is difficult at the best of times.

Nonetheless, there is always a small minority of restless males who insist on making small sorties into the frozen countryside. Sometimes up to nine males with eggs will leave the colony together and be found some four miles away. Cendron observed fourteen males with their eggs more than a mile from the colony, who by evening had managed to return through thick snow, their eggs precariously balanced. When it is snowing very hard, it is the rare hardy soul who ventures out. But there are always a few who do so. They no longer walk, but lie on their bellies and, using their wings, toboggan themselves forward, keeping the egg pressed against the incubating pouch with their feet. Even an injured bird will continue to protect his egg: One penguin had a bad wound on his foot that did not permit him to stand up. He kept apart from the other birds and managed to keep his egg balanced on his single good foot even without standing. Was he also doomed to remain outside the *tortue?* The report does not say. But whatever happens, the first concern of the male emperor is for his egg. As Bernard Stonehouse put it: "Birds have been known to fall over small precipices, roll down snowy slopes, trip over rocks, tumble heavily on slippery bare ice, or navigate their way among very rough sastrugi [ridges of hard snow] without releasing their grip on the eggs."

The only time a father will abandon an egg is if he has reached the maximum limit of his physiological ability to fast, and would die if he did not seek food. Not a small number of eggs are left for this reason, and it would seem that in each case the female is late in returning.

Nobody knows whether the emperor father "speaks" to the chicks inside the egg. I think it is possible, as do ornithologists I spoke to about it. Konrad Lorenz, in his beautiful book *The Year of the Greylag Goose,* noted that the mother goose communicates with her goslings before they hatch from their eggs by making very soft contact calls to them. They in turn are capable of making a number of different calls, which allow the mother to know whether they are developing normally. When they produce a plaintive call, known as "lost piping" (the same sound they will make later in life when they are separated from the family), the mother will respond with comforting contact calls, the equivalent of "I am here." The gander, a good father to his young, takes up a position by the nest and is on high alert as soon as he hears any sounds from within the egg.[5] A number of different birds (domestic chicks, Peking and mallard ducklings) call from within the egg, and it would be worthwhile attempting to discover whether the emperor penguin chicks are among them, and what response is forthcoming from their devoted fathers.

In July or August, after being gone for almost three months, the female emperor returns from the sea, singing as she penetrates various groups of birds, searching for her mate and her chick or egg. The males do not move, but make small peeping noises. When she finds her husband, she sings, she makes little dance steps, then she goes quiet and both birds can remain immobile for up to ten minutes. Then they begin to move around one another. Prévost describes how the female then fixes her eyes on the incubatory pouch of her partner, while her excitement grows visibly. Finally, if it is the right bird, the male allows the egg to fall gently to the ice, whereupon the female takes it and then turns her back to the male, to whom, after a final duet, she becomes completely indifferent. The male becomes increasingly irritated, stares at his empty pouch, pecks at it with his beak, lifts up his head, groans, and then pecks the female. She shows no further interest in him and eventually he leaves for the open sea, to break his long fast. The whole affair has lasted about eighty minutes.

How difficult it is for us to understand the emotions involved in these events. Yet it is hard to resist the anthropomorphic urge. Obviously the male emperor is aware of the loss of what has, after all, been almost a part of his body for two to three months. Is he disappointed, bewildered, relieved, or are his feelings so remote from our own (not inferior, mind you, just different) that we cannot imagine them? We would groan, too, under such circumstances, but the meaning of a penguin's groan is still opaque to us. Yet we, too, are fathers and mothers with babies to protect and comfort, negotiating meals and absences and other obligations, just like our Antarctic cousins. Sometimes, when we are overwhelmed by an emotion, we are hard-pressed to express ourselves. If penguin fathers could speak about this moment in their lives, perhaps they would be at a similar loss for words. Perhaps the songs and groans of the male penguin are all the expression they need.

How is it, one wonders, that the female emperor penguin is able to return just in time for the birth of her chick? As Alexander Skutch notes in his wonderful book, *The Minds of Birds,* it is improbable that she has consciously counted the sixty-three days or whatever the exact number is between the laying of her egg and the hatching of her chick.[6] "Only a most exceptional human could accurately time such long intervals without a calendar, notching a tally-stick or some such device. Some subconscious process, physiological or mental, was evidently summing the days to prompt the birds to start homeward when the proper number had elapsed."

If the egg has hatched and the male already has a chick between his legs, the female is even more excited to hear it peep, and quickly removes it from the male. She immediately regurgitates food to the chick. If she is late in coming (the miracle is that the mothers usually return on the day their chicks hatch), the male, in spite of his near starvation, has a final resource: He regurgitates into the beak of his peeping newborn a substance known as penguin milk, similar to pigeon's milk, or crop milk, which is secreted from the lining of his esophagus. The secretion is remarkably rich, containing essential amino acids, much like the milk of marine mammals such as seals and whales. It contains 29 percent fat and 59 percent protein (cow's milk contains just 4 percent fat and 3 percent protein). These feedings allow the young birds to survive for up to two weeks after hatching. Many of these males have now fasted for four and a half months, and have lost up to half of their body weight. It is a sight to see the well-nourished, sleek, brilliantly feathered, healthy-looking females arrive, and the emaciated, dirty, tired males leave.

Bernard Stonehouse, one of the first scientists to research the life of penguins, wrote an influential article in 1953 about the emperor's breeding habits.[7] But he did not know that females returned to the same male. He thought they took anyone, and wrote that "there was no indication in the rookery that any female returned to a specific male, or took charge of any particular chick; there is no family life." He was wrong on this point. As the eminent French explorer J. Prévost noted in 1963, it really makes no sense that the females are searching frantically unless they are searching for somebody specific. No matter how long it takes her, the female eventually finds her partner and therefore her own egg or chick. She does this through sound, through vision, and through memory.

The females have brought enough undigested food to feed the chicks every hour at first, then, once the chicks are bigger, two or three times a day. Penguin parents suspend digestion when bringing food home to their chicks by secreting a wall of protective mucus around the crop content. If prevented from feeding their chicks, penguins may discard the food rather than digest it themselves. (An emperor in captivity starved to death by feeding all his rations—about six pounds of fish daily—to an importunate chick.) Between twenty and thirty-four days later, the father returns, well nourished also, and now the two of them can take turns returning to the sea to feed. The chicks remain on the feet of their parents for about forty to fifty days from the time they hatch.

By September or October, the chicks have grown enough to run free. They then form what are known as crèches, penguin nurseries, consisting exclusively of chicks, with no adults present to guard or take care of them in any way. Why these nurseries form is not clear (for company?), but when the weather turns ugly, the crèches are quickly transformed into *tortues,* with the same function for the chicks as for the adults. Whether the ability to form *tortues* is innate or is the result of observing the adults is hard to say, but it is probably the former. Even when they are in the crèches, the parents still feed them, although more sporadically. On their return to the crèches once every week or two, the adults spend anywhere from a few hours to a couple of days with their chicks, which probably led earlier observers to believe that the crèches were guarded by adults. Why some adults stay longer there than others is not known, and perhaps there is some aspect of guarding to the behavior.

Early authors thought this feeding was communal or random: Any adult penguin would feed any penguin chick (the same mistake was made about bats). This turns out not to be true. What happens is that the parents join up and together approach each crèche in turn and sing. It is a little like human parents setting off to day care to pick up their children. This song may cause no reaction at all until one of the chicks approaches and gives an answering song. There are sometimes five thousand chicks to be examined. It resembles a test, since several chicks will often come forward. Before giving a second song, the mother or father penguins will rub their heads with the top part of their wings, just as they did earlier when they were courting. Then they will make a little dance step that encourages the chick to move away from the crèche, and only then will the adult feed the chick.

Stonehouse describes penguin chicks in their winter crèches when their parents return from the sea to feed them: "The parent stands at the edge of the crèche, which may contain two or three thousand tightly packed, sleeping chicks, and gives its own distinctive call. Immediately one little head shoots up from the mass, one piercing whistle sounds a frenetic reply, and the chick begins to fight its way through apathetic companions to meet its parent for breakfast." In spite of such care, he points out that a quarter to a half of the hatched chicks die, usually from a bird predator (skuas and petrels) or by wandering away and freezing or starving. What an awful feeling it must be for the parents not to find their chicks. We may well reject the notion of a melancholy penguin as human sentiment run wild, but I find the idea impossible to dismiss out of hand. After such care, why should a parent penguin not feel bereft at its loss?

Given penguins' concern for their own children, there are some disturbing observations, one of them made by Prévost. He noticed that giant petrels (the family of seabirds that includes albatrosses) will sometimes choose a small chick on the edge of the colony, open his abdomen with their beaks, and then eat the contents. The chick will only rarely cry out, "and the adults who are standing nearby are generally completely indifferent to his fate." This is one of those times when empathy or sympathy fails, and we cannot, or at least I cannot, imagine how one could be in the penguin's place as an indifferent bystander. Perhaps because the situation is so rare—penguins, as we have seen, have almost no predators on land—they are simply unprepared and therefore literally blind to what is happening in front of their eyes: We cannot see what we do not know. Perhaps the chick, by not singing, is not recognized.

One possible explanation comes from observation of kittiwake gulls. In a classic paper, Esther Cullen described her experiences with these birds over several years in the Farne Islands off the Northumberland coast.[8] These gulls, unlike any other, nest on tiny cliff ledges, about four inches wide. This gives them almost complete protection from predators and they have developed a number of interesting behavioral changes as a result. Since they are so rarely attacked, they did not swoop at Cullen when she climbed among the nests. She watched a herring gull catch a young kittiwake in the air: "Even when it did so only a couple of feet from a nesting cliff the adult birds left their nests merely to hover in a completely silent cloud over the scene without interfering, while the chick was screaming and trying to defend itself against the powerful beak of its attacker." The explanation is that the kittiwake is simply not prepared for such events and does not know how to respond, since the attack is so far out of its normal experience. I think this same explanation could apply to emperor penguins.

Mysteriously, it has been noted that most birds, including skuas, sworn enemies of penguins, will not attack crèches, even though the babies could do nothing to defend themselves and there are usually no adults nearby to protect them. It is not clear why this should be so. Is there a skua code of honor?

By December, the ice has begun to melt, so that chicks (whose thermal feathers had to grow in) and adults are able to ride out to sea on the ice floes. They might ride on the same iceberg, but it is not clear whether they are still a family. Nobody knows precisely what happens to the emperor chicks when they ride these ice floes with their parents out to sea. I asked Dr. Gerald Kooyman, of the Scripps Institution of Oceanography in La Jolla, whether the chicks stay with their parents when they are at sea, and he told me that they do not. We know that at least 80 percent of fledglings die in their first year at sea. The survivors will spend four to five years at sea before they return to breed when they are five years old. Since penguins are not sexually mature until they are between five and eight years of age, one wonders what their life consists of during the time before they take partners. Whether a pair stays together at sea is not clear.

What do penguins do when they are at sea? These remarkable birds (who seem more fishlike than birdlike) spend most of their time in the Antarctic Ocean fishing. Or so it would seem. We should remember that the sea is the natural habitat for a penguin. Even their feathers are made for water: Their short, slightly curved feathers alternate and overlap like tiles on a roof. The tips are oily enough to repel water and keep the sea out. A mat of downy filaments grows from the shaft of each feather, forming with its neighbors a dense undershirt lying close to the skin. This traps a layer of warm air, and acts as additional waterproofing in case the outer layer of feather tips breaks down. We often think of penguins as clumsy creatures when they are waddling along the ice, but in the water, it is a completely different story, for they are in their element. Adult penguins spend 75 percent of their lives (which, according to at least one report, can be as long as thirty-four years) in the water, where they literally fly through the sea, using their wings in this different habitat. It is as if they surrendered their ability to soar through the air in order to "fly" through the water better, as Edward Hoagland suggested when he saw them on a trip to the Antarctic, which he wrote about in *Tigers and Ice* (see Suggested Reading).

Since the adults do not return to land, or even to the Antarctic ice shelves, for months at a time, one wonders what they drink. At sea, penguins distill their own fresh water, using special nasal glands that lie embedded in the skull immediately above the eyes. Although they make hundreds of dives a day, they only spend about four hours a day diving. Nobody knows for certain what they do the rest of the time. Nothing, many people assume, which makes them seem stupid. Thus Robert Cushman Murphy says in his great 1936 book, *Oceanic Birds of South America:* "The corpus striatum, rather than the cerebrum, is the seat of their being, and the brain, for all its great expansion, is concerned far more with keen sensory susceptibilities and delicate muscular coordination than with any processes that might properly be termed 'mental.' Why, after all, should a penguin need 'brains' when its fundamental and inherited behavior pattern takes care of it through the seasonal cycle and the generations?"[9] But of course Cushman had no idea that these emperor penguins had such elaborate parenting habits. Nor did anyone know until very recently that they made such deep benthic dives, to the bottom of the sea, another remarkable feature of the emperor. When they move under water, their heart rate drops to five or six beats per minute (one twentieth of the normal rate). Dr. Kooyman tells me that these dives can be up to 500 meters deep, and last for up to twenty minutes. Only elephant seals can forage at such depths, certainly no other bird. Kooyman believes the function of these dives may be to provide their chicks with the gastric stones both male and females feed them back at the rookery, probably for digestive purposes.

If they do not stay with their mates, they do for certain meet up with other penguins. Bernard Stonehouse explains that "lone penguins of any kind seem restless, incomplete creatures; unless moulting or dying (when they prefer to be alone) their most pressing aim is to find other penguins, preferably but not necessarily of their own species, with whom they can stand in silent but satisfying communion." The reason, he says, for their conviviality is that "solitary birds are prone to dangers—getting lost, failing to find food when it is scarce or patchy, or being eaten by seals and other predators—which diminish when they travel in company." I think it is possible that they simply enjoy company.

I make no secret of the awe in which I hold the father emperor penguin; some, though, might argue against a heroic element to his parental solicitude. "But that is simply what emperor penguins do, there is nothing heroic in doing what you are programmed to do, whereas you make it sound like the penguin has made an individual choice," someone might object. There is some truth to this, for we tend to reserve the term "heroic" for an act that is chosen over other easier or more convenient ones. Nonetheless, human heroes, too, will often explain that they only did what seemed natural to them, or they had no choice, or they were brought up to behave in this way. So if emperor penguin fathers are simply acting as penguins, it is still impressive to our eyes.

Moreover, we are only beginning to learn of the astonishing paternal feats of emperor penguins. Few people have ever observed their fathering behavior closely for an extended period of time, for obvious reasons: The conditions of their habitat are extremely harsh, even perilous. Captive emperor penguins do not behave in a normal fashion when it comes to procreation and fathering. We might be surprised to learn that there is far more variation in paternal behavior than we assume, ranging from fathers who never abandon an egg or a chick under any circumstance to others who flee at the first sign of a bad storm. Perhaps the high rate of infant mortality (though the figures may not be reliable, based as they are on a relatively small sample) can be accounted for by this variability in paternal competence. Scientists find something disturbing in the notion that a penguin can deliberately choose his behavior. Similarly, the thought that a mother penguin at sea might suddenly *think* consciously about the birth of her chick, and *decide* consciously to return to land, is vaguely disturbing. It is easier to believe that some internal clock simply turns on and she finds herself heading for home for no reason that she can understand. But isn't it possible that she is heading back with a vivid image in her mind of her new chick driving her, hurrying her on? Similarly, the male emperor must feel relief when he sees her approaching. His hunger is extreme, his patience has been exemplary. Now it is time for him to head for the open sea as well and replenish his strength. These are the emotions that humans would feel under these circumstances; I can see no good reason to deny them to penguins.

When I visit the playground on a weekend and see all the fathers, many looking bored no doubt, but still there when they could be someplace else, I am struck by how children come into our lives and simply demand that we give them immediate priority—and we respond. There are many pleasures more exciting than sitting in a sandbox with a three year old digging holes, or sitting at the seashore building castles. More exciting, but in some absolute sense, less fulfilling. There is nothing that feels more remarkably right than being with our children, attending to their small pleasures, observing with satisfaction their joy. We may not be emperor penguins, but our embrace of our children is not totally unlike theirs in these moments of parental devotion. We too feel a devotion to our young that makes us forego ordinary pleasures to ensure that they survive and thrive.

One of America's great paleontologists, the late George Gaylord Simpson, was fascinated by penguins. At the end of a book he wrote about them in 1976, *Penguins Past and Present,* he said, "Finally, the question may be asked, 'What good are penguins?' It may be crass to ask what good a wild animal is, but I do think the question may also be legitimate. That depends on what you mean by good. If you mean 'good to eat,' you are perhaps being stupid. If you mean 'good to hunt,' you are surely being vicious. If you mean 'good as it is good in itself to be a living creature enjoying life,' you are not being crass, stupid or vicious. I agree with you and I am your brother as well as the penguin's."[10] I think we can go even further, and say that it is good to watch the emperor penguin, to learn from the emperor penguin, to lionize the emperor penguin as he proudly embraces the tiny ball of fluff on his feet.

TWO: Wolves Make Good Fathers; Dogs Don't

It is a mild evening in the Alaskan summer, and we can see a wolf pack in the distance. The alpha female has recently given birth to cubs. She is at the entrance to her den, a shallow cave in the side of a hill bordering a small bog, which is also a beaver pond. The sedges and grasses outside the den are ideal for sleeping and playing. There is a fine, unobstructed view of the entire area for more than a mile. Five cubs, six weeks old, are already climbing over one another, biting, playing, growling, yelping. The pack is returning from a successful hunt. The large male who is the father of the six cubs is in the lead. The rest of the pack lies down under the trees near the den to rest. The father walks straight up to the den, where he is greeted by his mate with enthusiastic wagging of her tail and moans and groans of pleasure: She is happy to see him return. But her pleasure is mild compared with that of the six cubs, who fling themselves upon their father, squealing with delight. They leap up to his face and kiss him wildly about the mouth, pawing, nuzzling, nipping his mouth and head. He backs up a few feet, then opens his mouth very wide and disgorges the food he has brought for them, in several little piles, to make it easier for them to eat without competing. It is fresh food, stored in his stomach as if in a shopping bag, and it is meant for both the mother and her young, all of whom have been waiting with keen anticipation.

This snapshot of life at a wolf den was hard to come by. True knowledge of wolves has been acquired only very slowly and with great difficulty. Progress has been hampered by the persistence of a false image of wolves. Men, especially, have drawn parallels between wolves and human males where they simply do not exist, or we have focused on an area that is easily exaggerated. Wolf as aggressor, wolf as dangerous. The lone wolf.

I, too, have felt the power of these prejudices. Although I knew that there has been no documented case within the United States of a healthy wild wolf attacking a human, ever,[1] the idea that a wolf is a dangerous animal dies hard. I was visiting the Czech Republic recently, and was taken to a remote area where a man has been living with a female wolf for the last seven years. The man, somewhat eccentric, had built a two-acre enclosure where he and the wolf spent much of their time. As I approached, he told me that he rarely allowed visitors to enter the enclosure, but he had read my book on dogs, and was delighted with my visit. He invited me to enter. My companions hesitated and made it clear they expected me to lead the way. As I boldly stepped into the enclosure, suddenly some primitive fear mechanism took hold of me, and I began to make feeble jokes about getting a better view from the outside. In fact, as I should have known, when I did enter, the wolf ran to the other side of the enclosure and nothing could coax her out to meet the visiting wolf "expert," for she was far more afraid of me than I was of her! The fear I experienced is no doubt rooted in our wealthy fund of false information and prejudices against wolves.

In contrast to the myth of the ferocious, aggressive lone wolf is the true picture of the wolf as good father and good mother, one that has been a long time coming. But while the genuine story of this aspect of wolf behavior is only recent, somewhere deep in the human unconscious it must have existed for a long time. How else can we explain the fact that humans have since ancient times held on to another wolf myth (though many people claim it mirrors historical truth): that wolves will raise our children? According to legend, the founders of Rome, Romulus and Remus, were wolf children. In the 1940s, the American public was startled to read about the one case of a wolf child reported in the literature that was assumed to be entirely authentic, and the only firsthand account by one of the major players in the story. No less an authority on child development than Arnold Gesell, professor of pediatrics at Yale, in his book *Wolf Child and Human Child,* vouched for the authenticity of the case. I have to agree with Ashley Montagu, who said that he was emotionally in favor of the story but as a scientist could not accept it. When I asked the great animal behaviorist Donald Griffin whether he believed it was possible for a wolf to accept a human infant, he said, "I don't think it is totally impossible." Marc Bekoff, an even greater authority on wolves, tells me: "I think it is entirely possible that a wolf could accept a human infant in special instances." From the point of view of the wolf, it might be acceptable, but pediatricians I have spoken to think it unlikely that an infant could survive with this care. True or not, the interesting fact is that humans have long believed that a female wolf would suckle a human child, and that a male wolf would permit this and protect the child from harm. I think this is more than fantasy. There is a profound similarity between wolf families and human families, and we seem to have sensed this for a long time. How remains a mystery.

What do we know about the social lives of wolves? Not as much as we would like, but one fact we know for certain is that wolves, and almost all the wild canids, are magnificent fathers. A wolf pack usually consists of eight animals or fewer, most of whom are related to one another. The breeding pair is the most important element in the pack. The male and the female have chosen each other, and the bond they form often lasts for many years, sometimes even over an entire life. This bond is only strengthened by producing a litter of young, which the pair frequently raise together. In the first weeks of their lives, the pups are intensely interactive with one another, and clearly it is this closeness early in life that acts as the glue that keeps a wolf pack, consisting mostly of brothers and sisters, together in later years. When pups are about three weeks old, they start interacting with other adult pack members. The emotional bonds are carried over into young adulthood, and give remarkable cohesion to pack life. At ten weeks, the pups begin to leave the den, generally at night, but come together at various temporary resting spots called rendezvous sites. Within six months, the pups join in the hunt and are able to travel long distances. After six months, except when they choose their own mates, the young do not form strong ties with other wolves. Almost everything that is important, from an emotional point of view, has already happened, and has done so primarily in the den.

It is in the den, or near the den, that we find the male wolf behaving as a father. The wolf father has hunted for his young (and his mate), he often licks the young, cleaning them thoroughly, he guards the den and protects the cubs inside, and once they are able to follow him, he teaches them how to be wolves. Wolves go through a socialization process, much as humans do. They need to learn rules, they need to learn about hierarchy within the pack, and discover where they fit into it. Most of this learning is facilitated by their father and mother working together. There is no indication that wolf fathers ignore their young or leave their raising to the female. Even hunting, which many people would regard as the ultimate instinctive activity, must be learned. People who raise wolves often remark that some of them never kill other animals. That is because they were not taught to. Learning to kill, for humans and for most wolves, is a cultural adaptation.

If I had to characterize the essence of the wolf pack in a phrase, I would say it consists in the joy of being together. Loneliness is not an intelligible concept for the young cubs in their parents' den. Young wolves are never without their mother or father or some other adult with whom they form close attachments. The baby-sitter might be an older sibling from the previous year's litter, and the young themselves stay in continuous contact all day and night. A young wolf, separated from his brothers and sisters for whatever reason, will howl. There can be no doubt in that case what the howl means. Even wolf researchers believe there is a strong connection between loneliness and howling.

There are many indications that young and even infant animals feel the same emotions that adult animals do. We know because they give all the same indications that they are subject to an emotion. When infant monkeys are separated from their mothers, they immediately begin calling in distress (even their hormonal profiles change). Ducks, when left alone, emit specific sounds designed to bring back their mothers. This may not be "language," but it certainly communicates what the duck is feeling. The same is true of greeting sounds. When geese imprint on humans, they greet them as soon as they see them with a very specific sound that clearly means, "Hi!" Elephants make trumpeting greeting sounds and their babies answer. Similarly, when an animal is hurt, there is rarely any doubt that the sound they make is the equivalent of "ouch," and signifies "that hurts" as clearly as do our words—perhaps even more so, since animals never make it up. The pleasure hums of many infant animals while nursing are sounds of contentment.

The feelings of young animals are accompanied by gestures as well. When happy, baby animals nuzzle. Wolf puppies, when they run to greet their father, lick his face. Yes, this is to get him to regurgitate the food he has brought for them, but it is also the general gesture for pleasure, signaling "I am glad to see you." This is why dogs lick our faces, something it is almost impossible to train out of them. If you get down on all fours and approach your own dog, it would be highly unusual for her not to lick your face in delight.

Once the young wolves are old enough to go along with the pack, the pack is rarely apart. Those of you who have lived with dogs will immediately recognize many similarities. You know how reluctant your dog is to leave you out of his sight. When we go on an errand without our dogs, they cock their heads, and look puzzled. Dogs wonder why we are leaving the pack without them. What could possibly be more important than the cohesion of the pack? They have a point.

With the emperor penguins, we saw how knowledge of their behavior has eluded us because of the difficult conditions of living in the Antarctic in their daily presence. The difficulties, however, are not due to the penguins themselves: They do not object to our company. Wolves, however, do. No human has ever been accepted by a wild wolf pack, though many people claim to have been so accepted. As with parrots and dolphins, it is rare for anyone to have lived with canid families in the wild. They are hard to find, and when we do find them, it is almost impossible to win their trust. This is probably because wolves have no predators in the wild; humans are the single exception. The wolf has learned to fear us and no amount of quiet observation seems sufficient to overcome this fear. As a consequence, our knowledge is meager and comes mostly from captive wolves, a severe limitation. So while we know that most wild canids have well-developed paternal behavior, and that coyotes and foxes, too, are active, loving fathers, there are almost no direct observations of wolves.

The most elaborate description I have been able to find is by Michael Fox, one of the world's leading experts on canid behavior and a vice president of the Humane Society of the United States. In the 1960s, he observed a male wolf and his mate at the Saint Louis Zoo. It was the first time either had raised cubs. During the first two to three weeks, the female did not leave the den. It was the father who brought food for both the mother and their cubs. He would disgorge the food and distribute it on the ground, but neither he nor the mother would eat. They waited until the cubs had eaten their fill before eating themselves. The mother nursed the cubs until they were eight weeks old, and then weaned them by disciplining them when they insisted on nursing. In this task, the father assisted her, and by the time the cubs were ten to twelve weeks old, they were respectful to both parents. When the cubs had reached four months of age, however, both parents were good-natured about allowing them to pull pieces of meat out of their mouths and would rarely snarl at them. As the father crushed marrow bones for the cubs once they were weaned, they would pull at his tail and ears, which he permitted without protest. The cubs would play with one another, sometimes quite roughly. When it got out of hand, the mother or father would walk over to the heap of squirming cubs and whine and lick them, which invariably caused the fighting to stop. Many people who live with dogs have noticed a similar behavior: When two humans are arguing in loud voices, the family dog will often whine, in an urgent attempt to restore harmony. At the end of her superb book *The Hidden Life of Dogs,* Elizabeth Marshall Thomas was able to answer the question of what dogs (and by extension wolves) really want: the peace and quiet of a lazy afternoon spent lying all together in the sun.

There is little doubt that wolves value good parenting. In an unusual observation, some wolf researchers studied a single female wolf who was very low in the hierarchy and constantly harassed by the whole pack. But one day, in spite of her rank, she was pressed into service as a "dry nurse" for a litter when the mother had to suddenly leave the den. As a reward for her good performance of the nursemaid role, she regained status in the pack, clearly a sign of how much importance wolves assign to the care of children.

Not so the dog. Although nearly everyone who has lived with dogs knows one or two exceptions, dogs make very poor fathers.[2] Male dogs appear to have very little interest in their own puppies. Why has the dog lost the ability to father? Darwin long ago noted that a wild duck is faithful to its mate, but the domestic duck is not: Something has been lost in domestication. Greylag geese choose a partner only after a long courtship and remain monogamous for their entire lives. Domesticated geese, on the other hand, pair, but they really don't seem to care with whom, nor are they monogamous. As far as I know, no domesticated male animal assists the female in raising young. He does not care for the young, he does not defend them, and he does not feed them. In domesticated animals we have succeeded in extinguishing whatever natural male parental behavior existed in the wild progenitor.

But when it comes to the dog, in my opinion, something else, something deeper, comes into play. Dogs are almost identical to wolves genetically (less than 1 percent difference) and also behaviorally. In some manner of speaking, a dog *is* nothing but a wolf. When it comes to the pack, though, there is a major difference between wolves and dogs. *We* are the pack for dogs; the human family replaces the wolf pack. The key point is that dogs are only bad fathers to their own children, not to ours. A male dog is very protective of human children, for as far as he is concerned, they are the cubs of the pack. Because typically no dog is ever the alpha male in a human situation, and is rarely permitted to form a monogamous bond with one female, it would be rare for a male dog to regard any puppies born to be his puppies. My speculation is that the instinct to father has not been entirely eradicated, it has merely been transferred to another species. Just as dogs will sometimes behave like our children, they will also sometimes behave like our children's parents.

Dogs are protective of human children, guard them, walk with them, attempt to teach them, and play with them in precisely the same way that a male wolf will protect and play with his cubs. Wolves make great fathers to wolf cubs; dogs make great fathers to human cubs.

Wild Dogs

Wild dogs, on the other hand, make fine parents. In dingo society, the Australian wild dog fathers make a point, as do mothers, of never hunting the rabbits that live near their den, leaving them for the pups to toy with when they are old enough to begin hunting.[3] The fathers regularly visit the den and are greeted affectionately by the pups, though only the mothers appear to feed them.

The distinction between a tame animal and a domesticated animal is an important one. Almost any wild animal, with patience, can be tamed. But this trait is not automatically passed on to the next generation. It applies only to a single individual. When an animal is domesticated, on the other hand, we have altered its genetic characteristics, and tameness will be one of the main traits we breed for. All domestic animals are tame, but all tame animals are not necessarily domesticated.

The dingo, which seems to have come to Australia about ten thousand years ago, was never domesticated the way the dog was. Accounts of the relationship between dingos and Aboriginals consist mostly of unsubstantiated claims. The Aboriginals do not use dingos for hunting. However, they often fondle them, never feed them, and use them primarily as warm blankets in the freezing desert nights; Aboriginals and dingos sleep huddled together for warmth. Konrad Lorenz, who tamed a dingo, points out that a carnivore that allows itself to be fondled and that sleeps in a huddle with humans must have gone through a long history of symbiosis with humans. It takes a great deal of trust to sleep together. Pariah dogs in Istanbul, Turkey, Lorenz goes on to say, live in close proximity to domestic stock, including small chickens and newly born sheep, but never harm them, no matter how hungry they become, even though the goats and other animals range free and are unprotected. Clearly they have learned, to their survival advantage, that they must not harm these animals. This suggests to me that at some point in their history dingos were tamed, but not domesticated. This would account for the fact that compared to wolves, they are only half as efficacious at fatherhood.

Unlike dingos, pariah dogs, which live primarily in India, can be trained, much like a domestic dog, and therefore may be animals who simply reverted to the wild from an earlier state of domestication. They may have retained some domestic traits and lost others. It would be interesting to find out if pariah dogs do any fathering, but I have not been able to gather any information on this point. If they make perfectly good fathers, it would indicate that reversion to a wild state carries with it the advantage of regaining old virtues lost in domestication.

How different is a pariah dog from a feral dog? Would a feral dog—that is, a dog who has left human control and lives in a semiwild state—revert back to behaving like a wolf with its young? Feral dogs are so little studied that nobody knows for sure. But they do form packs. Tom Daniels, who studied stable feral dog packs on a Navajo reservation for his doctoral work in the early 1980s, told me that he saw males who were solicitous of the pups, but only to some extent. On the other hand, Luigi Boitani, of the University of Rome, one of the world's leading authorities on wolves and feral dogs, tells me that in his studies of feral dogs, most females raised their pups completely on their own, without any support from the fathers or the rest of the group.

By definition, feral dogs are only domesticated dogs that have reverted, sometimes not even permanently, to a wild state. Over time, I would suspect that a truly wild pack of dogs would come to behave more like their ancestors, wolves, and would become once again the good fathers they once were. Here is the constant danger we face in domesticating any species: *We extinguish traits without any foreknowledge of what those traits are likely to be.* In our arrogance, we think we can control nature, but in fact we begin a haphazard and often unpredictable course of events that can have dire consequences even for humans—as we are learning to our peril when it comes to diseases and parasites in genetically altered animals. I love dogs, a domesticated species, but altering the genetics of dogs to create certain appearances that humans find attractive but harm them (causing hip dysplasia, blindness, deafness, weak backs, and so on) is cruel and unnecessary.

In the cape hunting dog, an African wild dog, adults typically wait until the juveniles have fed before eating, much like wolves. Not only the father but other adult males will regurgitate food for the breeding female. Red foxes make excellent fathers, even though they do not form packs and the young are driven away by the parents as they reach the end of their first year. Coyotes, who do form packs, make good fathers as well. Hope Ryden observed a den of coyote pups and two females who both took care of the young and a father who dutifully regurgitated food for them. Contrary to all expectations, she discovered a strange coyote who also brought food for the pups and even injured himself while protecting them against intruders. Perhaps the strange male was an older brother from previous years. Marc Bekoff, who studied coyotes for eight years in Grand Teton National Park outside of Jackson, Wyoming, told me that he observed numerous instances of paternal behavior and caregiving by male helpers, especially baby-sitting. There were no instances, however, in which an unrelated coyote acted in this way.

Leonard Lee Rue, who observed red foxes in Alaska in 1966, said he witnessed several meetings between male and female foxes that could be described with only one word: ecstasy. As the male approached the den with food he was bringing for the pups, the female would flop down on her belly, raise her tail up over her back, and wave it furiously. Then she would spring up and kiss the male all over with her tongue. This is exactly the greeting he would experience from the pups when he brought them their dinner. Red fox researcher David Macdonald describes a new father wriggling with eagerness to care for his children: He would warble at the entrance to the den, and if the mother did not respond, he would use his nose as a billiard cue, to poke the lumps of food through the entrance and into the den. His favorite occupation was to play with the cubs. When red fox researcher J. David Henry was observing dens in northern Saskatchewan, he moved in too close for a photograph of how the six-week-old pups were being raised, and the vixen decided she had had enough. She marched the pups in the middle of the night to a new den. The next morning, the father fox returned to the den with a rabbit in his mouth. He went to the main entrance and called the pups out with a chortle. When nobody emerged, he set the rabbit down and began to smell around the area. He figured out what had happened, detected the trail where the vixen and their four kits had traveled off through the forest, cached the rabbit, and tracked down his family.

Dogs

These stories give us a sense of how important canid fathers are. In no wild canid is "male investment" (as the animal behaviorists label it) completely absent. Dogs, on the other hand, exhibit little male investment, and yet dogs are direct descendants of wolves and not of any other species. Many authorities believe that domestication of the wolf took place only once. The fact that there is such enormous variability in dogs (at least eight hundred true breeding types in the world) need not surprise us. Darwin emphasized the extraordinary variation of domestic pigeons, which derived exclusively from the rock dove in a much shorter time than the dog has been with humans (at least ten to fifteen thousand years, and possibly much longer).

Besides having almost the identical genetic constitution, as I mentioned earlier, there are other striking similarities between dogs and wolves: Pregnancy lasts the same amount of time in dogs and wolves, a little over two months; the blind period in the young is the same, eleven to fifteen days; the order of appearance of milk teeth is the same, the first coming in at about two weeks. One could almost say that the dog is just a form of the wolf, not a separate species. They, at least, do not appear to consider each other to belong to a different species, as is demonstrated by the fact that wolves and dogs will mate, and the young are not barren.[4] On the other hand, obviously, a wolf is not a dog. This is the reason that people who work with wolves urge people not to attempt to keep them in their homes the way we keep dogs in our homes. It is dangerous and it is unfair. It is dangerous because a wolf is not a domesticated animal, and its "natural" needs may prevail over its feelings of friendship with us, a member of another species no longer in the wild; it can attack us or a companion for reasons that make sense in wolf society (challenging our dominant position, for example) but are intolerable in human society. It is unfair because a wolf is not meant to be walked on a leash or fed dog food in a bowl or be forced to obey human restrictions about defecation (rules that tame wolves ignore in any event). This said, it is nonetheless true that a dog tends to behave in almost identical fashion to a wolf. If we want to learn the significance of some obscure act of a dog, we turn to wolf researchers for answers. "Natural" behavior in the wolf corresponds almost exactly with "natural" behavior in the dog.

One of the most hotly debated topics in the social and biological sciences revolves around the question of what the term "natural behavior" refers to. The contrast between how dogs and wild canids approach fathering allows us to look at this question in new ways. By and large, I think attempting to determine what is truly natural is a worthy goal. We can then always choose to alter our behavior once we know what is natural, whereas if we don't know, we will make false claims that result in behavior that is much more difficult to change. Complications come in when we think about domestication. To the extent that dogs have been domesticated, they are no longer "natural"—an obvious point, but one with far-reaching repercussions. It is often said of humans that we are a self-domesticated species. I take this to mean that we have imposed certain restrictions on ourselves that do not correspond to our "natural" behavior. Obviously, we were not evolved to fly planes, drive cars, attach cell phones to our ears, or surf the Net. Strictly speaking, all of these activities are "unnatural," but few people would want to issue a blanket statement that all of them should be immediately abandoned.

While male parenting in wolves is partly innate, much must be learned. Wolves have their own experience as cubs of what a wolf father does, and later in life are able to observe other wolves as fathers to learn what is considered good paternal behavior. But dogs have been deprived of the learning that would be part of their natural life in the wild. When we consider what wolves do for their cubs, we realize that there is not much a male dog *could* do, even if he were so inclined. Significantly, we do not encourage female dogs to choose their own mates or permit them to live as a monogamous pair, not to mention the fact that we neuter (for good reasons) most male dogs in any event. But in the homes where we keep dogs, there is no den to guard. Even if a male dog defends a territory, *we* decide what that territory will be, and can arbitrarily alter it. And the mother dog does not depend on the father dog for nourishment, since we provide food.

Although a father dog probably has no sense that any puppy is "his" (there is no concept, among dogs, of "paternity certainty"; see chapter 6), I have seen male dogs who are extraordinarily tolerant of puppies, allowing them to chew on their ears and bite their tails exactly as wolf fathers do. (Others have seen male dogs guard "their" puppies from other dogs, though not from "their" humans.) Here is a behavior we have not been able to extinguish, perhaps because, as we shall see, it is not connected with sexuality. Dog pups are evidently unaware that their dog father is not a wolf father: Everyone has seen puppies mob the mouth of a male dog, eagerly licking around the corners, evidently hoping he will turn into a wolf and regurgitate his food for them. In fact, if you approach any litter of puppies on your knees, they will do the same to you. This expectation, this permanent hope, has not been bred out of dogs, and no doubt accounts for the intensity of a dog's staring while we eat.

These examples allow us to see what it is that we do to a wild species like the wolf when we turn it into a domestic species like the dog. This is very different from taming a wild animal. All mammals can be tamed if they are reared close to humans from an early age, and probably in the past individuals from most species that shared our environment were tamed and kept in captivity. Even reptiles and certainly birds can be tamed. It is not just that these animals learn to tolerate the presence of humans. There is pleasure for them as well in the association, especially for animals that are social by nature. Solitary animals are harder to tame, but many members of the cat family, including cheetahs, servals, and leopards, can become tame and learn to enjoy the pleasure of human company. But a tame socialized wolf is by no means a domesticated wolf (the definition of a dog!). A tame wolf, as I have said, cannot be housebroken, nor would most people leave their young child in the company of a wolf, whereas I would have no hesitation in leaving my three-year-old son with many dogs I know.

When we domesticate an animal, we alter its size, reducing it. We change the outward appearance; lop ears and curled tails, for example, are signs of submissiveness that we like and breed for. Docility is a trait humans favor in most domestic animals. We even alter the internal anatomy of the domestic animal; the brain is reduced in size relative to the size of the body and the sense organs become less acute, the domestic animal requiring less alertness to its surroundings. So we have shaped the dog deliberately to be a more docile creature, one that will easily subordinate itself to a human. We are mostly successful. Some dogs, such as Alaskan malamutes and huskies, remain much more wolflike (unlike the ever-friendly golden retriever) than others, but in general, dogs are reliably friendly toward humans while even the most tame wolf is not.

The most important single physical difference between wolves and dogs involves their sexuality. A wolf is sexually mature at two years, a dog at six months. The female wolf comes into estrus once a year, a dog twice a year. Male wolves produce sperm only seasonally, male dogs produce semen constantly. Even more important is the difference in the relationship between the sexes. Among wolves, the dominant female chooses her mate. While it would not be correct to say that choice is completely indiscriminate in dogs, it is much less specific than in wolves. In extinguishing this natural sexual behavior of the wolf, we have produced the greatest change in dogs. We have encouraged dogs to be sexually promiscuous because humans have specific goals when it comes to the kinds of breeds we want to create. Male dogs are ready to mate at any time of the year because this suits human ends—creating a certain breed of dog, for example, or seeking a certain temperament.

We have seen that in transforming the wolf into a dog, we have lost something valuable, the desire and the ability of the animal to be a father. Good fathering in the canid family means first of all being a good mate, part of a pair-bond, to use the animal behavior term. A dog who is close to one female is going to make a better father than one who is not. As in general among mammals, fatherhood and monogamy are closely linked. This is more than just pure speculation: Promiscuous behavior (including a lack of monogamous feelings for females) is what we demand from the dog, and what we get as a corollary is poor fathering.

What exactly a female wolf looks for when she is choosing a partner nobody really knows, except her. But certainly she wants a good father for her children. Since this means patience, tolerance, a willingness to forego immediate pleasures, to share food, and take risks in order to protect the young, I would not be surprised to learn that the female wolf is looking for kindness in the father of her cubs. What is in it for the father? We are guilty of narrow thinking if we confine the benefits to mere genetic continuity. We have direct experience of the intense emotional life of dogs around us. Since in every important way the behavior of a dog and the behavior of a wolf is identical, it makes sense to believe that wolves, too, are capable of feeling profound emotions. What better place for those emotions to achieve full play than in the den, in the presence of small cubs? The joyful licking and enthusiasm with which the father wolf is greeted by his young must provoke intense pleasure in him. The sense of security he is able to instill in them and in his mate must give him pride. The success of the hunt, which allows him to provide for his family, must bring him satisfaction. Humans are lucky: We have deprived dogs of their ability to feel these profound feelings where they belong, in the family den, and so they bring them to us. We are family for dogs, and we benefit from their loyalty, their courage, their joy at seeing us. The wolf father is filled with kindness toward his family. Is not another dimension of kindness a capacity for love? The family is surrounded by love (I see no reason to avoid the word, whether it be the wolf family or the human family greeted by its dogs).

A Wolf Says Farewell

Jim Brandenburg, a photographer for *National Geographic,* was working on a book, *White Wolf,* about wild wolves on Ellesmere Island, an untouched ecosystem in the northern Arctic.[5] At the end of the book, he describes how he was getting ready to leave this Arctic island, where he had been for months photographing the wolves who lived there. Just as he was loading the last of his equipment onto the plane, he noticed some movement at the distant end of the runway. He could hardly believe his eyes—it was the wolves, and not just the adults. They had brought the puppies the entire six miles with them. Could it possibly be coincidence that they had picked this day to take the pups on their first long-distance walk? "Surely it couldn't be happenstance—but the other conclusion, that they had come in some inexplicable way to say goodbye, seemed preposterous. All I know is that I found this gesture, whatever its origins, deeply moving. I still have a hard time even talking about it."

Almost all the major predators in North America, from mountain lions to grizzly bears, will occasionally attack a human, but wolves and orcas will not. Nobody entirely understands this mystery. I spoke earlier of the human fantasy of being raised by a wolf. While it may be a fantasy, it is based on a recognition of some deep psychological kinship. Is it just barely possible that a similar recognition is shared by wolves, that they regard us, too, as distant kin? Could it be that wolves sense something of our devotion to family, so similar to their devotion to the den? It is probably a question that can never be answered, but whether they know it or not, we have recently learned just how deeply similar wolf fathers and human fathers are. Human fathers, too, can know the delight of playing with their young, can lie side by side with an infant and feel the overwhelming contentment that comes with parental love. Some men may think it is "manly" to chafe at monogamy and grumble that we were not "made" to behave in this way, but that wolf we admire so much at the top of the hill, surveying his world, is about to descend to his den, where his life-long mate and his children await him. That is where his satisfaction is to be found. Are we so different?

THREE: Fine Fathers: Fish, Frogs, and Horses of the Sea

Most people find it difficult to identify with or to feel sympathy for fish. I suspect that this lack of compassion makes it easier for us to consume the billions of fish that are killed every year. Recently, I was observing Ligurian fishermen in a small village on the Italian Mediterranean coast haul in their nets and take out hundreds of gasping, writhing, dying fish, visibly in pain. When I asked the fishermen whether they thought these animals were suffering, they seemed astonished and perplexed by the question. I don't think it had occurred to them. How could it, when human culture is committed to the belief that fish feel no pain? I wondered when scientists who study fish were able to put this myth to rest. The great ichthyologist George Barlow, from the University of California at Berkeley, said that no scientist had ever doubted that fish felt pain, but they took it so for granted that they had never bothered to write about it. After all, the basic plan of the brain is similar in fish and humans, as are the neuronal pathways for pain. Scientists have even discovered endomorphins in fish, opiate-like substances released by the body to decrease painful sensations. The fact that fish have this mechanism to deal with pain suggests that they feel it. Whether this pain is accompanied by anything like subjective awareness is of course another matter.

People who fish for sport do seem to acknowledge that fish feel pain. When they catch a fish they either unhook it and throw it back in the water, or, if they plan to keep it, they often will render it unconscious by holding it by the tail and whacking it against the side of the boat—an act that seems cruel and that I find horrible in itself, but that is presumably meant to keep the fish from feeling the writhing agony of a death out of water. Patrick Bateson, from Cambridge University, pointed out in an article published in 1991 that fish are complex, long-lived animals who possess highly efficient mechanisms for avoiding injury. "For instance, some fish respond by flight when they encounter substances released from the damaged epidermal cells of fish similar to themselves," which certainly implies that they recognize injury and that they are aware that they, too, are subject to it. This is an altogether remarkable discovery (made by a Japanese scientist, T. J. Hara,[1] in 1986).

Humans are not exactly indifferent to fish. The number of fish tanks in American households is enormous, and fish are almost as popular as dogs and cats and birds as pets. What does it mean to have a fish as a pet? For some people with aquariums, it is no more than having a piece of the natural world, or rather something that is meant to simulate the natural world, in the background, that gives them, they say, a feeling of peace and tranquillity. People who like to watch fish are probably not the same people who like to kill them, although they may be the same people who eat them. Commercial fishermen, on the other hand, the last "gatherers of food from the wild," as the writer Mark Kurlansky calls them in his fascinating study *Cod: A Biography of the Fish That Changed the World,* probably are not terribly curious about the inner life of fish.

I have never entirely understood the psychological basis for the common legend, widespread in Europe, that fishes reach a biblical age. But I wonder if it does not have something to do with our hesitation about the ease with which we kill fish. Some fish do, in fact, live a very long life: Carp and pike, for example, can live to eighty years of age. (The elders of the cathedral in Mannheim, Germany, claimed not long ago to have found a pike that weighed 600 pounds, was 12 feet long, and died at the age of 267!) Why people should find it eerie to take the life of an animal who can live this long is puzzling, when you consider that every fish caught has its natural life span shortened considerably. I spoke with Donald Griffin about this. Among his many achievements is the discovery of bat sonar (which led to the discovery of dolphin sonar). He told me that in the 1930s (as I write this in 1999, he is a vivacious man of eighty-three) he caught bats and banded them. These were very small animals, 7 grams (about a quarter of an ounce), and it was just assumed they did not live very long. In fact, in captivity bats do not live very long. But he was astonished in the 1950s to catch the same bats he had banded twenty years earlier! This was the first time anybody became aware of just how long bats in the wild live— at least twenty years, and possibly longer. Somehow a fish like the goby from the Philippines, the smallest fish in the world, who lives less than a year, engenders less guilt when it is caught from the sea than a sheatfish, who, undisturbed, lives for almost a century.

Whether we can agree that fish have an inner life or not, scientists are coming to recognize just how complex they are.[2] One of the most interesting fish traits is that they can be very devoted fathers. Some people find it unnerving to be told that fish make good parents. Who wants to eat a solicitous father or a caring mother?

There are more than twenty-five thousand living fish species in the world, constituting more than one-half of all recognized vertebrate species. Aristotle (384-322 B.C.) attempted to organize fish phylogenetically, dividing them into cartilaginous fish, such as sharks, rays, and other marine hunters, as opposed to bony fish, the far more numerous fish who have skeletons of bone and gas-filled bladders that keep them afloat. This division is still in use today.

In at least 61 of the 418 families of bony fish, the males take care of their young alone or along with their mates.[3] One particularly impressive feature of fish parenting is the phenomenon of mouthbrooding. It occurs in a large number of fish that inhabit marine, brackish, and fresh water. Males (or females, depending on the species) hold the eggs in their mouths, give birth to the fry there, and carry them around the first few weeks of life. When I was living in Bali, we had a pond filled with large Japanese carp. From a distance, I could see the father fish swimming on one side of the pond and his babies on the other. If I approached too quickly, and the father sensed danger, he would race to the side of the pond where his fry were, just as they would be racing in his direction; he would open his mouth very wide, and in would swim the fry. With his mouth closed, he would swim frantically about the pond searching for stragglers, and when he found them, would suck them in. When I walked away, as soon as I was a sufficient distance to convince the father his young were safe, he would open his mouth and out would swim the babies. I wondered how often he would perform this fatherly duty, but did not have the heart to test him. I am sure I would have tired before he did, since for him it was a matter of life and death, for me merely a means of satisfying my curiosity.

Normally the fry of mouthbrooders also spend the night in their father's mouth, as in the *Geophagus jurupari,* a New World mouthbrooding cichlid (a kind of tropical freshwater fish). In many cichlids who are substrate breeders, which means that they lay their eggs on the bottom of the ocean, the father or both parents fan the eggs for weeks with their pectoral fins, making certain that the eggs receive sufficient oxygen and are kept clean. Watching this, one is struck by the concentration brought to the task. It is very serious business. Mouthbrooders achieve the same goal by a continual churning movement of the mouth, which brings the bottom eggs to the surface into the current of fresh water being drawn into the mouth, providing a constant supply of oxygen and the means to wash them free of waste material. Mouthbrooding may have evolved as the easiest way to avoid egg predation; after all, where could a small fish be more safe than inside its parent's mouth? Or it may have evolved because of a lack of suitable surfaces on which to attach the eggs, as is often the case in the open ocean. These conditions are known to scientists as "selection pressures" and could dictate the change from one way of protecting young (or even giving birth) to another.

There are numerous ways evolution has adapted the anatomy and physiology of fish for mouthbrooding. Some male mouthbrooders have special mucous cells in the oral epithelium, the tissue lining in the mouth, which increase during brooding and function as a lubricant. Another mouthbreeder, *Tilapia melanotheron,* never coughs, which is something nonparental fish do frequently because of irritation of the buccal (cheek or mouth) membranes. It has been suggested that the mucus prevents the irritation. Coughing, of course, would result in the expelling of the contents of the mouth, in this case, the fry, and then they would have to be retrieved. These fish stop eating while they have the offspring in their mouths, while the fry use the parental mouth as a food source, feasting on the tiny particles flushed in. The parental fish manage to avoid yawning as well, or, rather, they yawn without opening their mouths. The jaws are stretched, but their mouths remain closed. Swallowing, too, is carefully controlled. Once the young are born, they begin to breathe and swim within the parental mouth.

I found myself fascinated by mouthbrooding, and so, apparently, are others. Ichthyologists complain that the scientific interest in it exceeds its actual frequency among fishes. What makes mouthbrooding so compelling is that perhaps it represents a closeness that is more than we humans can achieve. All parents wish to protect their children from the dangers of the outside world. Mouthbrooding seems the perfect protective device.

Animal scientists who observe fish have a thesis that male fish are willing to be good fathers only when they can be certain that they are genetically related to the fry—that the fry are their children, and not the children of any other male fish. This is what animal behaviorists call piscine paternity certainty. Because the environment in which fish live is always wet, where eggs and sperm, once released from the body, do not dry up, it is easy for fish to fertilize eggs outside the female body. Among the sixty-one families of bony fishes in which care is given biparentally or by males alone, fertilization is external in all but one. Because the male sees the eggs, and fertilizes them directly, he can be absolutely certain that the resulting offspring are his own. He need not guess that the children are his, he knows it; he cannot be "tricked" into caring for the offspring of another male, and this encourages him to participate in their care. The general theory, one I find myself resisting, is that when a male cannot be so certain, he may be inclined to desert the young.

In fish, this theory certainly seems to make sense. However, what seems to make sense is not always what is true. A criticism of this hypothesis has been offered by Jeffrey Baylis of the department of zoology at the University of Wisconsin. His argument is based on the gonad size of fish. The more sperm, the larger the gonads. The more competition to inseminate females, the more important would be large gonads with much sperm. If there is not so much competition, one can expect to find small gonads. A male who fertilizes eggs internally is always competing with other males to be the fish who inserts the most sperm, thereby assuring his fatherhood. He can never be certain, however, and is always in competition. Males who fertilize eggs externally do not have to worry about competition, since they know that they are the fathers of the eggs they are fertilizing; it is right before their eyes. These fish, then, should have smaller gonads, because the lack of competition necessitates less sperm. But according to experts, exactly the opposite relationship has been found in fishes. Perhaps fish are less concerned with paternity certainty than the scientists who study them.

Do fish fathers think about what they do, can they have conscious experiences, especially when faced with a choice? The hard scientists say no, or at least that we cannot know. But the founder of ethology, Konrad Lorenz, thought differently, and his openness to these sorts of questions must account in part for his popularity with general readers. Thus in his book *King Solomon's Ring,* Lorenz tells of being astonished by what he observed in a jewel fish. He noticed that a pair of jewel fishes were retrieving their young for the evening, putting them in a nesting hollow over which the mother was hovering. Lorenz had forgotten to feed the fish that day, and they were ravenously hungry. The moment that Lorenz entered his laboratory late at night, he found the father frantically trying to retrieve truant fry into the nest. Lorenz dropped part of an earthworm into the tank. The fish swam up and grabbed the worm and was in the process of chewing it when he saw one of his babies swimming by itself on the other side of the tank. He raced after it, and took it into his mouth. But now the worm and the baby were both in his mouth. What would he do? One belonged in his stomach, the other in his nest. Lorenz was sure the baby would be devoured. But lo and behold, the fish stood still, his cheeks full: "If ever I have seen a fish think, it was in that moment! . . . For many seconds the father jewel fish stood riveted and one could almost see how his feelings were working." He found an ingenious solution: He spat out both the worm and the baby, and both fell to the bottom (the swim bladders of these cichlids contract when swallowed and they can be deposited like little stones into the hollow nests their parents make for them at night). He ate the worm, then inhaled his baby, and carried it home to its mother and its safe den. Lorenz and his students, who witnessed the whole event, applauded as one.[4]

Clearly Lorenz and his students believed that the fish was, in fact, deliberating, making a conscious choice to protect his baby. Why are we so reluctant to believe this? Partly because we see such a small section of the total behavior of fish in the wild, or of any animal, for that matter. (Is it possible that what Lorenz saw was the result of the fish being kept in an aquarium? It seems unlikely.) So we are used to seeing "average" behavior, and because it all begins to look alike, we think of it as being preprogrammed. But the same is true of human behavior: Notable instances of compassion, sympathy, or empathy are not seen every day. We have a tendency not to believe what is not in our direct everyday experience. What Lorenz observed, if indeed it was natural behavior, could not have been a unique event. He was just lucky enough to have been there at the right time to observe it. (Of course, this is an argument used by people who study infanticide among animals to suggest that the actual incidence is much higher than what is observed, but my argument for individual choice still stands.) We simply cannot know how many individual acts of heroism occur in the world of the fish. One father may flee at the approach of a predator, leaving his fry on their own. Another might fight the larger fish or put his own life in danger by wasting precious time letting his fry swim into his mouth. Can we be certain that there is no choice in the matter? Can we even be certain that consciousness is not involved? When we enfold our child in our arms when she is afraid, is this less an act of compassion because we did it so quickly, "automatically," as it were? If it is only later that we have the leisure to think back on the experience and understand her fear, who are we to decree that the paternal fish might not be capable of such reflection as well?

Is Fathering Instinctive?

In an early paper, Nikolas Tinbergen, who won the Nobel Prize in medicine in 1976, writes about what he calls "the curious behavior of the stickleback."[5] For Tinbergen and his colleagues, this little fish became what the rat is to many American psychologists. Tinbergen was particularly interested in the sex life of the three-spined stickleback *(Gasterosteus aculeatus),* and as it turns out, the stickleback is a particularly attentive father. Sticklebacks mate in early spring in shallow fresh waters. Each male stakes out his own territory, which he defends vigorously. Then he builds a nest by burrowing into the sand, lining the nest with algae and weeds, which he coats with a sticky substance he excretes from his kidneys, and making a small exit tunnel. Once the nest is complete, something odd happens to the male: He changes colors. He is normally a dull gray. Now his stomach becomes a bright red and his back turns bluish white. He is ready to court. He shows the female his beautiful colors (including his new blue eyes) as he slowly makes his way back to his nest. In this way he entices a female to examine it. Once she enters, he prods her tail with his nose, which causes her to lay her eggs. She then leaves the nest, and he quickly glides in and fertilizes the clutch. Then he finds another female and repeats the whole procedure. When he has up to five clutches in his nest, he watches over the eggs and fans water over them to enrich their supply of oxygen. He looks after them like this for several weeks. When the young hatch, he cares for them, keeping the brood together, pursuing stragglers, and bringing them back to the nest in his mouth.

The freshwater three-spined stickleback is a fine father. But Tinbergen was reluctant to concede this or even to think in such terms. He called the complicated pattern we have just examined "purely instinctive and automatic": The males protect and take care of their young because they have been instinctively primed to do so, not because they want to, and certainly not because they "love" their young. How did Tinbergen reach this conclusion? In his studies of instinct, he saw definite evidence that "red" (which normally signals the arrival of a competing male) was a flag for the aggression of the male. So much was this true, he wrote, that "even a red mail van passing our windows at a distance of 100 yards could make the males in the tank charge its glass side." In other words, the fish did not really see a rival, he just saw the color red, and was so primed to attack by instinct that he did so in spite of the red color belonging to a neutral van. To the mind of a scientist, aggression and love are similar, in that if an instinct triggers one, then it must trigger the other. The argument can then be made that if aggression is purely instinctive, so is love, care, sympathy, and concern. But we should remember that this oft-quoted example of purely instinctive behavior is taking place in an unnatural environment: a laboratory for which the stickleback was not evolved. Imagine studying natural human behavior inside a glass prison. In the real world that the stickleback normally inhabits, a red object coming at him is indeed another stickleback, perhaps coming to cannibalize his fry. He had better pay attention. Mail vans are rare in stream beds, but enemy fish are common. The red mail van does not only cause the fish to prepare for a fight, it also induces the good father stickleback to seek out his fry and suck them into his mouth, where they are safe. Both behaviors are based on instinct, but the fact that something is instinctive does not necessarily rule out feelings that accompany the instinct, nor need it mean that there is no variation and no choice involved.

I am not arguing here that we can safely ignore the fact that all animals have been evolved over generations to behave in a certain way. Surely deep inside the fish's brain, the significance of a red belly remains embedded over thousands of generations. I am reminded of an extraordinary observation by the great Harvard biologist Ernst Mayr.[6] In a population of sticklebacks on the Olympic Peninsula, in the Pacific northwest, the normal red color on the bellies of this fish have disappeared. This is because they are regularly attacked by a black predatory fish. As a defense, they have developed a blackish protective coloration, making it more difficult for the enemy to discover the male stickleback and his fry. Even in nuptial plumage, the male sticklebacks are black-bellied. Female sticklebacks, normally choose as a mate the fish with the brightest red belly. But here they have no choice. So, in the absence of other colors, they spawn normally in the nests of these black-bellied males. This population is now four to eight thousand years old. But somewhere in their central nervous system, the females have retained a somatic memory of the excitement of a red belly. If they are given the choice, in an aquarium experiment, they will choose the red-bellied males five to one over their less flamboyant black-bellied cousins. The males need to live, and cannot do so if they are red (since their predators will find them far too easily). Females adjust to this situation, but their "natural" behavior still lurks somewhere in their piscine atavistic memory.

We have, unfortunately, inflicted severe suffering on animals in experiments to discover what makes them depressed. For example, removing a child from a nurturing primate mother will cause her to become sad, sometimes terminally so. Nobody has thought to inflict this pointless experiment (I say it is pointless because we could figure out the results from common sense) on a male stickleback fish. But I have little doubt that if he were thwarted often enough in protecting and caring for his young, he might well survive, but it would be at enormous cost. He evolved to take care of his children; it is what he is meant to do.

We are not stickleback fish, but we are not completely unlike stickleback fish. We, too, have long memories. Human fathers did not evolve to spawn children and then walk away from them. It can be done. It happens, and far be it from me to suggest that we are less than human (being less than human is hardly an insult to me) when we do so, but we should not forget that to do so is always at a cost.

When scientists like Tinbergen argue that the entire behavioral repertoire of a fish is instinctive, they usually insist at the same time that these acts cannot be accompanied by emotions or ties of affection, say, between one fish and another or between parent fish and their young. I find this unconvincing. Consider the symbiotic relationship between a cleaner shrimp and its host, one that has fascinated ethologists for decades. The cleaner removes debris from inside the fish's mouth, picks its teeth clean, and performs other sanitary functions with impunity. Hans Hediger, for many years the head of the Basle Zoo, in Switzerland, raised a grouper in a tank by itself for six years, by which time the fish was four feet in length and accustomed to snapping up anything dropped into its tank. But when Hediger dropped a tiny live cleaner into the grouper's tank, the grouper not only failed to snap up the cleaner but opened his mouth and permitted the cleaner free entry and exit.

For the Lorenz-Tinbergen school of ethology, the paternal behavior of the male three-spined stickleback is a perfect example of purely instinctive behavior. But is it not possible that *even a fish* can develop affection for another fish to whom it is bound by ties of paternity or mutual benefits, as in these cleaner fish and their hosts? Of course it is to the genetic advantage of the stickleback to protect its young and bring back strays with his mouth, just as it is to the genetic advantage of the cleaner fish to service its host. But maybe along the way, over thousands of generations, it was also advantageous or adaptive for the fish to become fond of its host or children. If we see no apparent reaction in a fish to the removal of its young, we should pause before we so smugly assert that it is completely indifferent. After all, it evolved, exactly as we did, to feed and protect its young. Why would cherishing them as well be out of the question? We may not see it any more than we can see the female's longing for her original red-bellied lover. But it may well be there. Buried, perhaps, but not absent.

The Dance of the Sea Horse

Mouthbrooding is remarkable, but when it comes to being a father, there is no animal that can rival the sea horse. There are thirty-five kinds of sea horses, ranging from the thumb-sized "sea ponies," which live in the Gulf of Mexico, to the fourteen-inch giants of the eastern Pacific. But with all of them, it is the male who becomes pregnant. Yes, the male becomes pregnant, the only male animal that does so, and it is a real pregnancy, closely resembling human pregnancy. This occurs only after a long courtship. Amanda Vincent was able to show that male and female sea horses of an Australian species *(Hippocampus whitei)* are sexually faithful to one another in ways that would not be expected of a fish. Every morning as the sun rises they greet each other with an elaborate dance that lasts for six minutes. It is a reacquaintance ritual that is never absent. Both the male and the female sea horse change colors, from dull to bright orange (a kind of sea horse blushing) as they dance, often clinging with their tails to the stalks of waving seaweed that serve as their dens. One possible explanation for this behavior is that it may help the female determine when the male is ready to become pregnant. Just as mammalian males sniff the air around a female's genitals to learn from the chemical substances known as pheromones when she is ready to conceive, the female sea horse may have subtle methods of learning the hormonal and emotional state of her partner during the gentle dance.

The male sea horse has a small pouch on his stomach. When the female decides that conditions in this pouch are ideal, and that her partner is ready, she presses her belly against her partner and inserts what looks like a penis, her ovipositor, into the brood pouch on his abdomen and offloads her eggs into it. This is a prosaic description from somebody who has never seen the act (me). Listen to Amanda Vincent, who has observed it hundreds of times:

> As they ascend, the sea horses face each other with their tails bent back, and the female inserts her ovipositor into the open pouch of the male and releases her eggs in a long, sticky string. To transfer the whole clutch—which, depending on the size of the species, ranges from tens to many hundreds of eggs—takes only about six seconds, and then the pouch opening is sealed shut. The pair break apart, and the male gently sways to settle the eggs in his pouch. Both then settle down on the bottom with their tails wrapped around holdfasts. Each time I watch, I am newly astonished at the beauty and uniqueness of this graceful courtship and mating.[7]

The female leaves, and the father sea horse takes over. He seals his pouch, and over the next few weeks he carefully monitors conditions in it, providing oxygen and transferring nutrients as needed. He even secretes prolactin, the very same hormone that stimulates milk production in human women.[8] He is definitely pregnant by any definition of that term. Generally, the sea horse gives birth to a few dozen young, but one hero, James from the Caribbean, gave birth in his pouch—which held only half a tablespoon in volume—to 1,572 babies! After several weeks, they emerge one after another, in little explosive charges from the male tail, as fully formed, independent tiny sea foals. Once they leave his pouch, these miniature horses return to the male's nursery (a kind of oceanic playpen), where he feeds them with secretions from his pouch until they are big enough to find their own food. It is not clear if they ever see their mother. It appears that her duties ended when she handed over her eggs to her faithful partner.

I don't think there has ever been a male living with a pregnant woman who does not wonder what it feels like to be pregnant. Some, I am sure, go so far as to wish they could, like the sea horse, become pregnant themselves. Male envy of the female ability to give birth, to create life, to nourish it in her own body, is profound. Perhaps nothing on earth strikes us with such awe as pregnancy and birth. It is a mystery that of all species on earth, only the tiny sea horse has overcome whatever barriers evolution has placed in the way of male pregnancy. Perhaps a cult of the male sea horse is long overdue. Among its sacraments, men could do worse than to learn to imitate the early-morning dance ritual, greeting the sun and their spouses with delicate steps that tell them both good morning and how wonderful it is to see them.

Frogs

The physical anthropologist Frederick Hulse once said that humans are so profoundly mammalian in all observable structures that anthropomorphic explanations of mammalian behavior are less rash than similar explanations of the activity of snakes, snails, or spiders would be. In other words, we can see ourselves, or aspects of ourselves, in other mammals, especially in the great apes. He claims that people frequently establish empathetic relationships with other mammals, somewhat less with birds, and apparently *never* with fish or frogs.[9] I don't know about this. Since childhood I have found frogs fascinating to watch, and I think many children are transfixed when they are able to observe the transformation of a tadpole into a small frog (the change is usually rapid, a few days, but the green frog and the bullfrog may not change from tadpole to frog for one or two years). It is this metamorphosis, from aquatic to terrestrial (this is the reason we call frogs amphibians, not because they move back and forth between water and land), that, far from repulsing children, enchants them, corresponding, perhaps, to their own ideas of transforming or remaking themselves. This enchantment makes children feel friendly and attracted toward frogs; they find them beautiful. It was Voltaire who said, "Ask a toad what is beauty . . . he will answer that it is the female with two great round eyes coming out of her little head, her flat mouth, her yellow belly, and brown back." And Voltaire had not even seen the dazzling red-eyed tree frog *(Agalychnis callidryas)* from Central America, with spectacular vermilion eyes (with dark vertical pupils similar to those of a cat), a neon-green back, blue-striped flanks, cream-colored underside, and orange toe pads, who lives her gentle and nocturnal life as high as fifty feet above the ground in the trees of the tropical rain forests of Costa Rica. Alas, children are rarely consulted when harmful prejudices originate, and throughout the ages, frogs have been ill-served. It was the Swedish scientist Carolus Linnaeus who coined the term *Amphibia* for use in his new system of nomenclature, characterizing frogs as "abhorrent because of their cold body, pale color, cartilaginous skeleton, filthy skin, fierce aspect, calculating eye, offensive smell, harsh voice, squalid habitation, and terrible venom; and so their Creator has not exercised his powers to make many of them." In his charming book, *Frogs,* David Badger quotes this abusive catalogue and comments that "in that last bit of theological twaddle, Linnaeus was sorely mistaken. At last count, approximately 3,975 different species of frogs and toads have been identified worldwide."[10]

Very little, if anything, was known about the biology or behavior of frogs and toads (all toads are frogs, but generally the term "toad" is used for species with square bodies and dry, warty skin) until fairly recently. Even the fact that frogs hibernate in winter by burying themselves in mud was not known (the eminent Aristotle proposed that frogs were procreated from the mud). It was believed, right into the nineteenth century, for example, that frogs and toads could survive for centuries in stone or in the trunks of trees. In fact, gray tree frogs can withstand temperatures as low as minus 20 degrees Fahrenheit by manufacturing glycerol, an antifreeze ingredient, in their blood. When found frozen in blocks of ice, they thaw out and survive. Even the best informed and the least credulous of early observers believed in the therapeutic qualitites of the toadstone. The beautiful, gleaming eye of the toad was supposed to be an outward sign of the inward luster of the toad's jewel, supposedly concealed in his or her head.

In Pieter Brueghel the Elder's sixteenth-century painting *Seven Deadly Sins,* frogs are represented as obscene animals. That they are a common delicacy in France and elsewhere (the United States alone imports more than 1.25 million pounds of frog legs each year from Bangladesh, Southeast Asia, Australia, and New Zealand) does not encourage empathy in the popular mind. The Brothers Grimm tale "The Frog King" also has a dark underside, which we find explicitly recognized in Anne Sexton's poem "The Frog Prince," in which her father's genitals are compared to a frog. Dart-poison frogs are, of course, dangerous to handle, and most species of frogs and toads harbor at least a trace of poison in their glands. Skin rashes from handling frogs are not uncommon, although it is not true that frogs cause warts. No doubt, too, the frog's place as the victim par excellence in all high-school dissection classes has contributed to the ambivalence with which it is regarded today.

Most people would be skeptical if you told them that many frogs make attentive, careful, and devoted parents. But they do. Parental care has been documented in most frog families and in many frog species. You would probably encounter even greater skepticism if you put forward the thesis that male frogs can be very involved fathers. But it is nonetheless a fact that has been extensively studied. I don't believe that the unusual mating system among frogs accounts for the high percentage of paternal behavior, but fatherly behavior in frogs must have some explanation. Even some scientists, and certainly people in general, believe that frog mating is a very simple matter—again, totally instinctive: "If it is not small enough to eat or large enough to eat you, and doesn't put up a squawk about it, mate with it." (Sounds very male!) But in recent years we have learned more about the complexity of frog social behavior, especially their mating systems.

For most species of frogs, breeding takes place in water. The frogs migrate to their ancestral breeding ponds, using a navigation method that is still incompletely understood. The males croak during the night, to attract the females to their breeding sites. Of course, the choruses of frogs are themselves not without complications. When many male frogs group together to chorus, is it because they derive the benefit of easier mating, or because of the lower risk of being attacked by a predator? Some smaller frogs who are not very good at calling may just hang out in these groups hoping to intercept some unsuspecting female. When the female arrives, and exercises her choice (usually seeking out the loudest males; interestingly, mate choice can be demonstrated in female bullfrogs but not in female wood frogs),[11] the mating takes place, on the territory of the male. The male mounts the female, head to head, and the thumbs of the male swell into what are called his "nuptial pads," the better to grasp her slippery body. The clasping lasts anywhere from a few hours to weeks or even months—no doubt the longest mating act in the entire animal world.[12] Why it should take so long is not clear to me. Since male frogs lack a penis, fertilization is external: When the female frog extrudes eggs from her genital cavity at the end of her intestinal canal, the male releases sperm from his cloaca, covering and thereby fertilizing the eggs. What happens next depends on the type of frog.

In many frog species, the female, much like the sea horse, has now finished her maternal task, whereas the male has just begun his. Darwin was fascinated when he learned that the males of a species of tiny frog he discovered in southern Chile (and named the Darwin frog, *Rhinoderma darwini*) brood their young internally. Just two South American frogs do this. This is similar to the pregnancy of the male sea horse, although not a true pregnancy. When the female (sometimes more than one) of these species lays her twenty or thirty eggs, the male guards them for a few weeks. Then, with his tongue, he picks them up and seems to ingest them. But really he has only taken them into his large vocal sac, which swells like a balloon when he croaks, where they develop. In his mouth, they hatch into tadpoles and continue to grow, taking nourishment from their father's mouth. Eventually they metamorphose into tiny froglets, ready to jump out of their father's mouth, as fully formed as the sea foals who pop out of the abdomen of the male sea horse, able to manage their existence without the help of any adult frog. Researchers from the University of Chile captured several males bearing larvae in their vocal sacs. One of the males, they thought, was dead, and they squeezed eight live tadpoles out of him. But the next morning they found the father alive and well, and two of the tadpoles were back in his sac![13]

The male midwife toad is also pressed into paternal service, carrying strings of eggs around his legs, sometimes from more than one female, keeping them constantly moist with secretions from his porous skin, and then releasing the tadpoles into ponds when they hatch. The Australian pouched frog has an easier time: The tadpoles wriggle into the brood pouches on his flanks and later emerge as tiny froglets. There are species of frogs in New Zealand and Costa Rica in which the tadpoles wriggle onto their father's back, and he takes them on a journey that can last several days, until they reach the right body of water, where they can safely grow.

The male bullfrog is a particularly devoted father. He protects his tadpoles against enemies often many times his size. I saw one devoted bullfrog dad fearlessly chase away a poisonous snake ten times his size. I watched him shepherd his children, several thousand of them, into a small pond, where he remained in attendance, guarding them against the many dangers that threaten tadpoles. A few days later, the late-summer sun was quickly drying up the water in which they had been brought to safety and threatened to bake them. Their exemplary father used his snout, jaws, and powerful hind legs to dig a channel that allowed water to flow in and permitted the tadpoles to escape from the heat into deeper cool water. In spite of the care they receive from the male, however, or the female, few (less than a dozen) baby bullfrogs on average survive infancy. On the other hand, when we realize that a female bullfrog lays from six to twenty thousand eggs in a single clutch, it does not take much to achieve reproductive success, the goal of every animal, from frogs to humans.

In observations of a terrestrial-breeding microhylid frog from the mountainous moss forests of northeastern New Guinea, the *Cophixalus parkeri,* one parent remains close to its eggs during the 85–100–day prehatching period. In 86 percent of 72 clutches examined in detail, the male was the attending parent. In the remaining 14 percent of the clutches, females were with the eggs. The froglets remained with whichever parent took care of them for the full thirty- to forty-day period of absorption of the abdominal yolk mass. Newly hatched froglets sit on top of their father or mother. But the parents never stay together and have never been observed with the same clutch of eggs.

Recently, we have come to have a new respect for frogs, not for their extraordinary devotion as parents, but because we see them as harbingers of our own possible doom. Already the golden toad and the gastric brooding frog have disappeared completely and are presumed extinct. Much like the proverbial miner's canary, we focus on what the disappearance, death, or disease of these animals means to humans. The increased exposure of frogs' eggs to the ultraviolet radiation associated with the thinning of the ozone layer has significantly increased the mortality rate of frogs' eggs and therefore of frogs. But in an even broader sense, it is general environmental degradation that is causing the decline of frogs. This is a harbinger of terrible catastrophes looming for humans as well. The great herpetologist William E. Duellman says that "the loss of so many species not only affects the overall stability of ecosystems, but brings to an end evolutionary lineages that have survived for millions of years. The magnitude of such a loss is immeasurable."[14]

But I agree with a recent comment by the distinguished naturalist Edward Hoagland, author of *Tigers and Ice,* in which he reminds us that we should be worried for the sake of the animal itself, and not just for what it tells us about our own species. It is striking to learn about pregnant male sea horses, and discover the extraordinary devotion of South American male frogs. It is a good thing for human fathers to see the vast diversity of paternal behavior in the natural world. It is good to simply know that it exists, to learn about it, to honor the people who have brought this kind of knowledge back from the jungles and forests and oceans of the world. Immersing ourselves in the world of sea horses, mouthbrooding fish, and caring amphibians is a way of reminding us of what is essential in our own lives, but it is also a reminder that there is a larger world outside of us where many other species have faced the same kinds of problems we have, and often come up with novel solutions. We can imitate them, we can salute them, and we can just plain admire them.

I wonder about the fishes who guard their young in their mouths, and the frogs who worry about the sun being too hot for their little ones, and about the sea horse who herds his little foals into his corral in the evening—I wonder to what extent we are like them in our concerns about family and parenting and love. Like these fish and amphibians, we, too, evolved to have powerful emotions around what is important in our lives, especially when it comes to our children. The centers in our brain in which our emotions originate are remarkably old, "primitive," and not unlike those of these "lower animals." The term that biologists use to describe instances of identical behavior evolving in different species is "convergence." However, I think it is not mere convergence that humans and other animals love their children beyond everything else. I find it somehow comforting, as well as humbling, to see that, as different as we are, I have this in common with wild horses of the sea and pipefish and Darwin frogs.

FOUR: Dangerous Fathers: Lions, Langurs, and Bears

Franz Kafka, widely considered with James Joyce and Marcel Proust to be among the three most significant writers of the twentieth century, thought his father was a beast. But what kind of a beast? "It was just a metaphor," the literary critics tell us. I believe it was more than that. "Beasts" of every kind play a major role in Kafka's writings and the reason is not difficult to understand. His father, the formidable Hermann Kafka, was in the habit of using derogatory animal terms for his son. Kafka, a vegetarian who loved animals, fought back in the only way he knew: with words. His ultimate victory was assured when he wrote one of the greatest indictments of bad child-rearing in the history of literature, the "Letter to His Father" (*Brief an den Vater*, better translated, in my opinion, as "Letter to My Father"), in effect accusing his father of being the Abraham who really *did* want to murder his son, and not because God told him to. By writing about animals in his later work, Franz Kafka was able to explore the darkest and deepest aspects of human existence. But he clearly did not know about the reality of animal fathers.

We've probably all asked someone we know, "What was your dad like?" If the response is not often as eloquent as Kafka's, it is still not uncommonly, "He was pretty bad." Though we may want to learn the details, to know in what particular ways he was bad, we all have an idea of what a rotten father is. A bad father can be a father who is simply not there, or if he is, nonetheless has no time for you. If he refuses to provide food or shelter, is jealous of you, or verbally assaults you, beats you, sexually abuses you, or tries to kill you, we don't have trouble calling him a bad father. A human father can at some point reflect back on his life and think: "I was a miserable father" or "I was a complete failure as a father" or just wonder whether he was a good father, and how his children will come to think of him when they are adults, looking back on their childhood.

When it comes to animals, we do not consider this capacity for reflection to be part of their behavior. We do not believe elephants, bears, lions, or chimps can look back on how they behaved toward their young and feel remorse or a sense of failure. To speak of bad fathers among animals is problematic. Is not what animals do, by definition, natural? If all behavior in nature is the same as "natural" behavior, then how can natural behavior be considered bad? It is perfectly true that animal fathers can be absent, they can be neglectful, they can be dangerous, they can even be murderous. But we believe that the animals have little choice. It is a given of animal science that few animals can be other than who they are. We think of them as being hardwired, genetically programmed. So it is not surprising when an animal father is absent, since absenteeism is the most common form of fatherhood among mammals. The situation is different in fish, and even frogs, as we have seen, but most mammalian fathers are simply not there. We automatically assume that this absence is "natural," part of what it means to be that particular animal.

Elephants

I cannot help wondering, though, whether some of this absence is not imposed on the male by a wary female. Consider the example of elephants. I am a firm believer in the complexity of the inner life of an elephant.

Enough evidence exists to convince me, and many others, that elephants can feel forms of love that are remarkably like those displayed by members of our own species. The following observation was made by Katy Payne and her research partners while they were watching an elephant herd at a man-made watering trough:

> A very young calf fell into the deep end of the slanted trough and gave a wild bellowing scream. Instantly an aunt and two siblings ran to the calf's aid. They had just filled their mouths with water but had not yet swallowed it; as they ran, water gushed out of their mouths as if they were fire hydrants. Falling on their knees beside the frightened calf (who stood upright with her head, trunk, and shoulders exposed), they reached their trunks under her belly to try to lift her out. As they struggled, their screams, bellows, and rumbles were added to hers. Instantly more help came out of the forest. From an observation tower that we had erected near the trough, we'd been surveying the local wildlife all morning and had not noticed the thirteen mature female elephants who now ran forward and drew the infant with their trunks to the shallow end of the trough. Safe and pampered, she clambered out amid a pandemonium of reassuring rumbles.[1]

This is compassionate behavior, similar to (if not even more than) what one would expect from members of our own species. But note that all the major actors are females. Indeed, the elaborate inner life of elephants that we know about from the writings of the major researchers, Katy Payne, Cynthia Moss, Ian Douglas Hamilton, and Joyce Poole, revolve around females exclusively. The herd consists of families of related females and their preadult cubs, male and female. Once the males reach adolescence, they leave the herd and strike out on their own. For all intents and purposes, elephant cubs have no fathers, except in the purely biological sense. I am not certain why elephant society should have evolved in this manner, but I suspect it has something to with whether male care is necessary for elephant survival. It seems that an elephant father is simply not needed.

Full-grown elephants, male or female, have no natural enemies. They are too formidable and dangerous for any animal in the forest or the jungle to risk attacking them. Elephant babies are a different story: They must be constantly guarded against large carnivores—lions, tigers, and panthers. But they can be guarded by any adult (or even adolescent) elephant and remain safe. Elephants live in a warm matriarchal society, where brothers and sisters and aunts stay together in harmonious intimacy. The young are completely protected, unless, as rarely happens, they stray from the herd. What use could a father be in such a situation? He is not needed for gathering food, since elephants nurse for four years or more and are capable of feeding themselves soon after birth with plant life.

Moreover, as every elephant knows, the most dangerous animal in nature is a full-grown male elephant in musth. Musth is still imperfectly understood, and controversial: There are scientists who say it is nothing but rutting behavior similar to what we find in other ungulates, and there is another school that claims it is a phenomenon entirely independent of rutting. What is universally acknowledged is that a thick secretion, only very recently chemically examined, streams out of the temporal glands (an opening located midway between the eye and ear, which females possess as well) of the male elephant, rendering him wild by any standards, human or elephantine. In African elephants, only bulls over thirty years old come into musth, which can last two to three months. All animals, including other elephants, avoid these males, who are in what looks like a testosterone-driven psychosis. The male in musth is violent, unpredictable, and untrustworthy. No female, except one in estrus, wants such a male near her or her children. Since elephants continue to grow in size and weight for their entire lives, and since musth occurs in the oldest, hence biggest, elephants, and since females tend to choose these males to mate with, females in estrus do want to be around such males, albeit briefly.

It is telling that females select these males for the specific purpose of mating, but then seem to avoid them. As fathers, male elephants are not only not needed, they are not welcome. Females are simply too mistrustful of them. The extraordinary devotion of female elephants to the young in their families is legendary. It has been speculated that in the 1970–71 drought in Tsavo National Park in Kenya, many elephant cows died because they simply would not abandon their weak and starving calves to seek food for themselves, a kind of elephantine suicide. Because of such strong, lasting bonds, I do not find it surprising that unreliable males would be seen as a danger to the young.

I can think of little else that provides as much safety and satisfaction as belonging to an elephant family unit. Protection is certain, pleasures are manifold, including close physical contact among family members, and responsibilities are nil for many years. Both males and females experience this period of womb-like security. The female grows up to live forever in such an atmosphere, either in her natal herd, or, eventually, a herd of her own. But the adolescent male, when he is twelve to fourteen years old, begins to play more and more roughly, engaging in mock battles that seem to irritate the adult females. He is gradually but forcibly driven away from the family unit by the matriarch and other adult females, including his own mother. He follows the herd, but at an increasing distance. Eventually, he sets out on his own and thereafter winds up living most of his life as a solitary bull. Bulls rarely form any lasting companionship with each other. For short periods, the adolescent males will form gangs, and come together with other males, but by and large each male will spend most of its adult life in a solitary search for food and the rare opportunity to mate with a willing female. Such a life seems bleak in comparison with the warmth and comforts of life inside the herd.[2]

The common wisdom that elephants never forget—in other words, that they have excellent memories—is in fact accurate. Elephants remember well close relatives who have died. They delicately pore over the bones of the deceased, expressing obvious fascination and perhaps sorrow.[3] They seem to have the capacity to mourn. We have to wonder whether male elephants remember the mothers and aunts and sisters and brothers of their first ten to fifteen years, a time when they, like their sisters, lived in the midst of a warm, happy female family, and whether they mourn its loss.

From an evolutionary point of view, an elephant father may not be needed. But from an emotional point of view—and elephants are highly complex emotional creatures—elephant fathers lose out on the joys and rewards of family life. It appears that evolution does not necessarily care for happiness, as many scientists from Charles Darwin to Richard Dawkins frequently remind us.

Whales

Strangely enough (could size have anything to do with it?), the other species in which females play a lifelong role in the lives of their young is whales. Fathers have no part in caring for the young among cetaceans (whales, dolphins, and porpoises). In many species of whales, nursing is more prolonged than in any other animal, including humans. Short-finned pilot whales continue to lactate up to fifteen years after the birth of their last calf. The young of sperm whales, too, may suckle for ten to fifteen years. As with elephants, it is the matriarch killer whale who leads the pod. But in contrast to elephants, the males live with their mother, too, even after they are grown. I would hazard the speculation that male mammals who emigrate from home while their sisters stay (which is why biologists say that females in most species are philopatric, meaning that they have an urge to stay where they were born[4]), have a propensity for violence. Dolphins and sperm whales become independent at two years of age, but will stay in touch with their mothers for many more years, returning sometimes merely to suck at the breast (bottlenose dolphin calves nurse for three or four years normally, and sometimes much longer). Perhaps being in the mother's presence reduces an inclination to violence, or perhaps the prolonged nursing does this.

Female whales and possibly elephants are also the only animals besides humans to undergo menopause. Pilot whales can live up to sixty years, but the female ceases to ovulate after forty. Since she lactates up to fifteen years after the birth of her last calf, and the calf has normally stopped nursing, she is probably suckling other calves besides her own. No doubt, too, her wisdom is useful for all members of her extended family. The distinguished University of Michigan evolutionary biologist Richard Alexander, in his book *Darwinism and Human Affairs* and in his paper "How Did Humans Evolve? Reflections on the Uniquely Unique Species," points out that menopause in humans has nothing to do with the fact that women live longer now, the usual view. The maximum life span has not changed (despite medical progress) over the entire history of the human species. Premature mortality and accidental deaths affected the average human lifetime in earlier eras, "but the existing maximum life span is a product not of modern technology but of hominid evolution."[5] While menopause must have evolutionary significance—to help ensure that a mother will be alive to take care of her children—perhaps it is important in a spiritual sense as well, as a means of bringing wisdom about child care to a younger generation.

Bears

Elephants are absent fathers; they simply aren't there. But they are not dangerous fathers, perhaps only because they have never been given the opportunity to be dangerous. Bears, on the other hand, are dangerous fathers. I have never heard of an infanticidal elephant, but have read accounts of adult male bears who kill young bears. Male bears normally do not recognize their offspring, and are thus at least theoretically capable of killing and even eating their own young, something that is exceedingly rare in the animal world.

Bears have, as far as I know, almost no relation with their children and do nothing, ever, to make their lives or the lives of their mates any more comfortable, secure, or safe. Male bears seem indeed to be solitary, ill-tempered creatures when it comes to children. Every animal known wishes to spread its own genes and is eager to mate, and to mate successfully. Male bears, too, want to reproduce. But their contribution is limited basically to a brief copulation. How have female bears adapted to this?

Most animals cannot choose what strategies they use for survival. Evolution has chosen for them. Otherwise, they would all be conducting research on the best way to avoid becoming prey, and how to live well. Every animal species has devised some strategy to preserve the life of the individual and the lives of those closest to them, mates and children and often friends. Female lions, as we will see, devised a number of methods for avoiding infanticide by strange male lions who take over their pride. But the methods they found are hardly foolproof. Female bears, so I hypothesize, have fashioned a more clever strategy, one neatly adapted to their ecological niche: hibernation.

Bears are among the few animals who are not forced to hibernate, but choose to. Strictly speaking, the word "hibernation" should be reserved for those animals, such as bats, woodchucks, squirrels, marmots, and rodents, who go into profound, long-lasting winter sleep characterized by severe differences in body temperature. Since bears are easily aroused, and their body temperature remains the same, scientists who study bears prefer to use the term "dormancy" rather than hibernation.

An old Abnaki Indian sage once remarked that "a bear is wiser than man, because a man does not know how to live all winter without eating anything." Some scientists are troubled by evidence that bears elect to go into dormancy (they can postpone the time and even forego it entirely), since this implies that bears can consciously weigh information about their habitat, and perhaps even the state of their own bodies. And if they do this, then perhaps they are able to predict winter conditions based on cues in their environment. These are unsettling ideas for a traditionally trained animal behavior scientist. The generally held belief is that such behavior can only be the result of instinctive hard-wiring and not independent thought. In general, we like to reserve words like "choice" and "free will" exclusively for human use. We are, after all, the pinnacle of God's creation! Is it possible, though, that one of the factors female bears use to choose dormancy is their evaluation of the potential dangers posed by male bears at the time? I think it is possible.

Female bears often choose to den in areas that seclude them both from male bears and from humans, probably so that their

cubs won't be attacked. They often choose steep, sparsely vege-
tated, dry rocky areas, relatively inaccessible to hunters. Male
brown bears and male American black bears den too, but they do
so for less time, less than half the time of a pregnant female (male
polar bears do not hibernate at all, nor do nonpregnant females)
and never with females. Pregnant females den by early October
and emerge as late as the end of May. It is astonishing to learn
that some female bears hibernate for up to seven months without
activity, food, or water, and without urinating or defecating
(which is why bears are used as a model for the study of severe
renal failure in human beings), and that when they emerge, they
may remain in a state of semidormancy for up to another two
months, so that more than three-quarters of their life is passed in
some form of sleep. The bears eat indigestible material to form
an anal plug that lasts for the entire dormancy period.

Female bears are able to control the time when they give
birth. If for some reason—such as inadequate food supply—the
female is in poor condition, with insufficient fat reserves for her
pregnancy, she aborts by absorbing the blastocyst (the fertilized
ovum) into her body. Bear researchers have been able to predict
whether a black bear sow will give birth based on a correlation
between her body weight and implantation. Black bears breed
from mid-June to mid-July. But the implantation of the fertilized egg into the uterine mucus and growth of the embryo do
not occur until October. No doubt the reason for this is so that
the cubs can be born during the winter sleep. This usually occurs
in January, midway through the dormancy period of the female.

Although nobody has ever observed a birth in a den, it is
known that the female is not asleep during the birth (at other
times during dormancy, the sow is easily aroused and will attack
an intruder). At birth, the cubs are minuscule, weighing less
than a pound, measuring only eight inches long, and having no
fur at all. Blind, naked, and almost totally helpless, they are so

poorly developed that there has been a persistent folk belief that they leave the womb as undifferentiated lumps of flesh only to be licked into shape by their mothers. After the birth, she goes back to sleep, waking periodically to attend to the needs of her cubs, who spend their first months nursing and sleeping in comfort. Pregnant sows are the deepest hibernators, but become the lightest sleepers once the cubs are born. The cubs themselves do not go into anything resembling dormancy. Instead, they suckle and sleep, snuggled warmly against their mother's sparsely furred underside. While their mother sleeps, the cubs remain awake. As they nurse, they make a special humming sound, like a cat purring, a sound never heard at any other time. The mother licks the cubs to clean them and to stimulate them to defecate. She eats their feces, drinks the liquid they lose through urination, and positions herself to make it easy for them to nurse, guiding their little muzzles to her nipples even as she sleeps. The cubs grow quickly, and by the time they leave the den three months later, they weigh four to eight pounds. At six months, they already weigh between forty and eighty pounds.

We are fortunate to have the research of Lynn Rogers, whose official title is Wildlife Research Biologist with the North Central Forest Experiment Station in Ely, Minnesota, but to everyone else he is known simply as The Bearman. He earned this title by having lived with more individual black bears than anyone ever has before him. More myths about bears have been laid to rest through his work than through the work of any other researcher, in particular the portrait of the brooding, short-tempered aggressor. Instead, Rogers found that black bears are characterized much more by restraint than by ferocity, and that they soon learned to accept his presence without protest. He and his students have followed bears for the whole twenty-four hours of a day and have compiled the most reliable information ever recorded on black bear behavior.

Greg Wilker, one of his students, spent many hours around the clock with Patch and her two cubs in the bush at the southern edge of the Canadian Shield, in northern Minnesota. When the cubs and the mother emerged from the den in April or May, the mother would still live off her own fat for at least another week, even though she had lost up to a third of her body weight. This allowed her to give undivided attention to the cubs, and to make certain that their education could begin in earnest without concern for her own appetite. The cubs would play during the day just outside the entrance to the den, while their mother foraged in the vicinity. The cubs hurried into the den at the slightest sign of danger and their mother returned every few minutes to check up on them. For the sake of safety, the family unit remained close to the den. They would make short forays into the forest, but the small cubs would cling closely to their mother.

When Greg followed Patch, the bear and her cubs were taking a daylong walk into the woods. As Greg approached the bears, Patch halted, raised her head, and put her ears forward liked radar dishes, on the alert. There was a look of intensity on her ursine face. A predator was approaching. She blew out two loud woofs, and the eight-pound cubs bolted up a large aspen. When Patch realized it was Greg, who had followed her before, she relaxed, signaled the cubs with a different woof, and down they scurried to begin their leisurely walk. It was a feeding walk; the cubs were learning what they could eat. When Patch sniffed, the cubs sniffed too. They were less interested in eating (since whenever they rested they were nursing) than in playing. When one cub dropped behind, her brother ran back. The sow watched, waited, allowed them to catch up, and walked on. She was feeding almost continuously on hazelnuts that had been cached by squirrels during the fall. By the end of the day she would swallow more than 2,500 of them, one every twenty seconds while awake. She found them by sniffing the air, then mashing her nose to the ground. In June she would find ant nests in the same way. She also feasted on the large-leafed aster, and the flowers of the bear berry *(Arctostaphylos uva-ursi),* careful not to touch the blueberry blossoms (since she would harvest the blueberries themselves later in the summer). Her whole day consisted of a long, quiet walk in the shady woods, looking for water and plants, avoiding heat stress (with their heat-absorbing black fur, an evolutionary product of the cold woods, black bears must be careful to avoid heat exhaustion), teaching her playful cubs by example, and making certain that they never encountered danger. Greg was amazed to discover that the bear before him was an easygoing, vegetarian (insects excepted) pacifist.

The mothers are normally relaxed and even indulgent with their cubs. One researcher saw a young cub scramble onto some rocks and then hop onto his mother's back. He rode off in style, hanging on with paws embedded in his mother's fur. She did not object. But as with small elephants, this is also the time for a first spanking: It is crucial to the cubs' survival that they obey immediately. If there is any sign of danger, the mother cuffs her cubs up the nearest tree (they are natural climbers). The young cubs have much to learn from their mother, not only about danger, but also about where to find food. Sometimes they will return years later, by themselves, to an area their mother showed them only once when they first emerged from the den.

The cubs, who become self-sufficient at five to six months, do not attain sexual maturity until between three and four years of age. During their second winter, the family will all den together, and this time the cubs will hibernate as well. At their second emergence from the den, it is time for the bears to learn to get along with strange bears, to learn when to be polite and when to disappear. Except for humans, the greatest danger for any bear, especially for cubs, is another bear. A male bear in rut is a very dangerous animal. In black bears, the males and females are the same size, and so the female can easily defend her young. But male grizzlies and polar bears can be up to three times the size of the females. Yet so ferocious is the proverbial mother bear protecting her young that not even the much larger male bear is likely to risk a fight. The third winter, the cubs will den together with their mother for perhaps the last time. At three years of age, a bear is already an adolescent and ready to seek a temporary mate. It is not uncommon, however, for litter-mates to remain together for several years after they have left their mother.[6]

Clearly, female bears make gentle, nurturing mothers. But this doesn't address the reputation of male bears for being aggressively infanticidal. Now, I am as susceptible as anyone else to false information about animals. So I have assumed, along with the rest of the general public, that male bears, given the opportunity, will kill any cubs they encounter. My theory about hibernation—that it is an adaptation to avoid male bears and human hunters—grew out of that assumption. But how frequent, in fact, is infanticide in bears? The world's foremost authority on bears, Lynn Rogers, questions its frequency.[7] He told me that in all the many years he has been studying bears (starting in 1967 and continuing to the present)—and he has tracked and collared and radioed thousands of bears—he has never run across a case of a cub being killed by another bear. That does not mean it never happens. But surveying the literature, Rogers found only nine reported cases of cubs or yearlings killed by other bears between 1930 and 1978. Is it possible, then, that more bear cubs die at the hands of man than die at the hands of other bears? Most bears, Rogers pointed out to me, die from injuries inflicted by humans—gunshot, arrows, steel-jaw traps, and neck snares. "Eighteen out of twenty deaths of radio-collared bears in Minnesota were from gunshot," he said. "In the upper peninsula of Michigan, coyote bounty-trappers that I talked to in the summers of 1967 and 1968 said that they caught numerous bear cubs and that they usually killed them, rather than releasing them, in order to avoid possible problems with the cubs' mothers." So perhaps my theory of hibernation is only partly true; perhaps bears hibernate as an adaptation to avoid humans alone.

One question that intrigues me, and that I asked Rogers, is whether a male bear knows its own child. Since male bears have been observed to kill cubs, I also wanted to know whether cannibalism, which is not unheard of, ever occurs in the case of an adult male black bear eating its own child. There are, as far as I know, almost no recorded instances of a male animal killing its own child. *That* kind of infanticide seems reserved for humans alone. Do male bears, no matter how rarely, ever kill their own children? Rogers told me that we don't really know whether a male bear can recognize his own offspring, so even if the male does kill a cub, there is no evidence that he is deliberately killing his own child. There are some instances of females cannibalizing cubs, though never their own. Clearly, then, even cannibalistic females can recognize their own cubs and avoid harming them. Infanticide in animals almost always refers to a male killing the child of another male, not his own child, and so bears may not be the best animal to study if one is curious about infanticide, since it happens so infrequently in bears, and even when it does, it is not clear that the male who kills is seeking any kind of reproductive advantage.

Since male animals somehow refrain from harming their own offspring, isn't it parsimonious to think that animals are aware of whether and how they are genetically related to other animals? Might it not be possible that they think about this and make certain decisions based on their feelings in the matter? Why should we deny them the capacity to be aware of these feelings? I see no reason to believe that infanticide, when it happens, must be devoid of any thought, and driven only by blind instinct.

Lions

Infanticide is horrifying to us as humans, but it also poses certain intellectual puzzles. From an evolutionary standpoint, how can there be such a major clash of interests between males and females? Males want to procreate their own children, so if they encounter a female with children from another male, they will kill them, in order to accelerate her return to estrus. (The lioness will not go into estrus as long as she is nursing.) But females want to protect the children they already have. It cannot matter much to a female who the father is when the father is not there to help raise the children, as is the case with bears. But lions present a very different picture, and it is therefore not surprising that the earliest evidence about infanticide on the part of a male animal comes from the study of lions.

Female lions are well aware that any male coming from outside the pride represents a serious threat to her children. As soon as the females see such a lion approaching, they immediately move in the opposite direction, herding their young cubs out of danger. When they cannot avoid meeting a male, the females will threaten and even attack the invaders. They try to do this in a group, giving them a better chance of success. When alone, females who try to protect their cubs may pay with their lives. I am not aware of any other animal species in which the male and female fight to the death over the protection of the young. But we must beware of what we characterize as typical. The fact that something has been observed once or twice (though if we have seen it at all it probably also occurs at times when we are not present to observe it) does not make it routine behavior. As far as I know, only two such cases of a male-female fight to the death have been observed. Were these unusual, or, if we had better and more complete information, would we find this to be common behavior? One wonders how something like this, disadvantageous both to the female and to the male lion, could ever evolve. These are their potential mates: Why would a lion kill his future wife?

In general, the evolutionary explanation for male infanticide makes a kind of gruesome sense: In reproductive logic, it is to the male lion's advantage to kill the cub of a rival, thereby forcing the mother into bearing *his* cubs and propagating *his* genes. As a rule, males do not remain in a pride for much more than a year before they are ousted by a rival, or they simply wander off in search of a different pride. A female will not be ready to mate again until her cub is at least eighteen months old. So if a male arrives in a new pride where there is a young cub, he might wait in vain for the female to come back into estrus.

But how are we to account for those cases in which there is a takeover and there is no infanticide? And just how frequent is this circumstance? We should not lose sight of this simple but significant fact: After all, lions are nocturnal creatures, and can only be observed with great difficulty.[8] Can we really claim to have accurate statistical knowledge of the relative frequency or infrequency of infanticide? These are a lot of questions with few answers, I realize, but we must retain our humility in the face of the vast ignorance with which we approach these subjects. If we remain reluctant to even imagine other scenarios we are unlikely to uncover them.

In the most careful review to date of infanticide in mammals,[9] Anne Pusey and Craig Packer concede that "infanticide by males has only been observed a few times in lions." They deduce that it is a deliberate and efficient act and is probably how most cubs die following takeovers: "There is no doubt that male lions gain reproductive advantages from infanticide. Following a successful takeover, females mate with the infanticidal males, and

DNA-fingerprinting shows that all cubs born in a pride are sired by the males resident in the pride." But since direct observation of infanticide has only been made ten times in the Serengeti and once in the Masai Mara National Reserve in Kenya, at the northern edge of the Serengeti ecosystem, it is impossible to say how much a "natural" part of male lion behavior this really is. But let us not forget that the lion is not a bad father to his *own* cubs. He is tolerant to cubs in the pride, even if he is not certain they are his own, allowing them to clamber over him in play and often acting as a sunshade for them in the hot African sun. In behavior unusual for a mammal, the lioness will allow the cubs of other females in her pride to suckle her.

There are so many myths about lions that it would not be surprising for even scientists to become somewhat less than objective in the presence of these "fabled beasts." People have often acted strangely when face to face with a caged or dead lion: They have begged keepers or skinners for lion hairs to win love, lion whiskers to overcome enemies, lion claws for luck, lion hearts to become brave—scarcely any part of the lion's body has been thought to be without magic. It is odd how often we use wild animals to symbolize human preoccupations—bravery, war, romantic love, luck—but how rarely we actually look at the genuine characteristics of the animal. Sometimes, we observe one detail and then apply it promiscuously to the entire species. Many nonscientists, for example, are under the mistaken impression that a male lion kills its young. But the lion never harms its own young. The respected field scientist and authority on lions George Schaller wrote that, "While intruders into a pride area may kill cubs they find there . . . there was no evidence that resident males harm cubs." On the contrary:

> On one occasion an elderly lioness of the Seronera pride carried her three-week-old cub to the remains of a wildebeest kill and abandoned it there. It was so weak from starvation that it was

unable to suckle, apparently because its mother had no milk.
Two Masai pride males approached, attracted by the vulture in
the tree above the kill. One male found the cub . . . and gently
picked it up by the nape but then dropped it. He lifted it once
more, carried it 2 m, placed it on the ground, and after nuzzling it briefly walked off.[10]

When we observe lions, we are clearly not always certain
what to make of their behavior. Schaller gives us some startling
pictures that stay in the mind. After the gentleness seen in the
above report, one is stunned and chagrined to read a very different account of how a small cub was hurrying in the direction of a
kill and passed a nomad, a lion who was not part of the pride. As
if it were prey, the male lion pounced on the small cub, bit it
deeply, and shook it. A lioness—not the cub's mother—growled
and charged the male. He dropped the cub and ambled away,
passing within thirty feet of the male who was probably the
father of the cub. Though the father must have observed what
had happened to his child, he continued to eat, and showed not
the slightest interest in the commotion caused by a fatal attack
on his son. The injured cub, bleeding copiously from its side and
leg, sat in the grass and meowed pitifully, but none of the lions,
male or female, showed any response. The cub died. On a different occasion, a female nomad lioness killed three cubs, though
not her own, for reasons that remain mysterious. These images
are difficult to assimilate, because we simply do not know what
to do with them. We hunger for order and for explanations: Why
did none of the lions respond to the crying cub? How can we
understand adults not responding to a child in need? Why did
the female charge the male? If this was normal aggression to a
stranger, why did the pride male not respond similarly? Why
would a female lion kill three cubs if she stands nothing to gain?
It seems to me impossible to say which of these behaviors is

typical of lions and which is an anomaly, or if both are typical or both anomalous. We have no idea how many encounters are savage and how many are benign, and we must constantly bear in mind that these terms are human terms that may mean nothing whatever in the context of lions.

It is difficult for humans to regard lions or other animals as individuals. We look for preprogrammed behavior, innate acts that are not influenced by emotion, intelligence, learning, or experience. We are encouraged in this belief by accounts that seem to indicate a failure of insight. For example, George Schaller noted that lions are primarily visual hunters and ignore the direction of the wind. In spite of being three times more successful when stalking gazelles upwind, they do not seem to learn from their failures. If they were like us, we might reason, they would understand and alter their behavior accordingly. It would be in their interest to do so.

I am hardly the first to suggest that lions do not seem fully adjusted to communal life. Lions, of course, are not a solitary species, but neither are they a social species in the same way that wolves are.[11] It is as if they have not had much practice in living together, as if their present social system evolved only relatively recently. During the four years of Schaller's study of the Seronera and Masai lion prides, of the seventy-nine cubs born, fifty-three, almost 70 percent, died of starvation, predators, other lions, or unknown causes. In other parts of the Serengeti and in other parks in Africa, the survival rate is only 50 percent, or less. One cause of death that seems particularly repulsive to humans is female abandonment: If there is not enough food, the mother may simply walk away from her litter, or if there is only one cub left, she may abandon him or her, perhaps because it takes too much energy to raise a single cub. Schaller put it well: "The response of a lioness to her cubs is so finely balanced between care and neglect, between her own desires and the needs of her offspring, that the survival of the young ones is threatened when-ever conditions are not the optimum."

Hanuman Langurs

Lions are not the only infanticidal animals. Infanticide has now been described in a wide variety of animals: Hanuman langurs, mountain gorillas, baboons, redtail, blue, and red colobus mon-keys, howler monkeys, chimpanzees, lemmings, house mice, deer mice, wolves, red deer, bears, prairie dogs, golden hamsters, Mongolian gerbils, ground squirrels, lions, birds, and fish—the list is still growing.

But the infanticidal male animal about whom the most has been written is the Indian temple monkey, the Hanuman langur. Nobody has done more to raise this topic to serious scientific prominence than Sarah Hrdy. I read her book on the langurs of Abu with fascination. Anyone studying the topic of infanticide must turn to the body of information she has collected. At one point she says that she is no naturalist, and what brought her out of her room every morning was the intensely dramatic events that were unfolding—like watching a real-life soap opera with serious consequences. This was the only reference I was able to find in her first book about her own reactions to these rather sad events, in which males killed small infants. But a few years later, when she came to write her brilliant and influential second book, *The Woman That Never Evolved* (I wonder what happened to "who" in the title), she was much more reflective. Describing the killing of the infant langur Scratch by Mug, the invading male, she writes: "This is the only time in my career as a field primatol-ogist that I have ever cried while making observations." And in a footnote to this section, she says that she could not bear to write the same material in the same way still one more time, evidently because of the pain it caused her.[12]

But while we know that infanticide exists, we are still ignorant of the precise extent. How rare and how common it is depends not only on the species being observed, but also on the extent of our knowledge. Some of the most sophisticated research has been carried out by Paul Sherman, a leading animal behaviorist from Cornell, on ground squirrels (unlike tree squirrels, they nest in burrows in the ground). He attributes 8 percent of the deaths of all infants born (not all infants who die) to infanticide. At Jodhpur, in India, among Hanuman langurs, roughly one male takeover out of four is accompanied by infanticide, which is a high figure. But it still means that three-quarters of male takeovers occur without violence. What can be the explanation for this? And generalizing from all the studies, the frequency of infanticide among Hanuman langurs is only about 10 percent. I think the remaining 90 percent is worthy of some study.

Infanticide

In animal infanticide, the victims and the killers are almost always unrelated. The one exception occurs among prairie dogs, where the major cause of juvenile mortality is infanticide, which eradicates 39 percent of all litters born (only about half of all infants born live to emerge from their burrows). Unlike almost all other species, however, the majority of the killers are females, who are most frequently either the mothers or sisters of the victims. This is very odd. Except in rodents, exact figures and percentages are difficult if not impossible to obtain, but infanticide is never common, can rarely be predicted, and is almost never directly observed. Sarah Hrdy reports that langurs have been studied in thirteen locations, and only in six of them have male takeovers (the predecessor to infanticide) been reported. In the twenty thousand hours that they had been studied (in 1981), there were thirty-two takeovers reported. In twenty of these cases there were suspicious disappearances of infants. Based on this circumstantial evidence, infanticide was assumed to have taken place. What this works out to in percentages is difficult to say, but it is certainly not the high figure that is cited for squirrels and prairie dogs.

Many critics have claimed that infanticide is nothing but social pathology. But as Paul Sherman points out in his studies of ground squirrels, it seems inappropriate to dismiss the single most important source of juvenile mortality as a social pathology, especially when it occurs every year in a free-living population, when the behavior of the killers is predictable, and when related young are never killed. Sherman is quite explicit: "Belding's ground squirrels never kill related young." That is, they never kill their own children, or even children related to them, such as cousins or closer kin.[13] If this were a pathology, one would not expect it to obey a seemingly inviolable rule of this kind. I cannot see how researcher bias (preferring one explanation over another before investigating) could be at fault here. The figures have not been invented, and the explanation does seem to involve genetic relatedness. Nor is this a one-time occurrence: Undiscovered until the 1970s, infanticide has now been documented in eight of eleven ground squirrel species.

Early on in the discussions about infanticide, it was thought that it could be accounted for by simple overcrowding, or that it might be pure social pathology. While neither of these explanations has proven convincing, I can nonetheless imagine other naturally occurring factors that could help lay the ground for infanticide: stress coming from unknown sources in the environment, health problems, uneven food distribution (a drought in one season), all of which have nothing to do with the confounding variable of human intervention. But human intervention is inherent in all research and cannot be neglected, even if it is subtle. We need to be very persistent when it comes to searching for clues.

Consider the fact that all animals in the wild give birth. They have constraints, but clearly the vast majority of animal species have, undisturbed, survived and flourished. Many of these same animals, when they are captive, are such sensitive breeders that they give birth only with great difficulty or so rarely that when they do it is considered a major occasion and justification for the zoo. Some animals do not give birth at all in captivity, in spite of what researchers consider to be ideal circumstances: plenty of high-quality food, absence of predators, no parasites, good health care. Evidently the females have found something not to their liking, and we have not yet figured it out (it may be something as simple as a hatred of confinement). Think of how rarely and with what difficulty the following animals ever give birth in a zoo: gorillas, squirrel monkeys, black lemurs, red pandas, giant pandas, striped hyenas, many species of dolphins, and of course orcas, to mention only some of the animals who experience difficulty in giving birth in captivity. Some animals, it appears, would rather die without propagating their genes than give birth in a prison. And some animals in zoos kill their own young. When they do, maybe the reason for killing their own young could simply come from a loathing of being observed. Maybe to be on display causes an animal great upset.

We have a real opportunity to learn about how animals are altered by captivity, but this is not a subject dear to the hearts of zoo staff and it has rarely been addressed. It is interesting that the book by Hans Hediger still referred to as the locus classicus is already some fifty years old. And his major text, which tells us of the effects of human interference on zoo animals, has never even been translated from German into English.[14] I interpret this to mean that we do not like to acknowledge that we have an interfering influence on what we study. We are invested in the notion that we are objective, that we are simply observing what is there, not creating something, and especially not something that is deleterious to the species we are studying. Is it not at least a possibility that animals we are observing kill *because* we are observing them?

If we grant that 8 percent of ground squirrels are infanticidal, we are still left with a burning question that as far as I know has not been addressed by animal behaviorists: What about the other 92 percent? Why aren't they infanticidal? I asked this question of Richard Wrangham, a leading primatologist in the department of anthropology at Harvard. Is it possible, I asked him, that a langur, say, has the following internal dialogue: "I see my brothers killing infants all the time. I don't want to do that to a helpless infant. Every child is *somebody's* child, has some father who cares about him or her as much as I care about my children. No, infanticide is not for me, *nein danke.*" In other words, could an individual male langur simply opt out? "Surely not," exclaims Wrangham good-naturedly, but clearly impatient. He was not referring to the actual content of my invented dialogue, but to the very idea that *any* member of an infanticidal species would deliberately choose (whether consciously or not) to refrain from this behavior. What, then, I asked him, could be the reason that one monkey does ill and another does not? Only one, he told me: "The monkey simply doesn't have the opportunity. All data so far suggest that every male Hanuman langur would commit infanticide under appropriate circumstances; that is, when he could kill a helpless infant and get away with it." That is a rather depressing thought. But is it true?

I am constantly reminded, when reading about animals, that at some level, there is no such thing as a species: Every animal is a unique individual. If some Hanuman langurs commit infanticide—even if a majority do—some do not. Perhaps they even choose not to. Male lions are protective of their own children, even if murderous toward the children of other male lions. And not every male lion kills cubs. Individual behavior certainly suggests, to me at least, individual choice. Even the "lowly" California mouse, *Peromyscus californicus,* manifests some individuals who are good father mice and some who are bad father mice. The world's foremost expert on this species, Dr. David Gubernick, is doing his research on a free colony in Carmel Valley at the University of California Field Research Station. New fathers, he told me, sniff and lick the pups at the moment of birth or immediately after. Fathers will often retrieve a newborn pup, lick it, and huddle over it while the female gives birth to another young. They even show a "pregnancy effect," that is, they begin to act like dads toward other pups when their wives are within ten days of giving birth. So the father *Peromyscus* acts like a parent even before his pregnant partner does! Recently, David and I walked through the beautiful hills while he pointed out to me the various nests under the sturdy oak trees. His descriptions were filled with admiration for the mice. But he was particularly eloquent while discussing one champion devoted mouse father, who cared for countless generations without ever faltering. A mouse hero? I wondered aloud. David had no doubt.

The Nunamiut Eskimo, who live in Anaktuvuk Pass in Alaska, are fond of saying that there is no such thing as "wolf," only individual wolves. They often refer to *that* wolf or wolves under *those* particular environmental conditions, using the collective "wolf" much less often than does the modern wolf ecologist.[15] We can certainly understand this point of view from our own relations with dogs. Are male dogs aggressive? Some are, of course, and some are not. Can we even say that by and large they are more aggressive than females? My impression is that on the whole they are, but I cannot be certain. And I would say that so much depends on their individual history that a generalization of this kind is almost useless.

The brain weight of adult ostriches is low for their size, compared with other species. People tend to call them stupid, even if the people using this word know next to nothing about the life of these remarkable birds. Whatever their brainpower, there can be no doubt of the intensity of their emotional investment in their children. A father ostrich who has young chicks in a nest will often risk his life to save theirs. When a large and powerful predator, such as a lion, is close to the nest, the male ostrich will spread his wings and hold them low to the ground, his neck waving unpredictably, and then suddenly collapse on the ground. Intrigued, the lion will follow the ostrich, who will continue to collapse every few feet, a sure indication to the lion that the bird is ill, and easy prey. It is a risky display, but it often works: When the lion is far enough away from the nest that there is no chance he could find it again, the male ostrich is suddenly in excellent health, and running swiftly for his life. He has just risked it for his children. But not every ostrich father does the "distraction display." Since this is the case, I would hazard the guess that it is more often performed by an experienced father than a new one. He knows the joys of fatherhood and is willing to put more at risk.

Yes, some animal species, such as lions, are infanticidal. But even among lions, some males are never infanticidal, for reasons that have so far eluded our understanding. As far as I know, nobody has attempted to account for the variation, nobody has set out to explain the difference. I have a theory, and one that could easily be tested. My theory is that infanticidal males come primarily (though not exclusively) from the ranks of animals who have never been a father or have only recently become one. Is it possible that a lion who does not kill his own children but does kill the children of others has had less experience being a father, and that the more experience he has, the less chance there is that he will kill? Is it possible that once an animal has lived around children, especially his own, for a long time, whatever impulse he has to further his own genetic success by murdering the children of other males is lessened? He has had direct paws-on experience of the pleasures of being with children. He learns tolerance. Maybe he even begins to feel empathy. Is it so far-fetched to speculate that the peaceable kingdom is not exclusively a human fantasy, but is shared by some other male animals, even lions, bears, and Hanuman langurs? Perhaps it is, but we will never know if we never ask the question.

FIVE: Birds and Marmosets and Monogamy

In his new BBC television series *The Life of Birds,* David Attenborough describes the father sungrebe (also called a finfoot), a waterfowl from Guatemala and other tropical and sub-tropical zones. He has pouches like small saddlebags on either side of his body beneath his wings. His chicks hatch after only ten days, blind, naked, and completely helpless. Somehow they find their way into his pouches, one on each side, and he takes them with him wherever he goes in the water. Even when he soars into the air, they are with him, snug in their pouches.[1] There is no other bird who carries his chicks on flights. Suddenly I see the value of bird-watching. Imagine catching sight of this devoted father, with the tiny heads of his two copilots sticking out of his pouches, the wind in their faces, chirping ecstatically!

What do we mean when we say "I had a good father?" For many people, it means that their father was very much present, an integral part of family life. It is possible, of course, to be physically present and emotionally absent, but many people complain about the sheer absence of their father; he simply was not there. More than impressions are involved here. Statistics tell a dire tale: The average daily amount of one-on-one father-child contact in the United States is less than thirty minutes, and for dads who have divorced, more than 40 percent of them are no longer seeing their children five years later.

More depressing statistics: In a survey conducted by Sheila Kitzinger, 38 percent of the mothers questioned were alone with their babies for between eight and twelve hours every weekday.[2] Even worse, studies suggest that in the mid-1960s fathers spent, on average, 37.7 seconds per day interacting with their infants in the first three months.[3] Commenting on this in 1986, Charlie Lewis wrote that "there is no evidence to indicate that great change has occurred since this date."

It would be convenient to think that when fathers disappear or are not involved in the day-to-day care of their children, they are simply obeying ancient instincts, acting like their animal forebears (though human fathers spend less time with their children, in general, than do primates, who show intensive caretaking). If this were really true, any change from that behavior would be glacial, since we can expect evolution to proceed in terms of millennia, not years. And yet in a large poll[4] recently conducted by *Newsweek* magazine, 55 percent of men interviewed felt that parenting was more significant to them than it had been to their own fathers, and 70 percent said they spend more time with their children than their fathers did with them. In one generation, in other words, a major change in parenting is possible. Almost all my male friends agree that they are "better," by which they mean more involved, fathers than their fathers were. I am sure my son, Ilan, will be even more present to his children than I have been to him.

In thinking about wolves and dogs, we saw a reason to credit the common wisdom that fathers play a greater role the more monogamous they are. Less than 3 percent of mammalian species are monogamous. In birds, more than 90 percent of all species are monogamous. Therefore, one might expect fathers to play a more prominent role among birds than among mammals, and this is indeed the case.

Monkeys

In fact, there is no mammalian species in which the father takes the primary role of caretaker—except, occasionally, humans. Perhaps the closest we come to this occurs in families of tiny (as little as 3 ounces as adults) South American monkeys called marmosets, and also in tamarins *(callitrichidae)*. Marmosets and saddle-backed tamarins *(Saguinus fuscicollis)* are monogamous (mostly, the latest research shows cooperative polyandry) and very active fathers, carrying their children about from morning to night while the mother forages for food. Two scientists in 1981 showed that circulating levels of prolactin increased in male marmosets after they had carried their offspring. In this case it seemed that involvement produced the hormonal change, rather than the reverse.[5] Male tamarins also carry children that are not theirs. When the babies call out in fear or when they are in danger, it is the male who responds. One explanation for the role that males play in this society has been that the mothers generally have twins, and the physical burden is so great that she cannot care for them alone. The male takes care of the twins while she forages. It is significant that all group members share food with infants, at least in the golden-lion tamarins *(Leontopithecus rosalia)*. Is this because the monkeys in this family seem to have a concealed estrus, as do humans, and therefore no father can be certain of paternity? The ensuing strategy is to be nice to all children, since they could be your own.

One extraordinary behavior I read about is that in marmosets and tamarins the male will assist in difficult births with his hands. Spencer-Booth mentions an article written in 1937, in which the author, Lucas, claims to have observed a male assisting at parturition. The male received and cleaned the babies. But nobody I spoke to could confirm this.

As this book was going to press, I received a call from Richard Wrangham, chairman of biological anthropology at Harvard University. "I have some amazing footage for you; come over to the Peabody Museum as soon as you can." I went right away, and it was, indeed, amazing footage. In a film made for WNET *(Gremlins: Faces in the Forest),* the Dutch primatologist Marc van Roosmalen found an entirely new species of tamarin monkey in the Amazonian rain forest of Brazil. Somehow a camera was placed inside the tree-hole nest of this newly discovered tamarin, only to witness a birth. In close-up shots we see the mother begin contractions, and then watch the one-inch baby, no larger than a mouse, emerge. But the extraordinary thing is that the mother is not alone. Inside the tree hollow we see a companion, a male, her husband. He is right next to her, and while the contractions are an hour apart, he looks unconcerned, grooming himself in an offhand manner. But when the contractions come more frequently, and we see the concentration on the face of the female, he begins to monitor her as closely as any obstetrician, watching intently and patting her reassuringly. Then when the baby comes out he does something that, as far as I am aware, has never before been witnessed: He takes the umbilical cord in his teeth and severs it. And then he eats the placenta! This is the first time that this behavior, long suspected, has been captured on film in the wild. I watched it with Richard and several of his students, and all of us agreed that what we were watching filled us with awe.

The monogamous large gibbon known as a siamang, a

species distinct from smaller gibbons, is a so-called lesser (meaning smaller) ape, who, along with its cousins, comprise nine different species, including the white-handed gibbon, distributed throughout the islands and mainland of Southeast Asia. John MacKinnon, who studied siamangs in Malaysia in 1973, found that while the mother cares for the very young, once they become more mature the siamang father gets involved and carries his own children when they are between the ages of one and two and a half years. Once the juvenile is coordinated enough to walk by himself, he will again follow his mother.

In MacKinnon's study, Sam, a small, bright-eyed siamang youngster, was in the habit of clinging to his mother's belly as she swung through the trees of the Malaysian jungle. He was more than a year old, and began watching his father with increasing interest. One day, without warning, he suddenly leapt from his mother's arms onto his father's back. That night, he went to sleep, as usual, with his mother, but bright and early the next morning he jumped into position, ready for his morning ride through the treetops. His father seemed very pleased. From that day forth, he would ride about the forest from his perch on his dad, who took it all in stride. MacKinnon noted that by relieving the mother of this extra load, the male siamang gives her a chance to build up her strength again for the task of another pregnancy. David Chivers, who studied the siamang in Malaya, observed that the male carried the infant when it was alarmed, and that subsequently, as time passed, the infant increasingly followed the male rather than the female.

Is the explanation for male parental care here simply that having twins makes it impossible for the female to manage on her own? Evidently this is not a sufficient explanation. The primatologist Patricia Wright has pointed out that researchers had ignored two successful Neotropical families of monkeys who do not twin, but among whom both mothers and fathers take care of the children. According to Wright, one evening a mother in a Central American forest returned from foraging with a branch of ripe wild plums. Her infant sat by her side, begging for the food. She pushed her away several times, and only very reluctantly broke off a tiny bit of the plum and threw it in her direction. The little girl seemed scared, and ran off to her father, who was sitting nearby, also eating. He immediately handed over his entire cache of berries. As the sun went down, this same small girl ran up to play with her mother, who brushed her away. Her father, however, began playing with her as if he were her own sibling. There may be more such gems of unexpected behavior lurking in the forests and jungles, awaiting a sympathetic observer.

Although there is no evidence that they make good fathers, there is much evidence that a little-known South American monkey, the elegant tree-dwelling muriqui, the largest monkey in South America, found in the coffee estates of southeastern Brazil and extremely rare in captivity, is among the world's most peaceful citizens, making love, not war. Virtually nothing was known about this wonderful species until the 1980s. The muriqui exhibit some extraordinary qualities that have been admired by primatologists. The Harvard anthropologist Richard Wrangham, in his book *Demonic Males,* praises the fact that "females choose their mates at will. . . . During copulation, Muriqui males watch calmly, and sometimes they casually take turns. Up to four males may sit in line along a branch, patiently watching all that sex, and waiting their moment. While doing so they never show the slightest emotion— no aggressive displays at all." They are not jealous or aggressive; they are not competitive; in fact, they are complete egalitarians, as in an ideal society. Perhaps because they are not monogamous, when it comes to fathering, although they show no aggression, they do not show any great activity, either. Infanticide is unheard of. That is no small virtue, although I suppose a human father would be humiliated to be told: "Well, the best one can say of you is that at least you did not kill your child." Yet if we could say this of every father of our own species, it would be a considerable achievement.

Birds and Monogamy

However, monogamy and paternal care are by no means invariably linked. Many birds—including ducks and snowcocks, who are monogamous, do not show paternal care. Also, we must constantly bear in mind how little we actually know about the real habits of even the most studied birds. David Lack, who was one of England's great ornithologists,[6] claimed that cuckoos (*Cuculus canorus*) were monogamous, but he was contradicted by other ornithologists who insisted they are promiscuous. Nobody, it seems, has seen cuckoos mate. Lack was also surprised "to find that monogamy is the rule in many ducks and limicoline waders [shore birds], in which only one parent incubates and cares for the young, and in certain parasitic cuckoos, in which neither parent does so." In other words, the word from the birds is that we must not be fooled into making an ironclad link between monogamy or even love and paternal care.

This is as true for humans as it is for birds: There are couples who consciously choose not to have children (refuting the sociobiological claim that we all seek to propagate our genes first and foremost) and also have happy marriages. But it is also true that in kittiwakes, cliff-nesting birds, the main reason for separation is the failure to hatch eggs. Among humans, too, divorce is more common in parents with no children than in parents with children. This correlation ("We marry to have children") is one of those truisms of evolutionary biology that is useful because it can be examined and even tested rather easily in other species, even if it is somewhat of a cliché and even if it is, perhaps, offensive. The fact that the original evolutionary purpose of marriage (though it is a human cultural phenomenon), even of attraction to the other sex, was to have children does not make this necessarily true today. After all, all animals, including humans, have evolved to be more than merely a bundle of instincts. But even if procreation is not marriage's only purpose, certainly it remains important in the human institution of marriage. For humans, divorce also correlates statistically with an early death, especially for the male. This does not hold true in birds, though. Blue tits have a much greater divorce rate than do great tits, but they live just as long.

As noted earlier, unlike most other animals, some nine thousand out of the ten thousand bird species form monogamous pair bonds during the breeding season. Numerous male and female geese and swans remain close together every day and night of the year, even during migrations over thousands of miles. This kind of fidelity is found among fish as well: Pairs of butterfly fish, which live in coral reefs, have been recorded together for six consecutive years.

When we use the term "monogamous," we mean socially monogamous (that is, spending most of their time together), not sexually monogamous, since it has become clear that the first does not necessarily imply the latter. Ornithologists speak of "extra-pair copulations," meaning that the male or the female, who are normally a pair, each might seek an extramarital companion. In many bird species previously presumed to be monogamous, DNA fingerprinting has shown that the father of a given brood of chicks is not the mother's mate from the pair bond. Ornithologists believe that in many cases it is the female who initiates sexual encounters with other males (male sexual coercion is not as common among birds, except for ducks, as other animals, probably because it is easier for the female bird to escape into the air). Does the male know he has been "cuckolded" (a term derived from the cuckoo bird, of which there are 136 different species)? It is impossible to know. Does the male care whether the chicks are his or those of a companion? We assume that he does, and that is how we interpret many actions (bringing food, for example), but we can never be certain. If the male bird had doubts about paternity, would he decline to exercise the obligations of fatherhood? Male geese do not sit on the egg, but they guard the brooding female. Clearly they are helping her as part of their active partnership in raising the young. Both the male and the female protect and accompany their young goslings, who can fly shortly after hatching. They do not need to feed them, since the young are competent to find their own food, but they do teach them what to look for.[7] Migratory geese, who pair for life, take their young with them to their winter quarters. If the males had access to DNA fingerprinting, would they wait for the results before making this kind of commitment?

When it comes to the drudge work, like changing diapers, human mothers complain that their husbands find reasons to be otherwise occupied. David Lack noticed a similar pattern in birds: "Bright coloring tends to be present in the one which does not raise the family." In birds, the males wear the bright colors. How does this affect parenting? Some ornithologists believe that the male birds who have no role in parenting can afford to be colorful because there is no risk that they will lead nest predators to the brood, since the male himself does not even know where the nest is. When a female has to bring up the brood alone, she must be careful to do nothing that would increase their risk of being eaten. The females whose partners do not assist them are therefore usually cryptically colored. Does the male tendency to desert the female, or merely disappear from the family, have anything to do with doubt or suspicion about paternity, or are all males programmed to do as little as they can get away with?

In 1967, the biologists Robert Macarthur and Edward O. Wilson wrote a technical book on the theory of island biogeography (interpreting the geographic distribution of animals, plants, and people, both extant and extinct). In attempting to relate the properties of the life history of a colonizing species to its chances for success and, if it fails, to the length of time it persists before going extinct, they introduced the randomly chosen technical term *K selection* (in which K refers to the carrying capacity of the environment—that is, how many animals the ecosystem, usually a tropical island, can sustain) and applied it to species that mature slowly, which they called K-strategists. Opposed to this are *r-selected species* (such as insects who produce thousands of young without caring for them). The terms have been taken up and are often used by biologists as shorthand to refer to certain recurring themes. The Harvard biologist Stephen J. Gould summarized the differences nicely: "Some attributes of r-selected organisms might include: high fecundity, early maturation, short life span, limited parental care, rapid development, and a greater proportion of available resources committed to reproduction. K strategists might employ low reproductive effort with late maturation, longer life, and a tendency to invest a great deal of parental care in small broods of later maturing offspring."

Humans are the ultimate K-selected species. We have fewer offspring, high parental investment in each offspring, lower infant mortality, longer life, slower development, delayed reproduction, large body size; in short, we have evolved to pay very great attention to our children. Does this theory imply that we evolved to have both a mother and a father raise a child? Yes, this would be the optimum. When we look at other extreme K-strategists in the animal world (here is where such a shorthand proves useful), we also see this to be the case, as, for example, with penguins. In fact, many seabirds are extreme K-strategists, and put an enormous amount of effort into each child. This is true of albatrosses, petrels, and shearwaters as well. In spite of the fact that these birds have one of the richest habitats on the planet, the ocean, they still lay only one egg. This way they can concentrate on the single child that emerges.

Consider the extraordinary parental feats of the male and female wandering albatross. They breed on sub-Antarctic islands in the Southern Ocean. To find food for their chicks, they travel tremendous distances. A bird fitted with a radiotelemetry device tracked by a satellite showed that on each single foraging trip an albatross might travel 2,237 to 9,320 miles! Michael Bright, who reported this amazing feat, said that this particular bird flew at speeds of 50 miles per hour and covered 560 miles a day, flying day and night with few stops for two to three days. Albatross chicks, when they fledge, will spend from four to fourteen years circling the earth before returning home to breed. Their survival rate is much higher than that of penguin fledglings, 80 percent of whom don't make it beyond the first year at sea: More than 70 percent of the albatross chicks are alive after their first five years and more than 90 percent of these survivors make it to eleven years. Flying at such heights, over such vast distances, for such long periods, probably ensures that these large birds meet few enemies. No wonder humans have always felt a yearning to fly.

David Attenborough, in *The Life of Birds,* explains that parent shearwaters feed their young in their nest burrows for sixty days. On the sixty-first day, they simply stop. The chicks, who vociferously protest, are nonetheless able to go without food for days. They come to the burrow mouth for short periods to exercise their wings. Only after twelve days are they hungry enough, or strong enough, to take to their wings and fly. The parents' strategy is deliberate, it would seem; they must be well aware that no ultimate harm will come to the chicks from refusing to feed them, and it seems to be the only method to get them out of the nest and into the air.

Pete is a great-winged petrel, also called a grey-faced petrel (*Pterodroma macroptera*). He is a handsome bird, very dark, with a three-foot wingspan. Pete discovered his soul mate on Little

Barrier Island off the coast of Australia. They spent their time soaring over the subtropical parts of the Indian and West Pacific Oceans. They would feed mainly at night, looking for their favorite foods, squid and other cephalopods, by bioluminescence. But it seemed they were seeking something more. They found it when they reached the tiny, volcanic Whale Island off northeast New Zealand. Here they came across thirty-five thousand pairs just like them, who had all come for the same purpose. They were looking for a place where they could lay a single egg in a burrow, one that was not already occupied by the rabbits who had been introduced to the island and were fierce competitors.

Pete and his wife, Petra, found an empty burrow. At night Pete would go off fishing, and when he returned he would call loudly as he passed over his burrow. Petra called in return, and he knew, by her voice and the sounds she made that were unique to her, that he had reached home. He did not mind sharing the burrow with a neighbor pair. But the nest chamber was just for him and Petra. This is the place where she wished to lay her egg and she would be able to remember its location. She marked the spot with oil from her bill. Together they left for a honeymoon at sea. Pete, on his own, returned every few days to make certain that the nest had not been taken over by another bird.

Two months later Petra bid Pete farewell and returned to the burrow without him. She found it exactly as she had left it, the perfect spot to lay her single white egg, which was almost a fifth of her own body weight. A few days later, Pete returned to the island as well, and was happy to see the large egg. It was his turn to take over the incubation. Now Petra left to go to their favorite feeding grounds, almost four hundred miles away. Pete was on his own, sitting and fasting like our emperor penguins, for seventeen days. When Petra returned, Pete greeted her with an enthusiastic series of long calls, the same ones they used during their courtship. It was her turn to brood, while Pete went to feed for seventeen days. And so they continued taking turns until, after fifty-five days, their egg hatched.

Their son, Pedro, was covered in a coat of short, soft down, pure white. Proud parents, both Pete and Petra stayed with Pedro for a week. By then, Pedro could keep warm on his own, and so his parents left him by himself for four nights. On the fifth night they both returned to feed him a strange, green, oily substance, rich in fat, that they regurgitated especially for him. He did not seem to mind their absence, and with the feedings, he was gaining weight at an amazing rate. Three months later, Pedro weighed 20 percent more than his parents, and still did not have his feathers. A month later his feathers came in, and he was ready to fledge. That night his parents gave him his last free meal, and watched him get ready for his first flight as an independent bird. He has as much as thirty years of life in front of him, if only he can safely reach the ocean on his night flight to freedom. He does. And his parents have successfully fulfilled their role.

John Sparks, in his BBC-TV series *Battle of the Sexes,* points out that great-winged petrel "parents are condemned to rear their chick from a hatchling weight of 3 ounces to an 18-pound fledgling—a hundredfold increase. But this is not all. By mid-winter, the wanderer's gargantuan chick resembles a potbellied, furry bowling ball, standing over three feet tall and weighing 80 pounds—incredibly, three times as much as its father." (He will eventually shrink.) It is the only chick to grow so large so quickly, aided only by the faithful feedings of two truly devoted parents.

It is more than just curiosity that leads us to wonder why most albatrosses, petrels, Manx shearwaters, geese, swans, common terns, barn owls, Adélie penguins, and many parrots, who have long-term pair bonds, some of which last until death, nearly all make good fathers. Some of these feats of social monogamy inspire awe in humans. One might think that in birds that migrate, it would be easy to lose one another and therefore to separate permanently and seek a new mate. But barnacle geese, *Branta leucopsis,* are renowned long-distance migrants, who fly from the high Arctic in summer to winter on coastal marshes and pastures in temperate areas. After the journey, accompanied by their goslings, each pair spends the winter months in dense flocks of thousands of birds. In spite of the potential for losing contact in these flocks, each male-female pair remains together throughout the day, each season, *for life.*

Ornithologists have no difficulty in speaking of divorce to refer to birds who separate, but they avoid the use of the word "marriage" for birds who stay together, preferring the more scientifically neutral "pair bond," "mate," and other terms that do not threaten human prerogatives. I see no reason why we should not speak of birds getting married if we understand this to mean living together in intimacy. Nor should we shy away from believing that the reason birds get married is because they fall in love. Why should we be the only species for whom these words are appropriate? The noted biologist Bernd Heinrich, in a book just published on the mind of the raven (see Suggested Reading), writes: "Since ravens have long-term mates I suspect that like us they fall in love." To learn that the mate of a dying American black duck refused to fly out of gunshot range with the rest of the flock fills us with admiration, and wonder. If this should translate into resolutions of our own concerning love and fidelity, would that not be a marvel?

Marriage and Other Partnerships

Nearly every society known to us has had the custom of marriage. Currently, about 90 percent of people who *can* be married *are* married. Why? Common sense tells us that it must have something to do with children. In general, child-rearing is easier if there are a minimum of two people to share the burden of caring. Of course there are some marriages in which the soundest thing is to remove the child from the father, or from the mother. Homosexual marriages that include children are statistically safer for the child than traditional marriages. Lesbian households are notably secure and nurturing places with few dangers.

Among animals, we have only recently learned the full extent of homosexual raising of children from the remarkable book by Bruce Bagemihl, *Biological Exuberance.* He documents the fact that female grizzly bears sometimes bond with each other and raise their young together as a single family unit. He says that the two mothers become inseparable companions, traveling and feeding together and sharing in the parenting of their cubs (usually four of them). Sometimes the ursine friends will even nurse each other's cubs. How common is this? About 9 percent of all grizzly cubs are raised in families headed by two (or even more) mothers. We know that female bears sometimes kill cubs that are not their own, especially during the nursing period. I do not believe, however, that there is any case on record of a bear killing the child of her female companion. Whether the bears are together because they simply enjoy one another's company or because being together provides extra security for their cubs, especially from predatory males, is not yet clear.

It has been known at least since the 1920s that black swans *(Cygnus atratus)* from Australia and New Zealand make good homosexual fathers. About 5 to 6 percent of all pairings in black swans are of male couples. They often remain together for many years, sometimes for life. They will even raise young together. In fact, because the two males are able to pool their strength, they often acquire the best territory, sometimes the major portion of a pond, relegating the heterosexual pair to less favorable nesting areas. At times a male will seduce a female into building a nest with him, and laying an egg, but will then chase her away when the egg hatches, so that he and his partner can take over. Some homosexual couples simply drive off the heterosexual pair from their nest and adopt the eggs. They take turns sitting on them, and raise the chicks together as well. Bagemihil, who writes about this extraordinary behavior, says that homosexual pairs are often more successful than heterosexual ones at raising chicks, in part because they have access to the best nesting sites and the largest territories. He points out that on average, 80 percent of homosexual parenting efforts are successful, compared to only about 30 percent for heterosexual pairs.

Bruce Bagemihl provides an exhaustive list of alternative arrangements, many of which have been known but not properly assessed by other biologists. He points out, for example, that in some colonies of black swans, more than two-thirds of all cygnets are raised in broods that combine offspring from as many as thirty different families. So you may have a family of forty youngsters attended by a single pair of adults, who are not necessarily the biological parents of any of the cygnets.

Begemihl observes that female homosexual gray whale (*Eschrichtius robustus*) couples, when they are on their four-month journey from northern waters to the mangrove lagoons off Baja California, where their calves are born, often travel back and forth along the length of coastal inlets for hours at a time, "apparently with no particular purpose other than to be together."

We would also have to consider orcas (*Orcinus orca*). Although their family life is still little understood, the parenting system is definitely an elaborate communal one. A pod is made up of various matrilineal groups, led always by a matriarch. She is accompanied by her young and any adult sons. Her brothers, uncles, and even her mother and possibly her grandmother might be present. The matriarch, as long as she is breeding, only reproduces once every five years. So there is always a large pool of potential helpers in the population who are not themselves parents. Calves will be baby-sat by any adolescent or adult member of the pod at least once a day. These pods are remarkably peaceable and harmonious. This may be because the young get to know each member of the pod through their baby-sitting activities. I have not heard of a single documented case of aggression against a baby orca whale by another orca. On the other hand, it is very difficult for anyone to study the internal dynamics of orca society. I anticipate the day when a human diver will succeed in joining a pod. Only then will we have the detailed knowledge now lacking about these animals who may have evolved a culture superior to our own when it comes to raising vulnerable young.

Generally among animals, when the female can raise children on her own as well as she could with the help of a mate, there are no marriages. We have already mentioned the most prominent example, the elephant. Even though a baby elephant is dependent for a very long time (up to ten years) on its mother for survival, there are no long-term bonds between female and male elephants. Because elephants are precocial, as soon as calves are born they are capable of walking, following the mother, and while initially they nurse exclusively, soon they are able to feed alongside the mother. The father does nothing, and need do nothing, for the child. Neither the child nor the female requires the protection of a male from predators, nor does either need help in feeding.

Human children are dependent on their parents for longer than any other animal species. We are the most altricial species on the planet. It has been suggested that human marriage arose as a solution to the problem of this very long period of dependency in human young. But there are many counterexamples. Elephants have nothing comparable to marriage, yet young elephants are dependent for almost as long as human children. If anything, almost the opposite seems to be the case: The longer the period of dependency, the less likely is a tight bond between males and females. Young howler monkeys depend on their mothers for food for the first two years. Yet there are no close bonds between males and females. The same applies to Hamadryas baboons, lions, and the common langur. Could males simply be more impatient than females and not want to invest years of their lives in children?

If this is the case, though, what are we to make of the vast variety of homosexual behavior that has been reliably reported in many kinds of animal species, a few examples of which we have already seen? Male Humboldt penguins will often choose as a mate another male, and they have been known to stay together for up to six years, until the death of one of the partners. Like other married penguin couples, they spend much of their time close together, often touching. They will even live together in an underground burrow in a nest they have built together. Unlike male pairs in other birds, homosexual pairs of Humboldt penguins never acquire any eggs. They are together simply because they like each other. There is absolutely no reproductive advantage for them. Gentoo penguins have an equal number of exclusively homosexual pair bonds. But if one dies, the surviving male might well go on to pair with a female and even raise a family. One cannot argue that these homosexual unions, when they do involve coparenting, are made simply because it is easier to raise a child in this fashion, since the proportion of birds who participate in them is often relatively small, whereas one would expect them to be much larger if such unions were only a reproductive strategy. I agree with Bagemihl that animals, like people, form deep attachments to other animals and other people, often of the same sex, for reasons that have nothing to do with genetic advantage and everything to do with emotions, and one emotion in particular: love. Why it has taken two hundred years for biologists even to begin to recognize this is a comment on our species. In fact, there is a uniqueness to humans in this respect: We are the only species that humiliates, ridicules, tortures, and even murders members of our species because they love individuals of the same sex. Bagemihl points out that "almost without exception, animals with 'different' sexualities and/or genders are completely integrated into the social fabric of the species, eliciting little of the attention, hostility, segregation, or secrecy that we are accustomed to associating with homosexuality in our society."

Swans

In Britain there are three species of swan: the Bewick's and whooper swans, which are migratory, and the mute swan, which is not. The Bewick's swan, *Cygnus columbianus bewickii,* breeds on tundra in the Russian Arctic, and birds from western populations fly some four thousand kilometers each autumn to wintering sites located primarily in the Netherlands, Britain, and Ireland. (Will we ever know what these birds think about on their great migrations? I also wonder whether they are able to sleep at all.) All three swan species are monogamous, and have better luck with chicks when they stay together. Divorce was highest in whooper swans, who migrate short distances, and divorce was nonexistent in Bewick's swans, who migrate long distances. Bewick's swans are wholly migratory; the birds must breed, moult, and start their four-thousand-kilometer return migration in just four months, while the tundra is habitable. "No cases of divorce have previously been recorded for Bewick's swan pairs known to have bred. . . . None of the birds included in the analyses changed mates whilst the previous partner was known to be still alive." This is certainly superior to the human record. Precisely for this reason, some ornithologists argue, we can be certain that this trait is under tight genetic control, that is, that the trait of fidelity is innate rather than consciously (or even unconsciously) chosen. The individual swan can take no pride in fidelity, they insist. But it seems rather perverse to argue that the birds had no choice but to love one another! Female pairs, too, often come together in mute swans and in that case their clutches of eggs are entirely infertile. Knowing this, they still remain together, often for life. What is the driving force behind such behavior, which cannot be accounted for by the usual biological explanations? I do not see how we can escape the idea that swans, like people, can fall in love with a member of their own sex for reasons that have nothing to do with genetics and everything to do with feelings.

Imprinting

We have all become familiar with pictures of geese following a human (on land or in the air), a phenomenon known as "imprint-ing," a term coined by Konrad Lorenz, who described and explained imprinting, though he did not discover it.[8] There are a number of animals who, upon emerging from an egg or immediately after birth, form a strong and lifelong attachment to the first object they see. Obviously in almost every case the first object they see is their own mother, so this is a useful device. (Imprinting happens imme-diately in geese because they have such a short time in which to learn what they need to know before they are on their own.) Ducks nor-mally do not leave their nests for some twenty-four hours after hatching. So by the time they leave the nest, they are well past the critical peak period for imprintability, and have most likely already imprinted on the mother. Imprinting on the wrong object in the natural environment is thus very rare. But some species of birds (geese in particular, but many other kinds of birds as well) who for some reason first see a human being upon hatching imprint on the human being and follow her or him as if the person were the bird's mother.

Another form of imprinting concerns the later sexual preferences of the animal. Many experiments have been conducted in which domestic species of fowl, ducks, pigeons and doves, and finches have been reared by parents of a different breed and color. As adults, these animals prefer to mate with birds of their foster parent's color rather than their own color. It is significant that among some species of ducks in which the males and the females look very different (the males are brightly colored, the females are "drab"), only males imprint when they are fostered by another species; females do not. In species in which only the female cares for the young (for example, ducks and fowl), animal biologists believe there may be a strong selection pressure against female imprintability, since it would result in homosexual pairing among adult females, as the first object they see is their own mother. The homosexual bond may be so intense as to preclude fertile eggs and the raising of young. Females have an innate (that is, not learned) preference for the colors and elaborate courtship behavior and distinctive calls of the male. Males, on the other hand, must learn about the more subtle charms of the female, and perhaps imprinting on their mother at birth facilitates this. (Chicks imprint on one another in any case, which would explain why they remain so closely coordinated in their movements.)

In species in which the male is visibly different from the female, it is usually the male who is more conspicuous, having a distinctive color pattern or song. In these species, I have been assured, the females are less susceptible to imprinting. (I am not sure how one would determine this, however, since it must be very difficult to determine the gender of ducklings or goslings.) For example, among ducks and geese the sensitive periods for sexual imprinting correspond closely to the duration of parental care. So it is longer in geese than in ducks. This means that the infant bird is susceptible to imprinting only while it is a member of the family group. The sensitive period in some birds is over well before the chicks leave the nest and mix with members of other species, so there is little chance they would sexually imprint on a member of another species. Obviously, the fact that the sensitive period is *brief* evolved as a safety device so that the young will not form attachments where they do not belong.[9]

When I was a small child, I was present when two baby ducks hatched. They saw me, and for a whole year after that, they would follow me wherever I went, even to school. I was fascinated, but I was also proud, as if these ducks had recognized some special paternal (it was really maternal, but I did not know that at the time) quality in me. Only as an adult do I now see that these cross-fostering experiments, as they are called, have a sinister side. Birds were not meant to imprint on us. They do so not out of an excess of love, but faute de mieux—for want of anything better. Maybe we should not exploit this natural capacity to love, which was meant for their own species, not for us. I wonder how much of the bond between parrots and their "owners" is real as opposed to artificially induced by this sort of imprinting.

Ratite Birds

Among the male birds who take most responsibility for sitting on nests (brooding) are the ratite birds found in South America, Australia, and Africa—ostriches, rheas, cassowaries, and emus. The wild ostrich, *Struthio camelus,* is now found only in Africa. (Many people think of these birds as being from Australia, but they are an introduced bird there, raised only on farms.) These are huge, flightless, two-toed terrestrial birds with long necks and powerful legs. They are the largest living birds as well as the heaviest (at six feet tall, they can weigh up to 285 pounds). Each foot is armed with a formidable, sturdy, ten-centimeter-long flattened claw on the thick inner toe, making the birds strong enough to kill a lion. Given its stride of eight feet, it is not surprising that it is an extraordinarily fast runner. Both male and female ostriches sprint at up to forty-five miles per hour. Their huge eyes (the better to see enemies) are the largest of any terrestrial vertebrate. Ostriches are not sexually mature until they are three or four years old, and they can live forty or more years in the wild. When cornered, or when incubating, the ostrich tries to escape detection by remaining immobile, with its body, neck, and head flattened out on the ground. No doubt this gave rise to the popular (but mistaken) notion that ostriches bury their heads in the sand when alarmed. At night they roost in communal sites. Eyes closed, they sleep with their necks raised most of the night. For the deeper kind of sleep, which they do only for short intervals, they rest their heads and necks, stretched out on the ground in front of them. The male ostrich is one of the few birds (ducks and geese are the other two) to have a penis (unlike most mammals, the minuscule testes of male birds are internal; they have only tiny, poorly developed phalluses that are not protrusible, and fertilization takes place through a seminal sac everting into the female cloaca). The ostrich is so well suited to its arid environment that it does not even require drinking water.

The giant eggs, more than three pounds each, are laid in a communal nest by several females, including what is known as a "major hen" and several secondary females, or minor hens (sometimes they alternate; the designation has nothing to do with dominance). The major hen and the dominant male share the task of incubation and care of the young. The minor hens mate with several males and lay their eggs in different nests, but do not usually incubate. Before hatching, the ostrich chicks make a melodious contact call, which is answered by both parents.

Struth and Camela were two ostriches who had recently decided to raise a family together. Struth won Camela over by what is called *kantling*. He dropped to the ground next to his partner and rocked steadily from side to side, fluffing out his tail and sweeping the ground with his wings. He twisted his head and neck, inflating and deflating his throat, and singing to Camela a song that to humans would sound like a giant boom, but was obviously music to her sensitive ears. He found the nest for them, and as she began to lay eggs, they took turns sitting on the nest during the day, protecting the eggs, but not yet incubating them. But he alone was the one to sit throughout the entire night. His greatest fear was of the Egyptian vulture, the only bird to pose a real threat to his large and sturdy eggs. A human could stand on his eggs and not break them, so strong were they. But the clever Egyptian vulture had learned to throw hard quartz stones at ostrich eggs, and in this way was able to shatter the shells. Whenever Struth saw one of these birds, he would run straight back to his nest, something he didn't usually do.

Camela was not Struth's only love, but she was his main love. His other wives produced eggs for him, too, and together Struth and Camela collected seventy-eight eggs. Camela got on top of them and did her best to cover all of them. But that was impossible. Eight were likely to be her own, but she could only cover twenty altogether, which left many eggs that would never hatch.[10] She knew which were her own eggs, though, judging them by shape and texture, and moved most of the eggs of her friends to the edge of her nest, where they were doomed to remain unhatched. After six weeks, twenty eggs hatched. Struth was very excited, dancing and singing exuberantly, especially when he was able, just three days later, to accompany Camela and the twenty chicks on their first venture out. Did they think all twenty were their own? We don't know, but they took wonderful care of them.

The first day, there was a sweltering African sun, and they

both sheltered all twenty chicks under their wings from the heat. The next day there was a downpour, and they unfolded their wings like umbrellas for the whole family. A few days later they met up with another family group. The dispute that arose was mysterious. But at the end of it, Struth and Camela found themselves taking over the guardianship of the young birds from both groups. They were now almost a hundred, but this is not the record. Sometimes groups of up to 380 chicks have been recorded. For an entire year, the chicks were never without an adult escort, either Struth or Camela.

Struth was as active a father as Camela was a mother. He protected the hundred small ostriches with his powerful feet, and kept careful watch for enemies with his keen eyes. How much information he and Camela imparted to their young about the territory, its dangers, and its delicacies is still an open question, but the very fact that they remained close together for an entire year implies that some amount of avian culture is transferred to the new generation. The reason for communal guarding and communal nesting are not very well understood. If the ostrich is simply an unselfish parent, less concerned with enhancing his own reproductive success than with taking care of children, how can this be reconciled with Darwinian theory?

The rheas, *Rhea americana,* of South America are closely related to the ostrich. The male leads the female to a nest that he has previously prepared. He does this with several females. One after another, they lay their eggs in the hollow, and return every two or three days to deposit more eggs. The male alone incubates and rears the chicks. The chicks hatch synchronously, in a period of twenty-four to twenty-eight hours. After a few days, the male leads them away and then stays with them, constantly calling them with plaintive contact whistles. In danger, when it is too hot, or at night, the chicks hide under his wing. Lost chicks are always liable to be adopted by another male with his chicks and this can lead to a fair disparity in ages between the members of a crèche. The father takes care of them for six months, but the chicks stay together until they attain sexual maturity, at two to three years of age. They are easily tamed. When I was in the south of Chile, I saw great bands of them (called, in Spanish, *nandu comun),* and was able to approach them and stroke their long, elegant necks.

In parts of Asia (New Guinea and Irian Jaya), in the same family, are found the cassowaries, closely related to the emu. They have a curious structure on top of their heads, the casque, a tough, elastic, foamlike substance. Wattles, hanging from the birds' necks, unfeathered and brightly colored in different shades of gaudy colors—red, blue, purple, yellow, and white—are thought to act as a social signal of emotion in the dark rain forest, since the bare parts of the neck can change colors with the birds' moods, according to whether they are joyful or angry. Displaying a trait unusual among birds, the females are more brightly colored than the males. Only the male guards and incubates the eggs, but unlike the rheas and the emu, the male mates with a single female, who lays three to five eggs in a clutch. Because these birds are extremely difficult to observe, very little is known about them. They eat the fruit of at least seventy-five different varieties of fruit trees. The male prepares the nest, which is so well disguised that only very rarely have any been found. So hard are these birds to breed in captivity that huge sums have been offered for a clutch. The chicks can walk and feed by themselves a few hours after hatching. The father stays with them for nine months, protecting them primarily from their greatest enemy, feral pigs. To the Kalam tribe of the Upper Karonk Valley, in the Schrade Mountains, cassowaries are reincarnations of their female ancestors, for which reason it is forbidden to hunt or trade them or to keep them in captivity.

The emu, *Dromaius novaehollandiae,* is restricted to mainland

Australia. It is a huge, inquisitive bird that will follow humans, merely to see what they are up to. The emu is the only bird, I believe, that purrs during copulation. The nest is built by the male, but as with the cassowary, it is so well camouflaged that only rarely has anyone observed an incubating bird. The male and female stay together for at least five months before incubation begins. Only the male guards and incubates the eggs. Incubation lasts eight weeks and during that time the male does not eat, drink, or defecate, only getting up several times each day to turn the eggs and tidy the nest. After forty-six days the chicks are born, a maximum of four days apart. The chicks are able to walk after five to twenty-four hours. In a week they are competent swimmers and runners. Despite this fast maturation, the father stays with the chicks for at least five months. The fully grown adult emu has no enemies other than man, but the chicks are taken by dingos, foxes, and birds of prey. A male will allow chicks from other broods to join his group as long as they are smaller than his own offspring. Although the bond loosens, the male may stay with the chicks for up to eighteen months.

In 1932, the Australian government, under pressure from farmers, sent an army artillery unit to western Australia to exterminate twenty thousand emus that were causing extensive crop damage. The tactics for this emu war involved driving the birds along fences until they were within the range of machine guns and grenades. As soon as they were shot at, the emus dispersed rapidly into small groups. After a month of fruitless pursuit, the Royal Australian Artillery had killed only twelve emus, and had to withdraw in humiliation.[11] Unbeknownst to the soldiers, male emus sometimes coparent with each other: Two males will attend one nest at the same time, incubating all the eggs together. The two fathers then cooperate in raising their chicks together, calling to them with purr-growls and jointly defending them from predators. According to Bruce Bagemihl, emu coparenting probably occurs in about 3 percent of all nests. Would not those soldiers have been better off studying the parenting habits of these interesting animals?

Brooding

The fact that so many male birds participate in parenting must have something to do with their ability to brood (incubate) an egg (no bird is live-born) as well as the female, and, upon birth, to provide food along with the female, since no bird nurses. It reminds me of an excuse I hear so often (and use myself just as frequently) from men: They cannot be expected to be equal partners in caring for a nursing child, since the mother is indispensable and the man feels useless much of the time. One mistake we made with Ilan, who at three years old is still nursing, is that I did not give him an occasional bottle right from the beginning, so he could begin to see me, as well as his mother, as a source of nourishment.

While no human male has ever lactated, birds have no such excuse. In many species of birds, males and females take turns sitting on the egg. In more than half the species of birds, the incubation is shared by males and females; in about a quarter of them the females do this alone; and in just 6 percent it is the male who sits on the egg by himself. In some bird families, all three patterns coexist. When the duty is shared, one parent sits while the other brings food to it.[12] Then they reverse the order. The male hornbill, however, is an extremist. He does not sit on the eggs, his wife does. He walls her into a tree cavity for the six to seventeen weeks (depending on the species) of incubation by using his beak as a spade and plastering most of the entrance with mud (the irony is that his wife, sitting on the inside, helps him). Then he feeds her through a residual opening. She cannot get out, but neither can a predator of any size get in. Evidently he is a fanatic when it comes to protecting his wife and her eggs. During one season in East Africa, a male silvery-cheeked hornbill brought his wife 24,000 pieces of fruit in 1,600 nest visits during the 120-day breeding cycle.

Humans tend to think of brooding an egg as a purely instinctual activity. Is it then equally instinctive in both males and females? In fact, young inexperienced birds often lose their eggs. With experience, successful egg brooding improves. Males probably spend considerable time watching more experienced birds and learning the secrets of good sitting—the avian Zen of egg brooding.

In a few dozen bird species, the male provides most of the parental care. In those species, what biologists oddly call "sex role reversal" is quite common: We expect males to be bigger, more aggressive, and more interested in sex—and with these birds, the opposite is true. An example is the American jacana (*Jacana spinos*), a tropical shorebird that lives in freshwater swamps and marshes. The females keep harems of at least two males, and insist on mating with the members of their harem every day. The male makes the nest, broods the eggs, and attends and defends the young after the eggs hatch. It is of interest that in this species of birds, the females are almost twice the size of the males. If human males did more child care, would women become larger?

Wilson's phalarope (*Phalaropus tricolor*) is a graceful marsh bird resembling a sandpiper that breeds on prairie wetlands and Arctic tundra. The males provide almost all the incubatory care and the phalarope females are larger than males and more brightly colored. They are also highly aggressive toward each other when a male is present. When a female pursues a male, he will often swoop down over other swimming females, drawing them into the chase. The male then stops and hovers while the females fight in midair as he watches. The same is true for the red phalarope *(Phalaropus fulicarius),* a shore bird that nests on Arctic islands. Once the female starts laying eggs in the nest that they have both constructed, the dull-colored (he need not advertise himself, since he is already in high demand) male puts in the nest lining and then does all the incubation.

Pigeons

In pigeons, which are a monogamous species, the male does the parenting. He even has the ability to make milk in a gland in his esophagus in order to feed the young, just as the emperor penguin does. Pigeons are for many people practically the only bird that they ever see up close. But most people have almost no sense of what these birds are really like. Common wisdom has it that they are stupid, and this is a prejudice that has been widely disseminated, even by scientists. A famous anecdote (related by none other than Konrad Lorenz in 1935) tells of a cat killing a domestic pigeon and then the pigeon's mate keeping strictly to his schedule, roosting in his usual place at night beside the nest (in most species of dove, the female broods from the evening until the morning of the next day, the male during the rest of the time), and then brooding at the customary hour of ten o'clock the next morning. But we do not know enough about the circumstances to understand this behavior. As I said before, we know that experience makes birds more efficient parents; pairs nesting for the first time rear fewer young than do older breeders. Perhaps this was the hapless male's first attempt to raise a chick. These experiments with pigeons go back to the 1930s, and were specifically devised to show how stupid they are. One early experiment demonstrated that "a female pigeon would lay eggs quite readily if it were placed in a cage with a male pigeon; somewhat less readily with a female pigeon; and not at all if isolated completely from other birds. However, when it was accompanied by a mirror in its cage, it began to lay!" This is not amusing. Of course when an animal is wrenched from its natural home and tortured in an alien environment one can expect unusual behavior. That tells us nothing, absolutely nothing, about the real abilities or the real lives of pigeons.

The new respect for pigeons, unfortunately, derives from the same kind of human-oriented experiments. How stupid can a pigeon be, the new research leads us to ask, when they can be trained to peck at spots on their own plumage that they can see only in a mirror? Evidently they know that they are looking at images of themselves. Human children only recognize themselves in mirrors at about ten months old, and most animals (except for chimpanzees and orangutans) cannot recognize themselves at all. In addition, pigeons' ability to categorize is by no means limited to what is important to them in natural habitats (trees that give shelter and sites for their nests, and people who might harm them). Years of experimental work with pigeons shows beyond doubt that they can recognize the category "water," whether it is presented as a drop, a puddle, pool, or ocean. They can distinguish something shown to them on a slide as being either new or familiar. In fact, they seem to have an uncanny ability to understand precisely what it is that the experimenter is testing for. But none of this is any excuse for testing rather than simply observing. We know so little about the real life of pigeons in their natural world—why ask about their ability to count?

I am fascinated by pigeons and their unusual relationship with humans. They live with us in something resembling intimacy, yet we have never really succeeded in overcoming a certain wariness on their part. Many city people I know remark that they have never seen a baby pigeon. Where are they? I have my own hypothesis, which came to me after reading one of the great works of scholarship in our time, A.W. Schorger's 1955 book, *The Passenger Pigeon*. This remarkable bird *(Ectopistes migratorius),* also called the wild pigeon, with its small blue head, iridescent green and purple neck, massive breast muscles, and long, pointed wings commensurate with its speed and grace in the air, had an aura of uncommon elegance, to judge by the few photos that exist in the American Museum of Natural History in New York. As many as 6 billion of these spectacular birds existed in the Untied States in the last century. Even though each pair laid but one egg, at one time this pigeon formed 25 to 40 percent of the total bird population of the United States. They had coexisted for thousands of years with native Americans. But European settlers began killing them in unbelievable numbers, for sport and food. An Indian known as Leather-stocking said: "This comes of settling a country! Here have I known the pigeons to fly for forty long years, and, till you made your clearing, there was nobody to scare or to hurt them. I loved to see them come into the woods, for they were company to a body; hurting nothing." They were hunted mercilessly, and could not comprehend what was happening to them: "It was pathetic to see the efforts of the comrades of a wounded pigeon to support him in his flight. One after another would dart under the stricken one as he began to sink, as if to buoy him with their wings. They would continue these efforts long after he had sunk below the general line of flight, and not until all hope was lost would they reluctantly leave him and rejoin the flock." The year 1900 marked the end of this bird. Suddenly nobody could find even a single one. It was not possible, all the expert ornithologists agreed, that such a common bird could simply have vanished. The search for a living wild passenger pigeon began in all seriousness long after it had ceased to exist. Can anything be sadder? Huge amounts of money were offered for the capture of a single bird. The reward was never collected. On a bluff in Wyalusing State Park, at the junction of the Mississippi and Wisconsin Rivers, stands a monument to the passenger pigeon. The legend on the bronze tablet reads:

DEDICATED
TO THE LAST WISCONSIN
PASSENGER PIGEON
SHOT AT BABCOCK, SEPT. 1899

It is my belief that the humble street pigeon in New York City today somehow knows to avoid close contact with the murderers of his wild cousins. Perhaps that is why we never see their children: They don't trust us.

Building a Nest

Cooperation between male and female in nest building is the rule among birds, occurring in more than 80 percent of families.[12] Building a nest can be very hard work. Many species of passerine (perching) birds make more than a thousand trips to gather the materials used in making a nest. Often the behavior of the male bird during nest making gives a clue to the female as to what she can expect later in life. If he is diligent in constructing the nest, he is likely to be helpful to her in other ways when raising their children. She can expect him to brood the eggs and feed the chicks, too. Male birds often announce their suitability as fathers by their diligence in preparing a nest. Some will do it all on their own. The male village weaver *(Ploceus cucullatus)* hangs upside down beneath the bottom entrance of his nest, and then gives a display to unmated visiting females by flapping his wings to show their bright yellow inner lining. This display is an invitation to the female to come into the nest he has prepared, and the female will not enter without this invitation. When she does enter, the male begins to sing to her while she makes a thorough inspection of the interior of the nest, taking up to twenty minutes. As a test, she pulls and tugs with her beak at the materials within the nest. If she accepts him, she signals this by bringing soft grass tips or other lining materials into the nest and begins to line it as the male watches proudly. If the female does not accept, she flies away and does not return. If several females in turn reject his nest, a male will become dispirited and tear it down. "Dispirited" is, of course, an interpretation, but when I asked one of the legendary figures of evolutionary biology, Robert Trivers, whether he believed that weaver birds whose nests are constantly rejected by females feel anything when they tear them down to construct new ones, he told me, "I see no reason at all to assume that birds lack subjective experiences, including 'thoughts.' And I do think a methodology will someday be worked out. As you know, it is very unwise in advance to foreclose what science is capable of answering."[13]

Bowerbirds

The Australian and New Guinean bowerbirds construct such intricate and elaborately decorated bowers that many people find it hard to believe a bird has built them. In fact, the first European naturalist to find a bower, Odoardo Beccari, believed it to be of human rather than avian origin. The bower of the bowerbird is not a nest at all, but rather a site for courtship displays. There are two types of bowers, avenue bowers (with parallel rows of vertical twigs) and maypole bowers, in which the twigs crisscross and interlock around a small sapling. The male bird dances around this maypole and as he dances he raises and fans out a brilliant orange circular crest on his head. Some maypole builders, such as the gardener bower bird *(Ambylornis),* build a bower by piling sticks against a sapling on the floor of a mountain rain forest. Around the tower he places a kind of saucer made of moss. The towers are large, with roofs and internal chambers. The courtyards are made of moss and are decorated with snail shells of various colors, spider silk, and fresh flowers that are changed daily for months on end!

The striped gardener bowerbird *(Amblyornis subalaris)* builds a circular hut of twigs with a dome roof. He leaves a large opening at one side, the "forecourt," which he decorates with colorful fruits and fresh flowers that are also changed daily. Colors play an important role for many bowerbirds. The male satin bowerbird selects shiny blue objects that resemble the lilac-blue color of his eyes and the sheen of his glossy blue-black plumage. Gerald Borgia, one of the leading researchers of bowerbirds, has pointed out that "the male prunes the leaves above the platform, apparently to allow sunlight to illuminate the platform. The display of shiny blue objects, which are relatively uncommon, and their placement on a yellow background suggests an attempt to give an unambiguous and highly visible signal."[14] A brown gardener bowerbird will replace flowers in his bower with fresh ones, carefully inspecting each blossom as he puts it in place, shifting its position if he is not satisfied. Many observers have spoken about an aesthetic sense similar to our own.

Avenue builders actually *paint* their bowers: The male—taking a bit of fruit pulp, bark, chewed green vegetable material, or charcoal in his bill—stimulates the flow of saliva and applies the secretion with his beak to the inner walls of the avenue, staining them a different color. Some birds use a saturated wad of bark as a paintbrush. Nobody knows what the function of bower painting is. Could it possibly be a substitute for courtship feeding, or perhaps identification of the individual male owning the bower? Throughout this book I have tried to argue in favor of animals possessing subjective awareness, consciousness. Here is another instance: It seems to me the bowerbirds must derive some aesthetic pleasure from the bright colors. Darwin thought so, too: In *The Descent of Man* (p. 63), he wrote, "If female birds had been incapable of appreciating the beautiful colours, the ornaments, and voices of their male partners, all the labour and anxiety exhibited by them in displaying their charms before the females would have been thrown away; and this it is impossible to admit."[15] While these remarks apply to the physical characteristics of male birds, there is no reason not to extend them to secondary characteristics.

Some bowerbirds are exceedingly plain-looking. Which ones? Well, precisely those birds who make the most elaborate bowers. In bowerbirds, there seems to be an inverse relationship between the complexity of the bower and the colorfulness of the male bird. Species with sexual dichromatism (colorful males, drab females) build relatively simple bowers, while the males of the plain-colored species, in which the sexes are colored alike, build larger, more elaborate, and highly decorated bowers. The greatest painters, the most aesthetically sensitive, the birds who collect the most beautiful shells and build the most elaborate towers and tend the finest gardens, are the most dull-colored of the bowerbirds.

No doubt this was noticed for years without anyone thinking about it in depth, until E. Thomas Gilliard, the late curator of birds at the American Museum of Natural History (he died at the young age of fifty-three in 1965), made a series of trips between 1948 and 1964 to New Guinea. (He had been with the United States Army in the South Pacific during the Second World War.) He was an astute observer, a fine ornithologist, but he was also deeply interested in theory. Suddenly he noticed something that was extraordinarily simple, but profound: "These objects have in effect become externalised bundles of secondary sexual characteristics that are psychologically but not physically connected with the males. The transfer also has an important morphological effect: once colourful plumage is rendered unimportant, natural selection operates in the direction of protective colouration and the male tends more and more to resemble the female."[16]

I must say that I find this example of "transference" far more convincing than the psychoanalytic notion of transference (in which patients are said to transfer their feelings from their parents and other important figures from childhood onto the person of the analyst, an example of projection). It is rich in possibilities as well: Gilliard suggests that the bower building contains embedded in it many aspects of nest building. The wall of sticks, the lining of grass, even the way the male places egg-sized berries or pebbles near the center of the basketlike structure resemble what happens when a bird builds a nest.

Natural jewelry replaces brilliant feathers. The bower replaces the nest. What do they achieve? Well, the bird becomes the lonely eccentric artist, not expected to participate in daily household activities: He does not build a true nest, he does not take care of the kids. He is an artist, lost in his own world. He has more direct benefits, too: He need not call attention to himself with his brilliant feathers, making himself the target of predators. He is inconspicuous except when he is painting in his courtyard.

Evidently age plays a key role in building the bowers. Young and inexperienced birds build relatively rudimentary bowers with little decoration. Young birds watch older males and learn by imitating. So there is an important element of cultural transmission of bower-building "styles."

How did these remarkable behaviors evolve? There is a thesis that bowers evolved from arena behavior. Bowerbirds are arena birds: The males and females live apart most of the year. The males, during the breeding seasons, spend all their time at their bowers, in their courts (called the arenas) where they await the females.[17] These birds have no true pair bond, and the males play no part whatever in building or defending the actual nest or in rearing the young. But they do court. Arena behavior is found in any number of birds around the world. The courtship behavior, however, is in sharp contrast to the behavior of the other ninety-nine percent of the world's birds. The British ornithologist C.R. Stonor describes the behavior of the ruff, a sandpiper of northern Europe and Asia. The males and females live apart except for a few

minutes in the breeding season. In spring the males gather in isolated clans on grassy little hills in rolling meadowland. Each male
has a territory, an arena, that he defends. The clan waits as long as
necessary for the visits of occasional females in search of mates.
Gilliard, drawing on an earlier author, gives a vivid description of
the males on their mounds: "The clan waits day after day for the
visits of occasional females in search of mates. When one appears,
the males go to their courts and assume strangely stiff postures,
extending the colorful plumage of their neck ruffs. They look, says
Stonor, like a bed of flowers: The female wanders through this
cluster and pecks at the neck feathers of the bird she prefers.
Mating occurs immediately—whereupon the rejected males
immediately collapse on their courts as if in a fainting spell."[18]

The sage grouse and the prairie chicken of North America
have similar arena behavior. Gilliard also studied the magnificent
bird of paradise *(Diphyllodes magnificus)*. For months of the year
the male waits in his court. He spends countless hours trimming
away the forest leaves above his court, enabling a shaft of light to
enhance his iridescent coloring. Often these birds have what are
called "exploded" arenas, that is, the arenas are so large and far
apart that it is hard to recognize that they actually have boundaries that are maintained from year to year, boundaries from
within which the males keep in contact through loud powerful
calls.

Men, Women, and Monogamy

Is the quality of father-care better in birds for whom males and
females are the same size? It would seem so. Where there is
extreme sexual dimorphism, that is, where males are much larger
than females, there tend to be harems.[19] You see this in the gorilla,
in gelada baboons, in lions, and in elephant seals. Not only are the
males often twice as large as the females, but they also have larger

canine teeth, shoulder capes, manes, or large antlers. In these species, the alpha male acts as if birth and the taking care of a child are simply none of his business. Obviously these males are polygynous, not monogamous. They are concerned almost exclusively with mating success, not its aftermath.[20]

Many men like to think that we are such a species. And in fact, if one looks at the societies around the world today, probably the majority outside of the "developed" world are societies in which men take, legally or not, more than one wife when they can afford to. But since we also have many societies in which monogamy is the rule, one cannot simply say that our species is one way or another. That men do nonetheless say "we" are not a monogamous species is a commentary on their politics, not their knowledge. Many men, in describing the tendencies of human males, like to think of bears and lions and the silverback in a gorilla troop. But humans are only very slightly dimorphic in size. Men have more body hair, and deeper voices, but these are vestigial characteristics, serving no known function, and women, as we know, live longer. Across almost all animal species (certainly primates as a whole), the reduction of sexual dimorphism is commonly associated with monogamy.

I would venture to speculate (and it has to be speculation rather than fact, since we cannot know what the cultural influence has been on animals) that cultural values and pressures exert greater influence on humans than on any other species. Sexual mating systems, and how we raise our children, can be decided on the basis of our own thinking, rather than being driven by hormonal or even evolutionary forces. We can choose how we wish to live. Whether we live up to our choices is another matter. Once we have chosen, however, what we do can be more or less natural. For example, it is more "natural" to have your child sleep next to you than in another room, as we shall see in a later chapter, yet many people decide to put their babies in a crib in a different room. I think they are making a mistake, but that mistake is more understandable to me if the person is at least aware of the reason that sleeping in the same room is considered the more natural behavior.

What puzzles me about birds is that apparently in no bird species does the female inform her mate by voice or gestures that her eggs have hatched. When the father finally finds his eggs, by accident, it would appear, he examines them attentively, then leaves and promptly brings food to them. The great American ornithologist Alexander Skutch, in his book *Parent Birds and Their Young,* concludes that birds, "for all the satisfaction that constantly mated kinds appear to find in each other's company and the distress they show when separated, have not reached that higher stage of psychic development at which joy is enhanced by the sharing of good news. If they had attained this level of development, we would hardly expect a female bird to permit her closely associated mate to remain for hours, or even days, ignorant of the fact that their nestlings had hatched." It is hard for me to believe that there is not some explanation, but I would not want to disagree with so distinguished an observer.

I believe, as Meredith Small says in her new book *Our Babies, Ourselves,* that human infants were designed to be part of an intimate physical dyad with an adult. The very concept of "child" implies an other with whom the child interacts in an intimate, all-encompassing way. Our species did not evolve as a solitary species. Where monogamy exists, the child's close enmeshment becomes possible with more than one adult, perhaps not equally, but often with equal vigor or familiarity. Monogamy almost invariably implies family. It has always struck me that children almost never welcome divorce, and that once there are children, the very concept of divorce is odd. Even when we divorce, when there are children, in some sense we remain married, certainly in the children's minds. Divorcing the past is not really an option for children (divorce itself is not an option for them, either), and they can retain, even as adults, I believe, a wistful hope for reunion, a tribute, no doubt, to the ferocity of their feelings, but also to the remarkable intensity of familial bonds. Do other animals experience something at all similar, and if so, in what ways does it manifest itself? Could the very intensity with which animals invest in procreation be testimony to the force of their earliest happy experiences, a way of passing them on to their children?

six: Are You Sure He's Yours?
Who Cares about Paternity Certainty?

Why is there such a difference between birds and mammals when it comes to monogamy? Monogamy is only occasional among the four-thousand-odd mammalian species, while we saw that 92 percent of the eighty-six-hundred-odd species of birds are primarily monogamous. Is it all purely a question of strategy? All animals bear young and all of them must face the question of how to accommodate them in their lives. For no animal is this a matter of complete indifference. It takes energy to conceive a child or to raise it, and all animal fathers, the theory goes, want to be sure they are raising their own young. Is this true, though?

It does seem to follow from other, less contentious ideas about how animals recognize one another. There can be no doubt that animals do this reliably. Animal behaviorists place strong emphasis on the ability of an animal to know that it belongs to a particular species and not any other. This is important for many decisions that need to be made in the life of the animal, particularly mating and taking care of children. No wild animal mates with a member of another species, so clearly every animal knows something fundamental about who it is. How does an animal do this? Obviously to some extent there are innate factors involved. But far more important is experience.

Consider geese. Flocks in the wild consist of father, mother, and the young of the past two and sometimes even three years. During the years that the young goslings are following their parents, they are learning what it means to be a goose. Geese are highly social animals, and to them the flock is all-important (unlike ducks). The young watch the gander act as a good husband, protecting his mate when she is nesting. Even when he is some distance away, if he hears just one distress call from her, he will come rushing back, sometimes bringing other young males of the flock to help him. If an intruder is driven off, the gander gives a triumphant trumpet. He is also a protective father. These lessons are not lost on the young goslings, who grow up, generally, to be much like their mothers and fathers. They know they are geese, because they grow up as geese. Should something happen (say, a human interrupts the family unit) during the sensitive time when these important impressions are still forming, and a human is the first living being the gosling sees, she might come to believe she is a human, and will choose as her partner only a human, male or female. In the wild, such situations are so rare that they do not reflect a defect in the evolution of goose behavior.

These goslings know they are related to their parents and to their brothers and sisters because they are constantly in their presence. "Kin recognition," as animal behaviorists call it, is a topic on which many books have been written. Apart from their early experiences, animals use sight, or smell, or hearing to sense that another animal is like them, that they belong to the same species. To mate, it is essential that an animal recognize exactly how similar he or she is to another animal. Ideally, one animal chooses another that is similar to the parent of the opposite sex, but not too similar. Incest is to be avoided, since outbreeding is essential for healthy offspring. Young swans have certain beak details that are very like those of their parents. The dark patches on the beaks of the parental pair are similar in shape to those on the beaks of their own cygnets. When these cygnets are ready to choose a mate, they look for (consciously?) swans with different markings.

Humans do something very similar. The avoidance of incest was first noticed by Edward Westermarck, the great nineteenth-century Finnish sociologist. In a passage from his three-volume work, *The History of Human Marriage,* he wrote: "Generally speaking, there is a remarkable absence of erotic feelings between persons living very closely together from childhood. Nay more, in this, as in many other cases, sexual indifference is combined with the positive feeling of aversion when the act is thought of. . . . Persons who have been living closely together from childhood are as a rule near relatives. Hence their aversion to sexual relations with one another displays itself in custom and law as a prohibition of intercourse between near kin."[1] Westermarck's rule, as it has come to be known, has been demonstrated over and over, in such disparate places as Taiwan and Israel (children who grow up in the same kibbutz rarely marry).

Closely associated with reproductive success, kin recognition is equally important, according to theories from evolutionary biology, for care of the young. Animals must go further than simply recognizing the fact that they belong to the same species. They must be able to recognize that they are genetically related. And they do. Think about what happens to animals living in a colony, like ground squirrels, when an enemy, say a fox, approaches the colony. Certain members of the colony give out a loud whistle, a warning: "Predator approaching, watch out!" To whom are they addressing these warning calls? Are they telling the predator, "We have seen you," or are they telling other unsuspecting members of the colony that the fox is near? Do they risk their own lives by calling attention to themselves? Much careful research and elegant experiments (especially by biologist Paul Sherman) have been done to show that animals give predator warning calls more frequently when they are surrounded by close relatives than by relatives less closely related, and will do so even less frequently or not at all when surrounded by strangers. This shows that not only do animals recognize relatives, but that when they have a choice, to help a relative or a nonrelative, they will choose their relatives over other animals. This is what animal behaviorists call "kin selection," that is, we favor (select) those to whom we are related over those to whom we are not related.

But while the general point may well be true, we cannot know for certain when kin selection will come into effect or even *if* it will come into effect with anything remotely resembling precision. Will every animal really always prefer to help a related animal rather than, say, a friend? Are there some animals who will warn everyone, even if they risk their own lives? Will they keep silent if they think the risk to themselves is too great, even if surrounded by their own children? We have hardly begun to understand all the complexities of the sounding of the alarm. Think of humans: We, too, never know how we will react to danger until presented with the situation. We still don't entirely understand the reactions of many bystanders to atrocities during the Second World War. The great British geneticist J. B. S. Haldane, in his 1932 book *The Causes of Evolution,* was one of the first to explicitly formulate the idea that "in so far as it makes for the survival of one's descendants and near relations, altruistic behaviour is a kind of Darwinian fitness, and may be expected to spread as the result of natural selection." The story is that Haldane put this more convivially over a pint: He would be willing to risk his life for two full brothers, four half brothers, or eight cousins (since on average they would represent his own genetic endowment). But he was not entirely serious. And in fact we do not have any clear understanding of precisely how deeply our feelings are affected by our genetic relation to someone.

Kin selection and paternity certainty theory would predict that no bird would feed a chick that is not genetically related. But birds do this all the time. Have they been tricked? Are they just dumb? Or is it that the theory cannot really accommodate the great variety we find in nature? Scientists have outlawed the question of whether the birds know, in some sense of that word that we recognize, what they are doing when they feed a strange bird, or sit on a strange egg. The more fundamental problem is that biologists have shied away from asking any questions at all about the subjective experience of animals. Nikolas Tinbergen, one of the founders of ethology (the study of animal behavior, for which he was awarded the Nobel Prize along with his colleagues Konrad Lorenz and Karl von Frisch), warned his students in a passage at the beginning of his influential book *The Study of Instinct,* published in 1951, that "because subjective phenomena cannot be observed objectively in animals, it is idle either to claim or to deny their existence." This stern admonition took hold, and it was the rare scientist in this field who dared to declare even the slightest interest in what an animal might be thinking or feeling until the 1980s. Fortunately, today, many do, and the topic is now being addressed in a lively manner, but not in all fields.

Thus, the idea that birds might experience consciousness in some ways is not a topic addressed by ornithologists. I don't quite understand why this has been so. After all, if a cuckoo is being raised in the nest of another bird (something that happens so frequently there is a special term for it, "nest parasitism"), isn't it plausible that the father would recognize that one of his chicks looks very different from the others, when that chick might be five times their size—bigger, even, than the father? There could be many reasons that it would be interesting from a purely scientific view to ask whether the parents think about their chicks. But even from a purely speculative point of view, might these parents not simply be exercising individual preference? "This big chick may not be mine, but I like him, and I am going to feed him anyway." If we take the position that no two birds are identical (as anybody who has lived with birds on intimate terms, the way many people have with parrots, can confirm, their personalities range from wildly, possessively jealous to benignly, saintly tolerant, even of the dogs in the family), why not allow that some father or mother birds, even if only rarely, will make a conscious decision to raise a baby bird that they know is not their own? We will never know if we never acknowledge the possibility, because we cannot test what we cannot imagine.

Paternity Certainty

While evolutionary biologists tend as a group to shy away from questions that involve consciousness, awareness, and choice, they have no such hesitation when it comes to assigning primary importance to a more straightforward biological relationship, what they call "paternity certainty"—fathers will be deeply interested, the theory goes, in knowing whether a child is their own. How can a man be certain that a child is his? The mother knows: The child comes out of her. The man can only presume. Most people believe that monogamous species are monogamous so that the males can be certain that they are the fathers of the children born to the female they live with.

Animal scientists are intrigued by questions about whether fathers recognize their children as their own. No wonder this topic is fraught with difficulty, when even humans may be uncertain. The anthropologist Bronislaw Malinowski, in his book *The Sexual Life of Savages in North-Western Melanesia*,[2] the result of a four-year expedition from 1914 to 1918 in New Guinea, discusses the inhabitants of the Trobriand Islands in British New Guinea (now Papua New Guinea), who do not correlate intercourse with paternity. They told him three things that convinced him that they failed to make the connection. First, they pointed to a woman whom they claimed was so repulsive that nobody would ever, or had ever, slept with her. "Yet *this* woman has had a child, as the native would triumphantly point out, when I tried to persuade them that only by intercourse can children be produced." Another such woman had no fewer than six children, "all produced without the assistance of a man." The islanders castrated their male pigs, and the female pigs clearly mated with bushpigs. Not so, said the islanders, who despised the bushpigs and would never eat meat that comes from a crossbred animal— "the female pig breeds by itself." Finally, and most convincingly, Malinowski spoke of his friend Layseta, "a great sailor and magician of Sinaketa, who spent a long time in his later youth in the Amphlett Islands. On his return he found two children, borne by his wife during his absence. He is very fond of them and of his wife; and when I discussed the matter with others, suggesting that one at least of these children could not be his, my interlocutors did not understand what I meant." Malinowski tactfully did not enlighten him as to the fact that he could not have been the father of the child, having been away for several years.

Although Edward Westermarck, the Finnish sociologist, questioned Malinowski's data, suggesting that it may only have been that these people gave greater importance to the ties between mother and child than to those between father and child, it is significant that not all humans make the connection between sexual intercourse and fatherhood. Perhaps, though, Malinowski's magician friend did not care if he was the biological father of the child or not, but social custom prevented him from giving voice to such a heretical notion.

As for animals, in fact, we don't have any idea whether animal fathers understand the concept of "mine" when it comes to children. Jerram Brown, a leading biologist from the State University of New York at Albany, observed Mexican jays (*Aphelocoma ultramarina*) in the Chiricahua Mountains of southeastern Arizona.[3] What he found surprised him: 47 to 74 percent of all feeding visits to the young were what he called "altruistic," that is, they were carried out by unrelated birds. Apart from the unusual cases of nest parasitism, birds know that the chicks in their nest are their own. Brown found that at the time of fledging (when the birds have enough feathers to fly away from the nest) the feeding of the young becomes a completely communal affair and all evidence of parentage of particular young is lost. "The parents show no sign of discrimination between their own young and those of others. They appear to treat all young in their territory equally." It is not that their children leaving the nest confuses the birds, it is that they don't seem to care anymore. This is not what the evolutionary biologists expect. Brown concludes that Mexican jays just seem to be remarkably unselfish birds, more cooperative than any other bird so far studied. They could be. But maybe we simply don't know about other birds who are equally altruistic or helpful to their neighbors, to friends, to relatives. Maybe what matters to them is just what matters to us—how much they like somebody.

When I suggested to a group of primatologists that paternity certainty was not a matter of consuming interest to me or to many other fathers I knew, they looked positively shocked: What, you are kidding, aren't you? For some fathers, no doubt, the matter is pressing. When the novelist Frederick Exley *(A Fan's Notes)* saw his daughter Alexandra for the first time, he took one look at his child—"She doesn't look a thing like me," he said—and abandoned her.[4] So I thought further about this. Suppose, today, my ex-wife, Terri, were to approach me and say that Simone was not my biological child, but had been fathered by someone else. Would such a revelation in any real sense alter my relationship to Simone? No doubt it would be painful, and it might change how I think about my ex-wife, but I know it would not mean that I would love Simone any the less, or begrudge the time I had spent with her, the "investment," as biologists like to say, in her life. My feelings for her, I am sure, would not alter in the slightest. She would be the same person whether we were biologically related or not, and the past we shared, the emotions we felt together, the bond we had, would not change. The love between a father and a child is not a prisoner of genetics.

This view is not accepted by most scientists working in this field. According to many biologists, it is the doubt of paternity that explains the common behavior of people at a birth who remark on the resemblance of the baby to the father: "He looks just like you" is said far more often to a father than to a mother. People will even bring photos of the father (less often the mother) when he was young to match them with the baby. They are attempting to convince the father that the newborn child is his, that he need have no doubts, that he should care for "his" biological offspring. People assume, even if only unconsciously, that the father will be consumed by doubt and needs to be convinced, reassured, even placated. Sometimes the resemblance is indeed striking. But when it is not, do fathers really worry that they are being tricked into raising somebody else's child? I don't think so. For one thing, in reality infants rarely resemble either parent. A newborn's eyes are almost always blue, regardless of the color of the parents' eyes. The hair of infants often darkens as they grow older. Their noses are totally unformed until about age three. Some scientists have claimed that if we were asked to decide who the father was based on the appearance of a newborn, we would do better than chance. I remain unconvinced. One evolutionary theory goes so far as to suggest it is possible that human infants have evolved to look different from their fathers as a way to overcome or frustrate the male concern for paternity (and thereby assure their own survival). That may be a stretch (though I find it plausible), but what seems more likely is that the rule for our species may read: "If small and helpless, love whatever is presented," precisely in order to ensure survival of genetically unrelated infants.

Male sexual jealousy, too, has been explained as a consequence of the need to make certain that the children our partner bears are our own. It is part of our animal heritage, biologists explain. It is true that some animals, both male and female, go to extraordinary lengths to make certain their mates remain faithful. Most unusual is the female coral reef goby, *Signigobius biocellatus,* who lays her eggs in burrows excavated into sandy bottoms, then seals her mate into the burrow for the first three or four days after laying. That's one way to ensure monogamy. But there has been a proliferation of studies in the past ten years documenting the amount of "extra-pair copulations," as the biologists call them, that both males and females engage in, whether they be chimpanzees or long-billed marsh wrens. Why is it that nature so often frustrates what is considered to be an innate biological urge on the part of the male, that is, polygyny? In the case of nonmonogamous females, is it that they are looking for better genetic fathers, or is it that they just don't care who the parent is as much as males, who are supposedly obsessed with paternity certainty? And how much, after all, do male animals really care? It is almost exclusively human males who will kill another male out of sexual rivalry. Is this really the "animal in man" or is it rather the way a particular human male has been socialized into "male" culture? The fact that a man has an urge to do something does not automatically make it innate or confer the cachet of being biologically inherited. Too often this is merely the excuse that the man makes, more a legal defense than a scientific one.

Is there any equivalent to paternity certainty on the part of a child? When do human children first conceive of their "father"? Their use of the word (in its various equivalents, papa, daddy, dad, etc.) comes early, generally before the age of two (the distinguished linguist Roman Jakobson, in his article "Why Mama and Papa," pointed out that the first word of any child, anywhere, is invariably "mama," which is almost identical in all languages of the world, the nasal sound "m" originating when the child's lips are feeding at the mother's breast), but does a child have the same sense of father as of mother? Would this not depend entirely on the amount of time the child spends with each? Children, clearly, have no interest in a biological connection per se. It is the relationship they have with the person, and somehow the concept of "father" seems more abstract. This appears to be the case for animals. In monkeys, one expert said: "There cannot be any cognition of 'father.'"[5] But how about geese, or other animals for whom the father is an active participant in care? Do wolf cubs treat their mothers and their fathers differently, suggesting they have different internal images of each? We have seen some babies prefer one parent over the other at different times. Would this not suggest that infants, too, have some of the choices and individual personalities that adult animals do?

Adoption

It always amazes me that evolutionary biologists find certain kinds of apparently altruistic behavior so hard to credit. Scientists talk about "investing in offspring," and hold that males will be reluctant to invest in offspring to whom they are genetically unrelated. But we should remember that this is merely a theory, one that lives uneasily with the facts of adoption. The love of an adopted child and a parent who adopts is no less strong than the love felt by any biological child or parent. The sociobiologists think the fact that we tend to be secretive about adoption supports their view that adoption is not a natural behavior. But secrecy is a political decision, one that was in favor just a few years ago, but is less so today. In the 1950s, John Bowlby, for example, perhaps the most influential child psychiatrist of his generation, wrote in his book *Child Care and the Growth of Love:*[6] "Reputable workers usually preserve absolute secrecy on this matter [knowing the birth parents], and there seems no doubt that this is essential if the adoption is not to be endangered." Today, the opposite is generally believed: The more open the adoption, the better. Children want to know to whom they are related and deserve to know as well.

With hindsight it is easy to see some of the prejudices of people writing about adoption. Bowlby writes: "Race, and to some extent colouring, can be matched fairly easily, and by matching social class the securing of comparable intelligence is the more likely," as if intelligence were a matter of class, race, or coloring. Again, not so long ago, some experts in the field of adoption questioned whether the construct of "family" can even be rightfully applied to the parent-child unit created by adoption, since such an arrangement cannot provide "the essence of a normal family experience, which in the last analysis is immortality or at least liberation from the destiny of irrevocably coming to an end in one's own generation."[7] This attitude is certainly in keeping with the predictions of evolutionary biology, but it is an indication of how far we have come to realize how false it sounds today. Do we really only live on if we leave our biological children? Humility dictates that asking for immortality is perhaps unrealistic. How many people know much about their great-grandparents? Will our great-grandchildren even know our names?

Moreover, adoption may not be an exclusively human prerogative, as has been assumed. Among animals, it may not be so much uncommon as unknown. I am prepared to concede that we do not often see animals adopt unrelated young. But again this could simply be an artifact of what we look for: If we believe it cannot exist, there is no point in searching. And then when we do find it, we say it is so rare as to be without theoretical significance. Jane Goodall and her husband, Hugo van Lawick, followed a pack of wild dogs in Tanzania. One small puppy, Solo, was badly hurt, and when the pack set off across the Serengeti in search of food and water, she attempted to keep up with the frantic pace. For weeks she was helped by various members of the pack as the humans followed the drama by jeep. When she went into a coma, and looked ready to die, the pack abandoned her, and the writers saved her from hyenas following her trail. They raised her for the next month, but wanted more than anything to find her family pack. They did not succeed, but against all expectations, she was adopted by an unrelated male and female with pups of their own. The authors say that it was "an experience which can never before have happened in the history of a wild dog pack anywhere."[8] I wonder whether such adoptions, such moments of evident compassion that defy our scientific theories, are not more common than we know.

Male cape hunting dog pups have been reared solely by a group of males when the females died (after the pups were weaned). Male Japanese monkeys have been known to adopt young unrelated to them.[9] Cheetahs adopt strange cubs even when they do not stand to benefit in any way from the adoption. When the family of a herring gull chick is driven off by intruders, other gulls may adopt the chicks. If it is possible for us to be indifferent as to whether a child is genetically related to us or not, what implications does this have?

Investment?

If we believe that children are not just commodities, like money in the bank, talk of parental investment may be a misleading metaphor. The investment we make in our children is more like the investment we make in ourselves, it is more spiritual than material, more psychic than physical, more of an investment of the creative imagination than a sound fiscal plan. This means that a father can be as deeply invested in the child as can the mother; indeed, so can a grandmother, or even a godparent. We can even transcend the physical nature of our investment, and this gives us a freedom perhaps unique to our species. We can love a "damaged" child, a "defective" child, as much as we love a healthy child, and that love transcends the way in which we may have been programmed to feel. It forces us to ponder the very nature of love.

But can we be so certain that in this respect we are different from other primates? Perhaps I am falling into the trap of anthropocentrism, the prejudice called "speciesism" (to parallel racism), granting greater importance to my own species. We have frequently heard of babies who are born "imperfect" and immediately killed, both in animal species and in humans, often by fathers. What we don't know is the number of animals who were born this way and *not* killed, but protected by their fathers or mothers, or the number of children born with birth defects in earlier centuries who were not killed, but were, on the contrary, loved and sometimes perhaps loved even more deeply (or perhaps more purely, less selfishly) than other children, precisely because they were different and needed so much more protection.

Feeling special love for the runt of the litter may be something we share with other species. There are not many accounts of animals who protect and rear their children when they are born with serious birth defects, but there are definitely some: An entire elephant herd accommodated an infant with a clubfoot, moving more slowly for years so that he could keep up, a fact that was caught on video.

In her astonishing 1998 film *Baboon Tales* (which aired on the Discovery Channel and was produced by Tamarin Productions), Dr. Shirley Strum, a well-known baboon expert, shows us a small baby, Rama, who is badly injured in a fight with an invading troop of baboons, and then left behind when his troop leaves their territory. We see him sitting by himself, obviously in despair, crying out for help and comfort. Amazingly, a friend, a small juvenile, risks her own life to return to him. You can see on the film how frightened she is, and how wary. She tries to take Rama away with her, but he is too weak to move. She has to leave him. We assume this is the end of the tiny fellow, but that night the troop returns, and the next morning he is back with his mother, hurt, but alive. He makes it. There was nothing but danger for the adolescent female who helped him. Yet she did it, and it is captured in remarkable footage.

Also on video, and recently shown on the Discovery Channel, were images of an entire wolf pack mourning the death of the lowest member of their pack, the very wolf who was designated as the "omega." Yet when she was gone, there was undeniable sadness in the whole pack, who stayed by her body for days, at the expense of their own interests. Who can say how many similar cases have merely not been observed? If it goes against the grain of our thinking, then we will not even notice such cases when they are right under our noses. I am making a plea here for more imagination. Let us not pretend that we already understand what is bound to be obscure and difficult. We do not even have a handle on human love of this kind; why should we think we can rule it out among other animals? Sociobiologists who insist that animal parents are ruthless in the face of infants with poor prospects are failing to remember the great diversity that nature presents us with and also the mysteries we cannot always fathom with our theories. Again, let us keep an open mind in the face of some of these extraordinary tales and if they fit poorly with our theories, let us be prepared to jettison or at least broaden those theories to make them more accommodating to the richness of natural variety.

Too often explanations for certain behaviors in animals do not translate well into human terms. Indeed, such explanations are often counterintuitive when applied to human cases, as we see with adoption and the many moving accounts of parental love for Down syndrome children. The evolutionary biologists Margo Wilson and Martin Daly from McMaster University in Hamilton, Ontario, propose that parental/paternal love (in humans and in animals) may be expected to vary according to the answers a father gives to three different questions: (1) How certain can I be that the child is really mine? (2) Is my child likely to grow up healthy and reproduce? (3) What other chances do I have to marry and bear children?[10] Most evolutionary biologists would probably agree with this list. But there are innumerable examples, some of which we have just seen, that go against these seeming laws of biology. Indeed, is it not the case that love so often works against our own selfish interest, genetic or otherwise, that we feel compelled to reserve the word for precisely those situations? It may well be true, as Wilson and Daly observe, that "maternity is a fact and paternity an attribution," but I am sure I am not the only father who does not spend time worrying whether my children are "mine." How, in any event, can we possibly own another human being? And if we could, why would we want to? It will not confer love.

It seems absurd to claim, as some sociobiologists do (while admitting that no statistical evidence has yet been collected), that adopted children will marry less often and produce fewer children than nonadopted children (thus supposedly proving that they were less loved or cared for), or that people, like other animals, seem to be more deeply committed to their older offspring (since they are closer to reproductive age, ensuring one's genetic survival more quickly), and would grieve more intensely if an older child dies. How could one possibly undertake a study that could measure grief? How could the death of a two-year-old not be as unendurable as that of a twenty-year-old child, to mother and father? Living with someone, whether for two years or twenty years, especially children, whether our own or not, engenders love.

This is true even of dogs. We love a dog once we have bonded with him or her, and many humans find it unbearable to part with their dogs as they precede us to death. There is no genetic advantage to loving a dog with this kind of abandon and yet it happens. Over and over. Dogs, too, love us with equal infatuation. There is no genetic advantage for a dog to die of sadness when her best friend dies, yet many such accounts have reached me. I believe them. There are an increasing number of stories (scientists dismiss them as mere anecdotes, but when enough of them accumulate, they can serve as data—in any event, why should an event that is observed in a laboratory be dignified as data and one observed in a home become just a story?) of animals who form deep friendships across the species barrier and pine away with mourning when the friend dies. These tales run counter to kin selection and fly in the face of reproductive success as the only goal of animals and humans alike. They remind us of the primacy of feelings, of the powerful forces mobilized by sorrow and love and compassion, a power that can even defy the very bedrock of evolutionary logic.

Sometimes acts of compassion that appear to be "contrary to nature" are to be found across the species barrier. Sheila Siddle, the director of the Chimfunshi Wildlife Orphanage Trust in Zambia, sent me a video of a remarkable event that was captured purely by chance on film.[11] It occurred at a watering hole in Kruger National Park, one of the world's oldest and largest animal preserves in South Africa. An impala calf was attacked by a pack of African hunting dogs. Running for her life, she leapt into a river, where she was promptly seized by a seven-foot-long, gray-olive Nile crocodile. He grabbed her in his jaws and dived under the water. Suddenly a female hippopotamus charged the crocodile, who quickly let go of the impala and swam away. The hippo pushed the wounded calf toward the river's edge, then used her muzzle to help the impala climb onto the steep bank. She limped away, then collapsed on the grass. The hippo climbed out of the river and walked over to the impala. She opened her enormous jaws and breathed warm, moist air on the calf. She did this five times. She was trying to save her life, in vain, as it turned out, since the little calf was mortally wounded. Animal experts, viewing this footage, have struggled to understand what was happening. It was hard to accept what they were witnessing, but here it was, captured in black and white on film. What possible benefit could there have been for the hippo? We can only guess why this particular hippo showed what looks to us like unusual kindness and concern. I believe it possible that the hippo was touched by the suffering of the impala; that she acted as she did out of compassion.

People who study hippos say they have never before seen a hippo do anything like this. They go on to say that compassion from one wild species to another is wildly improbable. But why should humans be the only species able to feel compassion for other creatures, ones not like us? Maybe many animals do, and there is just no filmmaker around in the forest to record it. Maybe animals and humans are not so driven by purely biological needs, urges, and impulses as we have been led to believe. Maybe every animal, human or not, is capable of transcending its own gender, and even its own nature, from time to time. That's a nice thought.

SEVEN: Playful Prairie Dog Fathers

Good fathers can come in many forms. A father can be directly helpful, by protecting the mother, feeding the baby, or feeding the mother, or he can protect the territory or simply be tolerant. Gorillas make very tolerant fathers (when they are not killing the infants of another father). We have seen one form of good fathering, in which ratite birds brood, protect, and stay with their chicks. But something that bird fathers rarely do is play with their young. The great paleontologist George Gaylord Simpson, in his charming book *Penguins Past and Present,* notes that "many mammals, especially young mammals, behave in ways that can be interpreted only as playful. That is not characteristic of birds, and young penguins, even after leaving the nest, do not do anything much more interesting than chasing about screaming for food or just standing with (one feels) empty minds. There is, however, an eyewitness account of adult adelies hopping onto a passing ice floe, taking a ride, then hopping off and running back to repeat the performance on the next floe that came along. If humans did that, they would be playing. I don't know what, if anything, the adelies thought they were doing."[1]

In almost all mammalian species, the young play. Humans stand fascinated at the bars of cages where monkeys chase one another in mock battles. We can read their signals almost as easily as they can, and seem to know what is only play, not aggression. Researchers have noted that among chimpanzees, a juvenile male will often allow an infant to chase him around a tree or another chimp, and then suddenly change direction, chasing the infant.[2] They are playing tag. Either party may hold a twig or leaf between the lips or in one hand; I believe this serves a function similar to the dog's play-bow, as a visual signal that everything that takes place from that moment on is pure play, and is not to be interpreted by the rules that normally apply. But note that the chimp who is playing with the infant is not an adult male. Father chimpanzees rarely play with their children.

Many people have observed that human fathers, on the other hand, even those who do little else with their young children, nonetheless play with them, and there has been considerable controversy over whether fathers' play differs from mothers' play. The roughhousing often characteristic of male play is said to be sex-specific. I notice that I am far "rougher" with Ilan than I was with Simone when she was his age. I throw Ilan high into the air, and he demands that I become a dinosaur to frighten him. With Simone, we would sit quietly on the floor and build imaginary ant houses together. And both Leila and Terri, my first wife, are and were more gentle with our children. But this could merely be an example of cultural prejudices at work. A lot of the differences (the kinds of games they play, the objects they seek out, whether dolls or guns) we see between one child and another do not deserve to be given theoretical significance, especially when we get into the dangerous territory of what is "male" and what is "female" when speaking about small children. Erik Erikson's views about little girls building "contained" spaces and little boys making phallic rockets seem dated when read today. But even if the way fathers play with their children is different from that of mothers, it is still almost universally true that human fathers do play with their infants. This is not always the case with other primates.

Prairie Dogs

Some adult male gorillas may play with infants. In fact, some of the great apes seem to have no other paternal function beyond play, when they have that. But there is one species in which fathers seem to play so indulgently and so frequently with their young that it deserves special mention. I am referring to the black-tailed prairie dog *(Cynomys ludovicianus)* from the Black Hills of South Dakota, a member of the order Rodentia. (The prairie dog, of course, is not a dog, as the name indicates, nor is it a mouse, but rather a marmot that derives its name from the barking-like sound it makes when it detects a predator.)

For many years all our knowledge of these remarkable animals came from a 1955 Ph.D. dissertation by John A. King of the University of Michigan.[3] These plump, tawny rodents, weighing about two pounds and measuring fourteen to seventeen inches, make their own towns, which contain more than one thousand individuals and cover seventy-five acres, sometimes even square miles. Their burrow entrances are surrounded by mounds one to two feet high and five to six feet across. On top of these mounds sit sentries, scanning the skies and the surrounding countryside, on the lookout for enemies. Prairie dogs have evolved eyes that are set up very high on their foreheads so that when they emerge from their burrows they can immediately see a hawk or eagle overhead. When they do see one, they give out a sharp bark, warning the community. The call is then taken up by other prairie dogs. King claims that when the danger has passed, there is a special sound, indicating "all-clear," that the prairie dog makes by throwing itself into an upright posture, a kind of defiant and joyous "yes." Recently, a scholar from Arizona, Con Slobodchikoff, has discovered that prairie dog calls are in fact far more sophisticated than even Dr. King (who seemed to adore them) thought. He has demonstrated that not only do they have distinct calls for their different enemies (much like vervet monkeys, whose varying signals have been intensely studied), but they also have a special sound made only for human beings approaching their territory, and yet a different sound for a human male armed with a gun. Moreover, if the same man returns, months later, without his gun, the prairie dogs remember that he once came by with a gun, and give the warning sound of "man carrying gun." Such complexity was never imagined possible, and even now there are many scientific skeptics who find the idea of such sophisticated communication oddly unsettling.[4]

In the nineteenth century, prairie dog towns were commonplace, and people imagined that they had elaborate social systems. Washington Irving wrote in 1832 that the animal "is, in fact, one of the curiosities of the Far West, about which travelers delight to tell marvelous tales, endowing him at times with something of the politics and social habits of a rational being, and giving him systems of civil government and domestic economy." Early travelers spoke of towns stretching for many miles across the prairies, and in Texas one such group was said to cover an area of 25,000 square miles and to house some 400 million animals. (This led, needless to say, to a more or less successful campaign to completely eradicate this wonderful creature from the West.)

The prairie dog town is divided into wards. Within wards there is an even more significant division, one invisible to the naked eye: a coterie, the territory of a clan. This consists of an adult male, several adult females, and their offspring. We cannot call these male harems, since sometimes there is more than one adult male. One coterie that King observed consisted of only two old males and a barren female!

Whenever two individuals from the same coterie meet in a prairie town, they turn their heads toward each other, open their mouths, and kiss. Even if they are racing back to their burrows to escape danger, they will still hurriedly give each other a kiss. At other times, though, the kiss is more prolonged. King tells us that "two animals will meet and kiss; then one will roll over on its back, still maintaining oral contact. Often the kiss ends with both animals rapturously stretched out side by side." It appears that this kiss is a means of identification, much the way dogs smell each other, to find out who they are, how well they know each other, what their past relationship has been. But the kiss, King tells us, is only a preliminary. What is really aimed at is the grooming experience, engaged in by all the animals of a coterie, especially the pups, who chase adults in order to crawl under them and encourage them to groom. They nibble and paw and lick and expose their whole body to the ministrations of their grooming partner.

The odd part of prairie dog life is that this friendly state exists only among the members of each coterie, and does not extend between coteries. "Clans" is therefore a well-chosen designation. Prairie dogs love their own coterie but not the coterie of a neighbor. However, aggressive encounters between coteries seem to have, much like wolf aggression, a ritualized aspect (involving exposure of the anal glands under the tail), and real damage is extremely rare. But, like wolves, prairie dogs do not have an entirely peaceful nature, as we shall see in a moment.

Curiously, the grooming obsession of the pups seems to play an important role in emigration. Pups seem never to cease their desire for adult attention. Prairie dog etiquette does not permit the adults to rebuff the pups, and sometimes, to escape their continuous and tireless pursuit, the adults pull up stakes and simply emigrate. King thinks this forbearance accounts for the extremely low mortality rate among the young. He observed only one pup out of fifty-eight who died during the time of his observation. The pup is king in prairie dog town:

> After leaving his birthplace the emergent pup meets his father and other members of the coterie and enters a pup paradise. He plays with his siblings and the other young. All the adults kiss and groom him as his mother does, and he responds to them as he does to her. He readily accepts foster mothers and may spend the night with their broods. He attempts to suckle adults indiscriminately—males as well as females. A female will submit quietly; the male gently thwarts him and grooms him instead, rolling him over on his back and running his teeth through the pup's belly fur. The pup's demands for this treatment increase as he grows. He follows the adults about, climbing on them, crawling under them, doing everything he can to entice an adult into a grooming session. Sometimes, if he fails to win attention, he may playfully jump at them, and they may enter into the game. Only on the rarest of occasions is he rebuffed by an importuned adult; seldom is he kicked or bitten or drubbed.

It is easy to feel a fondness for these playful creatures, seeing them as miniature people. Which one of us would not like to be the object of such warm affection for much of the day?

But it seems that the more we learn, the more some of our ideals, or, in any event, fantasies, about the harmonious life of animals are toppled. Today the world's leading expert on the black-tailed prairie dog is Dr. John Hoogland, at the University of Maryland Appalachian laboratory. He is the author of the standard book on the subject, *The Black-Tailed Prairie Dog: Social Life of a Burrowing Mammal,* published by the University of Chicago Press in 1995. When I called Dr. Hoogland to discuss prairie dog fathers, he confirmed that they were active fathers indeed— defending the territory, giving alarm calls, making mounds and rim craters around the burrows to protect them and provide observation towers, playing with and kissing the babies, and even sleeping with them. I asked him if he liked prairie dogs. He responded: "Do I ever! I am crushed when they die. They are like little people." But Dr. Hoogland discovered, much to my chagrin, that like other animals in their family (ground squirrels and marmots), prairie dogs are infanticidal, both males and females. The infanticidal males, however, are almost always yearlings, and males never kill their own juvenile offspring (this is true of males in general, and of male Belding's arctic and thirteen-lined ground squirrels in particular). Whereas Dr. King, years earlier, had not seen a single baby harmed, Dr. Hoogland's research shows that in fact about 10 percent of all babies die because they are killed by an adult prairie dog. However, in his investigation of another prairie dog species, the Gunnison, he did not find a single case of infanticide after watching them for seven years (which is still not proof, of course, that it never happens). How are we to account for such differences between almost identical species?

I was curious about what Dr. Hoogland considered the most important thing he had learned about prairie dogs, assuming it would have to do with infanticide. Instead, he told me something that has become the leitmotif of this book: "One of the most important things that prairie dogs have taught me is that individuals vary tremendously." So, yes, prairie dogs can kill helpless infants. Dr. Hoogland would not, I am sure, agree with me that they have a *choice* in the matter, and yet he must agree that not all of them do it. Some do, some don't. He and I agree that prairie dogs, like humans, are individuals. Each one has a life history, with its accidents, its incidents, its lows and its highs. Each has its own personal traits and childhood experiences, and each one can surprise us. Every life story would be particular, unique to that one individual. No two stories could possibly be identical.

A distinguished animal behaviorist at the University of Michigan, Barbara Smuts, reminds us of this in an unusually personal account of her relation to the baboons she has studied for many years, each one of whom she came to know as a highly distinctive individual: "Every baboon had a characteristic voice and unique things to say with it; each had a face like no other, favorite foods, favorite friends, favorite bad habits."[5] It is sometimes hard to remember this, especially when human attempts to destroy an entire species weigh heavily on our conscience. (We will probably never again, thank God, hear the comment "They are only animals, for heaven's sake" in an attempt to justify our role in the extinction of a species.) When we destroy a species, we also destroy the library that contains the unwritten books about their lives, each of which could have brought us closer to a deeper understanding. A *complete* understanding we will never have, of prairie dogs or of any other animal, including the individual human animal. Had you asked somebody, even a zoologist, fifty years ago about prairie dog fathers, he would have looked at you blankly. But because of people like Dr. King and Dr. Hoogland this is now a valid field of study. The future will bring many treasures, I am sure.

Beavers

How little we know about animals. For hundreds of years we have lived next to prairie dogs, and until recently knew next to nothing about their actual lives. (Indigenous people have lived more closely with, and therefore have a more realistic assessment of, other animals. Nonetheless, I think distortions have entered into their accounts by the mere fact that so much of their knowledge, even when accurate, has been based on the desire to kill them for food rather than to observe them for fun or for knowledge.) We can say the same about beavers. We know very litle about beavers and have garnered very little information about them after watching them for hundreds of years. I wonder if beavers seem less studied than other animals because of what author Hope Ryden calls their innate good nature and sociability. In the past we seemed partial to nature "red in tooth and claw" and liked to hear about dangerous carnivores. European authors admired speed, strength, courage, and whatever qualities could be ascribed to the monarchy, which many authors were all too eager to please with praise from the natural world. Georges-Louis Leclerc de Buffon, the foremost zoologist of the eighteenth century, moved in aristocratic circles (he was made a count), and in his influential writings dwelled on the "noble" beasts, such as the lion: "His figure is striking and respectable; his look confident and bold; his gait stately, and his voice tremendous."[6] The French monarch approved.

Although beavers were common in Europe, they almost never appear in fairy tales or fables for reasons that remain obscure. The only story of the beaver that was widely known in Europe is nonetheless an interesting one for what it reveals about human guilt about the use we make of animals. A medicine called castoreum was believed to be contained in the testicles of the beaver. When hunters chased him, the beaver was said to bite off his own testicles and throw them to his pursuers. (Greek writers such as Aelian and Pliny the Elder used this story and it was then taken up by writers of the medieval bestiaries.) In reality, of course, the beaver did no such thing, it was the hunter who tore off the beaver's testicles. But about the real life and the real abilities of beavers, almost nothing was known.

Native Americans held them to be people from a separate nation. The French priest Chrestien Le Clercq noted in his 1691 account of life among the Micmac Indians: "The Indians say that the Beavers have sense, and form a separate nation; and they [the Indians] say they would cease to make war upon these animals if these [beavers] would speak, howsoever little, in order that they [the Indians] might learn whether the Beavers are among their friends or their enemies."[7]

When Buffon himself became fascinated by accounts of the beaver that were reaching France and Europe from American explorers, it is not surprising that he saw them as contented artisans or peasants:

> However numerous the society may be, peace and good order are uniformly maintained: their union is strengthened by a common toil, and confirmed by the conveniences they have jointly procured; and the abundance of provisions which they amass and consume together, render them happy within themselves. Having moderate appetites and an aversion to flesh and blood, they have not the smallest propensity to hostilities or rapine, but actually enjoy all those blessings which man only knows how to desire.

That they could be devoted and playful fathers is only becoming clear in more recent times. Like parrots, wolves, dolphins, and whales, beavers are difficult to observe in their moments of intimacy and so we do not have a full portrait of family life. The clues so far, though, indicate that they have evolved a most remarkable family intimacy. Why? Well, their teeth are so large and powerful (they can cut through a tree as fast as an electric saw) that they have had to devise reliable means of curbing any aggressive use of such deadly weapons, much like wolves have had to do with their canine teeth. It is extraordinary that colony members almost never use their teeth as weapons, either against one another, or even against other animals. In fact, it is well known that beavers live in notable harmony with one another and with muskrats, whom they appear to welcome into their homes (or just tolerate?) much as badgers have been known to receive, and make friends with, coyotes and foxes. Also, in northern climates they are forced to live under ice for the whole winter, sometimes two or three generations together, in very close proximity, with a very limited supply of food (whatever they have cached under the water before winter set in) in a very small space (sometimes just three or four feet in diameter). They are pure vegetarians, and so unlike wolves they do not need to hunt cooperatively, but they do need to cooperate in building their remarkable dams and lodges.

Donald Griffin, who after discovering bat sonar went on to start an entire new field in animal behavior, cognitive ethology, told me that he has become interested in beavers for precisely these reasons. He has devised a special video probe that attaches to a pole, which he places in the middle of a beaver lodge in a pond near the Harvard Concord Field Station. He uses an infrared light so as not to disturb the beavers, and has now filmed hundreds of hours of their behavior. Before he had done this, only one other researcher, from Quebec, had any footage of beavers in their lodges, and this was twenty-five years ago, when video quality was poor. Recently Professor Griffin was astonished to see a video of three kits, about a month old, and a male (he could tell because he had no nipples, whereas the female, who was still nursing, clearly did) who looked as if he were trying to drown his kits, dunking them, dowsing them while the kits were screaming. Actually, it soon became clear, the parents were getting ready to move them to another lodge, probably, Griffin speculates, because of the disturbance his instruments had created. Since the kits were too buoyant to dive, the father had to push them into the water to get them out of the exit of the lodge. Beaver kits, Hope Ryden explains, are precocial, and can swim perfectly well when only four days old. But they are not allowed out of the lodge during their first month of life. Since beavers are nocturnal animals, when members of the colony swim out into the pond at night, one family member remains with the young to guard them. The only entryway into a beaver lodge opens under water. I watched the videos with Professor Griffin, and I can attest that to me the tiny kit sounded exactly like my son, Ilan, shouting, "No, no, no, no!"

I called Hope Ryden, the author of the marvelous book *Lily Pond: Four Years with a Family of Beavers,* and she told me that father beavers are extremely active and immensely tolerant. She then sent me the following account:

> There were eight members in the colony, including two kits of the year, and winter food was going to be in short supply. In the fall, five of the beavers, including the colony patriarch, began to create a new pond much higher on the watershed. Lily, the matriarch, remained behind, for she was very ill and badly crippled and could not scale the seven dams leading up to the new pond. Nor did the kits of the year take part. They remained with their mother down in the Lily Pond Lodge.
>
> I was concerned for the three of them. Upstream five healthy adults were completing a new lodge and putting in a huge food raft, but at Lily Pond, Lily and the kits made no provision for the winter ahead—Lily being too weak and the kits being too young to do so. Well, nature is cruel, I mourned. The three of them will starve.
>
> Meanwhile, none of the five grown emigrees had bothered to revisit their home pond, so I was surprised when, one evening, the patriarch showed up and entered the Lily Pond Lodge. Seconds later, he emerged, followed by the kits. What was he up to?

By some means, he must have signaled his youngsters to follow him, for the three headed toward the pond's inlet at such speed that the two kits had difficulty keeping up. Paddling as fast as they could, they sometimes had to grab onto their father's fur or tail to keep from falling behind. At the first dam, I anticipated trouble, but the three clambered over it with ease. They then proceeded to navigate the first of seven terraced ponds, which connected Lily Pond to the colony's new home. One, two, three, four dams they scaled, but with each effort the little beavers seemed less able to keep up the pace. Still, the patriarch pushed onward. At the fifth dam one of the kits stumbled backwards. Then, on a second try, he again failed to make the grade. Oh no, I thought, he'll be left behind in no man's land. He can't possibly find his own way to an unknown destination.

But I underestimated the perceptiveness of the father beaver. Somehow he must have sensed that only one kit was following in his wake and he stopped and floated for some time, while the second kit repeatedly tried and failed to surmount the dam. Finally, however, the little kit did manage to heave himself over the top, and immediately the three set off again and continued on until they reached the beaver colony's new quarters.

I marveled at the intentionality of the father beaver's behavior. He must have had some aim in his beaver mind when he embarked on such a long turnaround journey to collect kits he hadn't seen in some time so that he could lead them to a new site. Obviously, there is survival value in paternal solicitude. Had he not undertaken this task, the kits soon would have been left to their own devices and likely died, for as things turned out, their mother's life was fast running out.

She also told me a story about how the beaver dam was broken by vandals and was in a state of complete collapse. It was a near disaster, and the entire beaver clan began feverishly working to repair the damage. Even the two small kits worked, though they were too young to be very good at it. The father would come along after they had put their sticks in and would quietly rearrange them so that they were properly fitted. Could he have felt some satisfaction at seeing his youngsters work on the dam? In any event, he was tolerant of their clumsy efforts.

When I wrote *When Elephants Weep,* I was not aware that according to some scientists, beavers, when caught in a trap, cry real tears. Hope Ryden noted that in a report before the World Symposium on Beavers, the scientist L. S. Lavrov verified that the North American beaver does indeed produce "a copious emission of tears" when under duress, and is likely to do so when "manually restrained." Hunters say that while awaiting the blow of a club about to be lowered on its skull, the beaver covers its head with its forepaws.

The beaver is one of the few mammals who is not just monogamous, but mates for life unless one dies. As Hope Ryden points out, beavers form their lifetime alliances months before mating season casts its heady spell on both the sexes. "Beaver pairing is based on an attraction that is as mysterious as it is compelling, one that is unrelated to any immediate urge to copulate," she says. This is unusual in the animal kingdom.

There are very few reports of male animals who assist in the birth process, but Dorothy Richards and François Patenaude have witnessed the father beaver present as an attendant. Hope Ryden witnessed the deep involvement that male beavers bring to parenting. This is contrary to the myth, often repeated, that after his kits' birth, the father beaver is relegated to a bank burrow and only returns to the lodge when the babies are several weeks old. On the contrary, the father resides in the lodge, helping in a very active manner during these early weeks. He brings solid food for the kits, shovels in roots and sticks for them to chew, grooms fussy babies, keeps the dam and the lodge in good repair, and all sleep together, mother, father, and the kits, in a monkey pile.

Beaver kits are well developed at birth, even though they weigh but one pound, with their bodies already covered with fur, their eyes open, their sharp little incisor teeth fully erupted, and they are able to swim within a few hours of birth. They nurse for as much as two months, an unusually long time for such a well-developed infant. The kits usually stay with their family for a year, even two, and sometimes much longer. Hope Ryden points out that two-year-olds have been known to remain at their birth pond for an extra year and sometimes longer, and that moving out seems to depend entirely on the inclination of the offspring. The reason for their long childhood is similar to the reason for ours: The baby beaver has a great deal to learn, and learns it by observing older siblings and parents. Maybe this is why certain Native American tribes viewed beavers as "little Indians" and did not kill them.

It is very unusual for any animal to allow grown kin to return to the natal den after years away, be recognized, and be accepted, not just tolerated. But this behavior has been documented in beavers by Harry Edward Hodgdon and others. Hope Ryden expressed admiration for the fact that beavers not only can recognize their grown children after a long separation, but that they are willing to share their limited resources with these same children even when they are of breeding age, unusual among nonhuman animals.

Like human families, beaver families revolve around their young. Beavers resemble us in other ways as well. I attempted to show in *When Elephants Weep* and *Dogs Never Lie About Love* that many other animals experience profound feelings of pleasure in their natural world. Hope Ryden captures this in a beautiful passage in her book:

I cannot help but believe animals experience joy. It seems so obvious. When my dogs celebrate my return with high leaps, or bolt from my car and race madly about the yard of my weekend cabin, I am entitled to believe what my eyes and common sense tell me: they are expressing joy. Their behavior is so analogous to our own (jumping for joy or wildly running down a beach) that it would seem sheer sophistry to pretend they do not actually feel the emotion they so vividly portray.

People who have seen beavers cavorting about their ponds in the spring gain the definite impression that they are rejoicing in their ability to once again play in the water. Housebound for the winter, they become delirious with the celebration of spring. A father beaver will porpoise over the body of his young kits and then all will swim back and forth across the pond very swiftly as if they were delighted to be in the same world with the willow trees in leaf. You can observe a father beaver floating on his back during this time while his kits plunge and surface over and over. They experience pure animal pleasure in their release. The whole family can be seen rolling, porpoising, and somersaulting. It is possible to spot a father beaver swimming with great speed across the lake with one of his kits hanging on, then turning around and swimming back, sometimes out of sheer exuberance.

Both male and female beavers allow their babies to hitch a ride on their backs. Both mother and father work very hard, and their kits get involved from an early age in the building of dams. For animals that work so hard, it seems that play is essential to their health and certainly to their happiness. Clearly much of the time the young kits are learning to be beavers, but at other times one cannot avoid the feeling that they are playing with their father because their little hearts are filled with the special joy that beavers feel when they have been confined for half a year to a small underwater home and are bursting to greet the green world above once again.

Independence

The human species, perhaps like all other animal species, displays a certain ambivalence when it comes to independence: We fear it and we long for it. And this is true for both children and adults. The fear of independence is probably a carryover from the normal fears of early childhood, being lost, being abandoned, being left behind. If we consider our development as hunter-gatherers, there would be many occasions when these normal fears could easily be realized: A child wanders too far off, or the extended family or band needs to move on, and he cannot be found. A two-year-old alone in an African savanna would not survive very long. The development of fear in the first two or three years is universal, and seems to have nothing to do with the way a child is raised. Fear of strangers is found in British and American children, among the Kung Bushmen, the Hopi Indians, Guatemalans, Ganda infants, and Zambian infants.

When Ilan was two, he was very fond of the phrase "Ilan do it alone." He wanted to go down stairs, push his Baby Jogger, and open doors by himself. It strikes me that this desire for independence is one of the few areas in which many fathers seem to have some advantage over mothers. Fathers as a rule seem rather more eager to foster independence in their children than do mothers. When Ilan first announced at the end of his day in preschool that he did not want to come home, but wanted to stay there, I felt proud, whereas Leila looked crushed. Symbiosis is a powerful gratification, and what mother would willingly give it up? Then again, the father is eager to reap the benefits of the child reaching out. The lesson for fathers is that independence is a relative term. There are times when it should be encouraged, fostered, admired. But there are also times when a naturally occurring caution is to be respected. Some fathers have problems with this, forgetting their own histories. They can mock the child, especially a boy, for being timid, or use absurd gender insults—"Don't be such a wuss"—when all the boy is doing is behaving like the young child he is. Respect, humility, a recognition of how little we understand about what is "normal" and what is "pathological," and a willingness to celebrate the diversity of animal and human nature are always called for.

Play, we have seen, is the major motor for independence. Children playact what they see adults do, naturally, but they also seem to play out of a developmental plan that helps to prepare them for later adult activities. Playing at being a mother or father (some birds who help at the nest and older wolf siblings who baby-sit the pups in the den may be doing this) is learning to *be* a mother or father.

Anne Rasa, who spent years observing a family of dwarf mongooses in the Taru Desert of Kenya, said that they were the most playful animals she had ever encountered. Even after he is supposedly independent, the male often cannot resist joining in the play. Like a little rubber ball, he will bounce around the kits, "beeping loudly" with pleasure. And when in wrestling with the youngsters he grasps one on the neck with his teeth, his playmate turns into a limp little bundle, ready to be carried. The male is startled by this and drops the baby, at which point the baby staggers around, beeping the play call again. But the kits turn most of their charm onto their own father, not so much to get him to play with them as to encourage him to take them on a food-foraging trip. Here we see play merging into the beginnings of a desire for independence. The pups emerge from their mounds early in the morning and give their father no peace until he sets off with them on an excursion. He digs out tasty grasshoppers for them, holds them in his mouth, and gives a call as they mob him to take the hapless victim. Rasa noted that the mongooses were invariably followed on these excursions by yellow-bills, who hop behind the procession, attempting to seize the insects from the youngsters. But in spite of the birds' formidable bills, Rasa never saw one make a stab at the young mongooses themselves, only at the insects. She concluded that "mongoose and hornbill really did seem to be friends." These "baby-breakfast-finding" excursions were also occasions for the fathers to teach their small ones how to hunt and how to recognize prey that could serve as food. This seemed to be exclusively the job of the father. He is the one to foster independence, not the mother. Or perhaps mothers are simply too exhausted for yet another task. Of course, human mothers do more than their share of teaching their children to be independent, but perhaps the "play-teaching" excursions of the dwarf mongoose reflect an approach that human fathers are more likely to adopt.

It is considered to be one of the primary roles of the human father to prepare children for independence, for taking their rightful place in the world of adults *without* recourse to Mom and Dad. I can remember my own father telling my mother that what looked harsh to her in his treatment of me was simply his way of assisting my transition from childlike dependence to full maturity. I believe that he did what he did with the best of intentions ("You will not always be there to prepare his food the way you have taught him to like it" and so on). But now I wonder about it. Maybe the human species is more like the orca and we were really meant to spend our entire lives near, or in contact with, family.

Sometimes when I am at a playground with Ilan, I become acutely aware of the fact that I have done exactly the same things with him, at the same place, in the same way, at the same time, more often than I can count. Sometimes as I sit watching him it feels unreal, and I ask myself, What I am doing here, what has any of this to do with me? The answer is swift and merciless: This has nothing to do with you. Or, rather, it has to do with my beginning to fade for Ilan, to recede into the background.

Imperceptibly at first, Ilan moves farther away from me at every play session, establishing his own ground. This is a long and slow process that will take many years, even decades, not hours or weeks or months. But I am struck by the thought that when it is accompanied and facilitated by play, it is easier, more natural, less decisive or even traumatic. Will this allow Ilan, when he is fully adult, to maintain a playful relation with me, something that it seems other adult male animals rarely achieve? Perhaps when adult fathers and their children play they are remembering childhood, celebrating equality, or some of both.

EIGHT: Leaving the Nest

In avian research there is something called the
"Concorde fallacy."[1] This refers to the amount of effort and money
that was put into creating the Concorde supersonic transport air-
plane. After a certain point there seemed to be no way back, even
though the results expected were meager, simply because so much
time and energy had already been expended.

The Concorde fallacy is often applied to a group of birds, the
megapodes, also called incubator birds, a family of gallinaceous
birds, which include domestic poultry and pheasants. Their twelve
species are distributed over the Indo-Malaysian and Polynesian
islands (New Guinea) and the Australian continent. We call them
mound builders, because they build the largest moundlike nests of
any bird: up to fifteen feet high and fifty-four feet long! Jared
Diamond, professor of physiology at UCLA Medical School (and
author of the popular book *The Third Chimpanzee*), points out that

when accounts of the habits of these birds reached Europe in the early sixteenth century, the stories were dismissed as false, fabulous, and fantastic by "biologists willing to accept accounts of mermaids and sea monsters."

Unlike almost any other species of bird, mound builders do not sit on their eggs and give no direct care to their young. Yet the amount of time and energy they *indirectly* spend on their offspring is far beyond that of any other species of bird. Where they can, these birds use "natural incubators"—a hot beach, volcanic soil, or hot springs—to keep their eggs at the right temperature. But those that live where this is not possible have evolved a far more elaborate strategy: They build their own heat-conducting mounds. Reptiles hatch their eggs in a similar fashion, not in mounds, but usually in holes, among rotting vegetation or buried in the soil (sea turtles dig nests on sandy beaches and lay up to one hundred or more eggs), and most show little parental care of the emerging young (male cobras, however, watch over the eggs).[2] Since birds are descendants of reptiles, perhaps the mound builder's behavior is a carryover from its reptilian past.

Two species of this bird, the Australian brush turkey and the mallee fowl, are capable, to the astonishment of everybody who has studied them, of detecting and regulating the temperature of the mound. The male builds its mound with different kinds of vegetation, sand, and soil. One species, the mallee fowl, spends an average of five hours a day working on his mound. Mounds contain an average of almost eight thousand pounds of collected material. To open a mound for egg laying or to test its temperature, a male must remove and replace nearly two thousand pounds of sand. This is 472 times the bird's mass, equivalent to a human moving seventy thousand pounds of sand.[3] In the winter months the male opens the mound and fills it with organic matter. In the spring this matter ferments and creates heat, which reaches the eggs. If there is too much heat in the mound, the male bird opens the mound at dawn to allow sufficient heat to escape. (He regularly checks the temperature inside the mound by testing the soil in his mouth; the male mallee fowl uses his tongue, the brush turkey uses his whole head and neck, for they are bare of feathers.) In summer, as the fermentation decreases, solar heat is more important, and so the male bird leaves the mound open during the day to expose the egg chamber to the sun's rays. Later in the summer, he opens the mound early for cooling purposes, but restores it to its full height toward the evening for insulation. In autumn, with no heat from the organic matter and little from the sun, he opens the mound late in the morning, when the sun is shining directly onto it, and rebuilds it again with heated soil in mid-afternoon.[4]

Most ornithologists would not be prepared to accept the possibility that the male mound builder makes any kind of conscious calculation to determine his actions. But how can something as complex as this, in which there are daily variables that need to be monitored, be done without awareness? The bird needs to wake up in the morning and feel the sun to assess its heat and what effect that will have on his mound. He does this for months on end; how could it not be in his consciousness at every moment? I am not sure that a skeptic could ever be convinced otherwise, but it is interesting to me that animal behaviorists increasingly are inching toward the view long proposed by Donald Griffin and his students, namely that animals have awareness. They are doing so precisely because the information coming in from the field gives evidence of greater and greater complexity. It is fascinating to note that as observations improve (via the simple technique of sitting patiently in the field), the complexity of what is seen increases, which in turn allows scientists to entertain the possibility of ascribing ever more complex "thoughts" to animals.

The mallee fowl constructs mounds that are normally fifteen

feet across and two and a half feet high. The male works at this mound every day, for several hours, ten to eleven months of the year. The Concorde fallacy (large investments and small returns) is applied to these birds because of the way their behavior originated. Initially, the female bird simply dropped her eggs in hot soil. This worked well as long as conditions cooperated. To hatch, the eggs had to be kept at about 92 degrees Fahrenheit. But when these birds moved into other, cooler areas, where the temperature was less reliable, how were they going to keep the eggs at the required temperature? Mounds had to be built, and these eventually became increasingly elaborate, allowing the temperature to be regulated more precisely. In the end, the birds (or more often, the male alone) wound up spending enormous amounts of time on the mound.

But now, after having spent such inordinate energy incubating the eggs, once the chicks are hatched, the parents do not care for them at all. Neither the male nor the female does anything for the young. They are the only group of birds—indeed, the only group of warm-blooded animals at all—that does not care for its offspring after birth. In some mounds, there is only one egg, which hatches in about two months (from forty to ninety-six days, depending on the heat). The eggs are surprisingly thin-shelled. If they were thicker the chick would be unable to escape. (They are the only chicks lacking an egg tooth, and instead use their extremely strong feet to break the eggshell.) When the chicks work their way to the top of the mound (they can spend up to fifteen hours digging to the surface), they simply take off. They are born with a full set of flight feathers, and on the very first day of their lives are able to roost on a nearby tree. Unlike all the other chicks from this family of birds, they are able to forage for themselves immediately.

Such odd birds, with so many unique characteristics. A final one: They have no following reaction. Every other bird follows one or both parents, but the mound builders never see them, nor do they seek them out. Nobody knows for certain how they learn the necessary social signals, how to behave like a megapode, how to so carefully build the mounds and regulate the temperature depending on external circumstances. Maybe they learn everything they need to know as they are momentarily exposed to their parents in walking away from the mound, or maybe there is some acoustic contact between parents and chicks while they are still sheltered in their eggs in the mound. We are becoming increasingly aware of how much information is actually passed between parents and chicks while they are still inside the egg. The behavior of the megapode chick is undoubtedly a strong argument for the existence of animals who possess inborn, preprogrammed information that is accessed automatically—in other words, animals in whom learning plays no role whatever. We must be careful, however, not to apply this too promiscuously: Many birds require exposure to the songs of their parents to learn to sing properly, as was noted earlier.

How I would love to inhabit the mind of the male bird at the moment all his vast effort comes to fruition, as he watches his son or daughter walk away without so much as a backward glance. Does he feel cheated, or proud? Does he expect gratitude? Is he disappointed? We like to think that, being programmed to do what he does (just as the chick is programmed to do what it does), he feels nothing. I wonder. After all, when we come up with a term such as the Concorde fallacy, we had something like disappointment in mind, or an emotion in birds that is not entirely unlike disappointment.

Moreover, why not ask if *any* animal expects or feels gratitude? This is one of those anthropomorphic questions that biologists almost never ask themselves (at least in print), probably because it appears to demand pure speculation, anathema to a scientist.

I think, though, that we are not forced to rely entirely upon speculation. I have argued, in *Dogs Never Lie About Love,* that dogs, for one, very definitely feel disappointment. All of my readers who have lived with dogs have seen this over and over: When we tell a dog, "Yes, you can come for a walk," and the dog rushes to the door, a look of eager anticipation on her face, and then we change our minds, or something intervenes, and we have to say, "No, I am sorry, but you cannot come," the look that comes over the face of the dog is unmistakable. First she cocks her head, as if to make certain she has heard correctly. Then when she realizes that she has, she throws herself onto the floor, her ears droop, her eyes roll up, she sighs audibly, and lying there, in a state of abject dejection, she is the very picture of disappointment in its purest state. Nobody could possibly mistake it for any other emotion. Conversely, when we relent, and tell the dog, "All right, you can come along after all," she bounds to the door (all is forgiven) and on her face, beside anticipation, joy, and excitement, we read, correctly, I believe, pure gratitude.

Well, you may argue, it is fine and good to assign such emotions to dogs; after all, they have lived among human beings for ten to fifteen thousand years, small wonder that some of our emotions would have rubbed off on them (though I wonder if it really isn't the other way around: Maybe we humans developed some of our capacity for emotional depth from having watched and been associated with dogs—our emotional superiors). But birds? Can we really believe that birds, too, are capable of emotions like ours? I see no reason why not, and many reasons why. And I am not alone. In the last few years, many authors have begun to discuss the possibility that birds are far more complex creatures than we have ever given them credit for. (Consider the injurious insult "bird brain.")[5]

Now, if dogs can feel disappointed because we did not take them for a walk, why would a male bird not feel disappointed after all the effort he has gone through on behalf of his chicks to watch them walk away without the slightest regret? In fact, I agree with just about any scientist that in reality no megapode father has spent an evening agonizing about how ungrateful his chicks are. Dogs, having lived with us for thousands of years, have learned to be cued in to our plastic behavior: On one occasion we take them for a walk, and on another we don't. No mallee fowl chick ever turned back to spend time with his father, so no father has ever learned to expect any other kind of behavior from his young.

We are preprogrammed to find interesting facts significant. We search for a theory, a reason behind the facts. Birds completely lack viviparity; that is, there is no instance, among birds, of a chick born alive. They all hatch from eggs. What can possibly be the significance of this? By the same token, no bird ever lactates (penguin and pigeon's milk is a misnomer, it is not real milk). Is this because the milk would be so heavy that birds could not fly? In fact, the largest birds, like ostriches and cassowaries, are flightless. Similarly, it is hard for me to relinquish the belief that to be born precocial (a miniature adult) or altricial (needing prolonged care) is in and of itself significant. I keep looking for a pattern: Precocial birds have a shorter infancy. The growth of myelin sheaths around nerve fibers—a sign of maturation—is at hatching much further along for these birds than for altricial birds. So precocial birds have alert senses and are able to run; the altricial birds, on the other hand, are born sluggish and have a longer period of infancy and are therefore protected for more time.

But very similar species can vary: Rabbits are altricial, but hares are precocial. Environment certainly plays a key role. A baby rabbit is born in a nest, hidden from predators, and can afford to remain immobile for some time, whereas a hare is born in the open field and must be able to run away from predators almost as soon as it is born. Fawns can run almost as soon as they are born because they need to. Mice are altricial because they are protected by a hidden nest. Altricial birds (they are called nidicolous, or nest dwellers), such as pelicans, hawks, pigeons, parrots, cuckoos, owls, hummingbirds, woodpeckers, and most songbirds, all have hidden nests that protect them. The precocial birds (called nidifugous, or nest fugitive), such as ducks, geese, swans, quail, kiwis, and shorebirds, have no nests, and must be able to fly immediately. A young osprey, on its first flight over a lake, looks as if it is about to splash into the water, but gains altitude until it can disappear over a far horizon, and this just days after it is hatched. We do what we can afford to do—is that perhaps part of the underlying general principle? Consider sleep: The top predators, humans, lions, wolves, all sleep long and well. On the other hand, animals that are primarily prey, and need to be alert, sleep very little and are easily aroused: deer, rabbits, mice. Does the albatross, which can spend weeks in flight without ever landing, sleep at all during this time? At least one animal, the Dall porpoise, a river dolphin, never sleeps at all (no surface sleeping, not even catnapping).[6]

I don't know if there is a real correlation, but I am tempted to speculate that the differences between altricial and precocial birds have something to do with fatherhood. A bird with an active father can afford to be altricial, because help is present. So human infants are altricial in the extreme because as a rule a human infant, who is vulnerable for almost eighteen years, can count on the help of a father or other adults who will play a major role in their lives.

All animals feed, or help feed, their young. But we are probably the only species, besides whales, that continues to feed its young well into adolescence, and even beyond. Becoming independent is almost an oxymoron for human children: They are almost never entirely independent. We can define independence as the time when the young leave the family home to start their own families. Marriage seems to be part of our definition of independence. (Which is not to say that an unmarried person is never independent—in fact many people stay unmarried precisely because they wish to remain independent.) On the other hand, marriage is, in some profound sense, merely an extension of the pleasures of childhood: We become intricately enmeshed in the life of another person. Instead of being dependent on an adult for food or clothing or shelter or protection we are now emotionally dependent on another adult. Perhaps it is not so much dependent as *inter*dependent. Adult married couples depend on each other at the level of the psyche, both mentally and emotionally. I suspect that people who have had miserable childhoods have a tendency to avoid marriage, or else they see it as an opportunity to make up for the intimacy they did not find during their childhoods.

Intense and extensive parenting, as many evolutionary biologists have noted, is characteristic of the human species. But it is not exclusive to us. What is exclusive, as I have said before, is our curiosity about the parenting of other species, our ability to learn from other species, even one so different as birds.

Can we learn from the emperor's embrace? I don't see why not. After all, learning is often nothing more than being shown the existence of something we had not thought about ourselves. Fathering has been learned in this way, even among animals. There are certain populations of Japanese macaque monkeys, for example, in which adult males take care of children. But in others this care is entirely absent. The only explanation can be that it was acquired by some individuals or troops and not others. Maybe one Japanese macaque, seeing a friend take care of his child, thought it was a wonderful thing, and that he would like to try it as well. Maybe he just needed to be shown. Biologists balk at explanations of this kind. But the richness of behavior in the natural world, the sheer variety of it, works against their narrowness.

Certainly I believe that fathers, human fathers, especially, can learn from watching other fathers and mothers take care of children. Not only that, but it is a central theme of this book that we can learn a great deal by watching other species, and by examining in detail the solutions they have found for raising children. If they have found solutions better than ours, why not copy them?

But there is one area in which I am afraid that human fathers are on their own. When it comes to taking care of older children, adolescents, for example, we cannot turn to animal fathers because, as far as I know, no male animal takes care of his children into adolescence (and beyond) except the male human animal. Why is that? I have attempted to explain some things by the fact that human babies are so altricial, and by and large this succeeds. But in this case I cannot pretend that a sixteen-year-old is still helpless and would expire without parental help. Moreover, our species is moving toward longer and longer dependency, not the other way around. Children in the United States leave home later and later, marry later and later, and have children later and later. Of course there are historical and cultural explanations for this, but I also wonder if it might not have some evolutionary significance. Could it be that it really takes that long for a child to learn everything necessary to be a good parent? I think it may. We get to watch the successes and failures of our own parents for so long that we learn what to imitate and what to avoid. Not that we always implement these lessons, but in theory we can.

It is one of the enduring mysteries of psychology that some badly abused children turn into exceptionally loving parents. I think this is the case only when that child has been able to look, clear-eyed, at the horrendous mistakes of which he or she was the victim, and was able to vow never to inflict those mistakes on his or her own children. Here is where the kind of reflection that seems unique to humans is most valuable: We *can* look back, and say: "I will never do to my child what my father did to me." I don't think any other animal is capable of this.

So I see that I too have succumbed to the same ethnocentrism I have so often criticized in these pages: looking for what is uniquely human. Isn't it enough that we are different? At least I am not claiming that it makes us better. After all, one reason that no emperor penguin chick has to look back on his childhood and vow to do better for *his* chicks is that no emperor penguin father ever deliberately tormented his own son or daughter. That seems to make them not just different from us, but better.

What seems odd to me is that animal fathers who have been intimately involved in the infancy and rearing of their children do not conform to what humans expect of a father whose children have left the nest: permanent interest without interference in their lives and a successful transition to being a grandfather. Consider the male wolf. The males rarely use the den during the daytime. Instead, they choose a high point, a lookout, where they can act as sentinel. Many people have seen father wolves standing on a high ridge over the den, attentive to any possible danger. If a human approaches, the father wolf will make himself conspicuous by howling, then move off a distance, howl again, and continue to do so until he is several miles away from the den. The obvious purpose is to distract the human from finding the den. He is willing to risk his own life rather than see his children come to harm. By wolf standards, another wolf is an adult when it is able to breed, generally by about twenty-two months, certainly by the time it is three years old. Until that time, there seems to be cohesion of various kinds among members of a pack. But once they are at most five years of age, wolves go their separate ways, and form or join another pack. The question that I have is, Why don't the ties that bind a father to his children remain for the duration of his life? Why would he not experience joy in meeting his long-lost children? Might it have something to do with the fact that males need to migrate out of the family territory to ensure outbreeding? Most animals, though not all, avoid incest in this way. I have no doubt that a wolf, just like a dog, will recognize a mate, friend, or child from years before. But I have failed to find any stories about wolves finding each other after years and showing their happiness. Is it possible that we simply do not know enough about wolves to be certain that this never happens? David Mech, the world's leading expert on wolves, in his recent book *The Wolves of Denali,* tells of a puzzling phenomenon: He observed seven cases of male wolves one to four years old who joined long-established packs. Three of these might have involved a wolf returning to his natal pack after an unsuccessful attempt to find a mate. Mech was puzzled by the social tolerance of these wolves, especially since he had established the fact that as much as 65 percent of the mortality in the population he observed was probably due to other wolves, the highest ever reported in any wolf population.

With humans, it is not only common to welcome our children after a long absence, it is almost a hallmark of our species. In fact, some parents find it much easier to be grandparents than to be parents. We are almost always delighted to see our children again after an absence. The emotions, and the memories of emotions, are intense on both sides of the divide.

Nor do humans, once parents, ever cease to be parents. Simone was an adult at eighteen, but she was still my child. She remains no less my child at twenty-five. In fact, I think I can safely say that the bond between us has only deepened as time goes on. For one thing, Simone nursed until she was three years old, and while I was delighted with this (Ilan is still nursing at almost three), I was to some extent excluded from the particular kind of bond she had with her mother. Once nursing ended, I was able to play a much greater role in Simone's life, and did. The nursing dyad is certainly a unique image, and I derived enormous pleasure from watching it. But my playfulness brought something precious to Simone, and I loved the new-found interest in me that she was obviously showing.

Is it possible that we have our psychological inhibitions against incest to thank for our prolonged contact with our children? At the later stages of life, fathers (and mothers as well, of course) have the chance to share their own life histories and experiences with the developing child. This is the advantage that speech gives the human animal. Even though Simone lives on her own now, and is an adult in every sense of the word, we can continue to share this bond, and indeed it is one of the greatest pleasures of my life. I can talk and tell, recite my stories to Simone, and listen to hers in a way that presumably no other animal can. Maybe a wolf stays together with his children as long as they have *work* to do together, but once that is over, they cannot reminisce about the work in tranquillity the way humans can. A wolf does not sit around the den and trade memories and experiences. At least I don't think so. But he raises his pups to leave the den, and with our children, this is the goal, too.

Epilogue

In the 1960s, Robert Ardrey, the playwright-turned-anthropologist, wrote a controversial best-seller, *The Territorial Imperative,* in which he argued (not very persuasively, I thought) that the territorial instincts of animals apply equally to humans (or, as he called us then, "man," which, for a change, might be actually accurate). Describing the instinct, he wrote: "'The place is mine; I am of this place,' says the albatross, the patas monkey, the green sunfish, the Spaniard, the great horned owl, the wolf, the Venetian, the prairie dog, the three-spined stickleback, the Scotsman, the skua, the man from La Crosse, Wisconsin, the Alsatian, the little-ringed plover, the Argentine, the lungfish, the lion, the Chinook salmon, the Parisian." Can we draw up a similar scorecard for fatherhood? "This child is mine, I will take care of her," says the male emperor penguin, the male sea horse, the Scottish father, the Jamaican father, the father wolf, the male mouthbrooding teleost fish, the Indonesian father, the male tamarin, the father from Berkeley, California, the father from India, father beaver, father prairie dog, the male Darwin frog from Argentina, the Chilean father, and even (back into our past) the ancient Egyptian father, the Sumerian father, the Neanderthal father.

There are not so many human universals, fewer than we thought just twenty years ago: We all die, all women eventually undergo menopause if they live long enough, men cannot give birth, only women lactate, humans can't breathe under water, we all need to sleep, and all babies need to be taken care of to survive. We have no choice; no amount of expertise will change these universals. But when we were very young, in fact, on the day we were born, we were able to make certain decisions on our own: when to eat, when to stop eating, when to sleep, and when to wake up. This is natural knowledge. The less we interfere with such knowledge, the better. A good father knows this, a good mother knows this. They don't need an expert to tell them. For what experts generally do is to interfere with natural processes. The baby will eat when hungry, which is most of the time. If she demands food, of course she should be fed. To tell her that an expert has decided that it is best to eat every four hours, and when she cries to further tell her that this expert has decided it is good for her to cry, is to mock mother/father nature.

In the preceding pages I have sometimes spoken about instinct with derogation, as if the mere mention of the word were the first steps on the path to biological determinism. But there are times when it seems right to call upon instinct. I have noticed that fathers invoke instinct as an explanation for what they do far less frequently than mothers do. Fathers rarely claim that they simply know in their bones what to do for their children. This is what women often say, and so often it is true. And yet men tend to pose as "experts," pointing to what they claim is objective science and insisting that what they are saying is free of bias. The dean of American behaviorist psychology, John B. Watson, in his widely influential 1928 book *Psychological Care of Infant and Child,* warned mothers:

> There is a sensible way of treating children. Treat them as though they were young adults. Dress them, bathe them with care and circumspection. Let your behavior always be objective and kindly firm. Never hug and kiss them, never let them sit in your lap. If you must, kiss them once on the forehead when they say good night. Shake hands with them in the morning. Give them a pat on the head if they have made an extraordinarily good job of a difficult task. Try it out. In a week's time you will find how easy it is to be perfectly objective with your child and at the same time kindly. You will be utterly ashamed of the mawkish, sentimental way you have been handling it. . . . In conclusion won't you then remember when you are tempted to pet your child that mother love is a dangerous instrument? An instrument which may inflict a never-healing wound, a wound which may make infancy unhappy, adolescence a nightmare, an instrument which may wreck your adult son or daughter's vocational future and their chances for marital happiness.[8]

Astounding as this piece of nonsense is, parents at the time believed it to be true. Such is the power of "experts" and our own timidity in the face of them. Nor should we think this example unique. Expert advice, almost always, comes in the guise of omniscience. It is, of course, easier to recognize in hindsight that supposed wisdom of this kind is false.

When we watch other animals be good fathers to their children, it is with a jolt that we realize they do so without the benefit of expert advice. They do what comes naturally to them. Does fatherhood come naturally to human fathers? I think it does, as long as there is no interference and our minds are not cluttered with harmful prejudices, among which is the mistaken idea in the popular imagination that no other animal is ever a good father. This false fact is then used as an excuse for why men cannot be expected to act as loving and responsible fathers: Since men are animals, it is "only natural," they say, to disappear after copulation. We talk about men as "lions" or "bears"—but we also think of them as "wolves," and wolves *are* good fathers. There is also the bad advice of the experts of previous times who told us that parenting was a woman's job, that it came naturally to her, not to men, that it was instinctive with her and only learned (or better not learned) by men.

I have never spoken to a father of grown children who did not wish he had spent more time with his children when they were young. If he could change one thing, it would be that one. The old cliché that nobody dies wishing he had spent more time at work is true. We die wishing we had been closer to our children. Yet male remoteness, even absence, is sanctioned by our civilization; it is expected, it is even rewarded. This goes contrary to nature.

Human fathers evolved, like many animal fathers, to care for and feed their partners and their children, to love and protect their partners and their children, to stay with and not abandon their partners and their children. I realize that the mere fact that we evolved to do a certain thing does not make it right or wrong. Nonetheless, I believe we must remain informed about our own evolutionary history. We do not come into the world completely de novo. There are certain lessons we can learn by watching natural behavior in other species, and by wondering about just what it is that we evolved to do. As I've said before, if we decide to go against this, our consent to do so should be completely informed.

Too often human arrogance has interfered with natural design to our detriment: Think about how tonsils were routinely removed a few decades back. Many doctors still argue that the appendix is completely unnecessary. But a friend who is a medical doctor, Jerry Tsagaratos, tells me that it contains lymph tissue that is part of the immune system. Female circumcision, widely acknowledged to be a barbarity, is still practiced in many countries of Africa. We rarely improve on evolution. (We were not evolved to have babies so late in life, either, but infertility treatment can add something precious to our lives; it doesn't remove what is already there.) I am sure some things that have survived are purely maladaptive anachronisms that may have been adaptive in the past, but are no longer so. I recognize some things are the result of genetic drift, that is, random changes in gene frequencies. But those are not what I am talking about. I am talking about behaviors that evolved over the last two and a half million years that we tinker with at our peril.

We are the only mammal who gives birth to a naked (which is why we cannot groom our children, but can kiss them), single offspring. The little girl or boy is altricial in the extreme, and stays that way for longer than any other animal. So children need from us warmth (the human body), comfort (touch, the sounds of soothing speech), protection (from other animals or humans who mean them harm), food, cleaning, shelter, clothing, education, and medical attention. This is not so daunting if you think that we evolved to be this way.

We evolved (this means that historically we come from an ancestral environment where it was adaptive to do certain things that have had an impact both on our biology and on our psyche) *to share a bed with our infants.* In no higher primate species do infants sleep alone. They were never meant to sleep alone. Why should it be defined as normal for an infant to sleep by itself, when it never, ever did so in the entire history of the human race until recently? It was Dr. Spock who told parents that "it's a sensible rule not to take a child into the parents' bed for any reason."

That is precisely the problem with "rules"; they are so often wrong. There was nothing sensible about that one at all. For father and mother to sleep with a child provides safety (protection against sudden infant death syndrome, for example), comfort (night terrors are far less frequent in cosleeping babies), nutrition (the baby can breast-feed through the night), and the even more important memories of smell, touch, and sensation that give one a feeling of security in later life. Fear of the dark is only natural in a world where a predator has a better chance of stealing the young when it is dark and adults might be asleep. So every infant is hardwired to resist being separated at night. That is why whole books are needed to teach us a very unnatural thing: to make our babies sleep by themselves. It is true, of course, that we are no longer hunter-gatherers sleeping in a forest teeming with predators. But we are working against two million years of evolution in attempting to make a child adapt to this entirely new world, to no advantage.

We evolved to feed our infants whenever they are hungry. We did not evolve to feed our children secretions from another species. We are the only animal that takes the milk of another animal for our young. Cows' milk was designed for calves, not human babies. The fat content of human milk is very low, which means babies were meant to nurse frequently. Other animals, like rabbits, are able to feed their young sporadically because the fat content of their milk is so high. But if cottontail rabbits feed their young only once in twenty-four hours, we must remember that rabbit babies are in a draft-free, fur-lined nest (the rabbit is the only mother who uses her own fur to line her nest). Unique among mammals, the male tree shrew builds a nest for its young, but then the female feeds the infant for only five minutes once every forty-eight hours (and certain Alaska fur seals visit and nurse their children only once in eight days!). Human infants, on the other hand, were meant to have access to the breast more or less continuously. Human milk contains more than one hundred amino acids, vitamins, and minerals that provide the best food for the human infant's health. There is no substitute. This is the way babies were fed for 99 percent of human history. Prolonged (at least two years) breast-feeding is good for the baby, good for the mother (good for the father, too, since what is good for his children is good for him), and provides essential nutrients. The peace and attachment that come from the hormonal storm of oxytocin and prolactin in the mother can never be replaced by any supplement.

We were evolved to respond quickly to the cries of a baby. A baby is not meant to cry for very long: In Pleistocene days it would have called the attention of a predator. Crying is a signal of something amiss. Primate babies almost never cry, unless they are left alone or fear that they have been abandoned or are hurt. Simone, my first child, would cry at night, and we wondered why. Our pediatrician insisted there was no reason to change anything; learning to sleep by herself, he said, was important. Now the reason she was crying is clear to me: She did not want to be alone. She was right and our pediatrician was wrong. Ilan never cries at night, because he sleeps with his mother and me. In many cultures crying is considered a normal part of infantile behavior and supposedly good for the lungs. Thus in Holland, Dutch mothers sleep in separate rooms from their infants, and both doors are kept closed, so that the cries of the baby are not heard. When thinking about practices of this kind, it is a good idea to bear in mind what John Bowlby has called the "environment of evolutionary adaptedness," that is, the characteristics of our earliest environment. This is where the human race evolved, and anything that goes counter to it is going to meet with resistance. The infant who cries in this case knows more than the pediatrician who insists on ignoring the cry.

Fathers evolved to stay with their children throughout their entire childhoods, eighteen years or longer. Staying is good for the baby, good for the mother, good for the father, and provides essential emotional nutrients that give the child a feeling of self-worth and self-value that can never be replaced by any achievement or recognition in later life.

We evolved (especially fathers!) to play with our children on a daily basis. Prolonged play (many hours of it every day) is good for the baby, good for the father, good for the mother (it gives her a break), and provides essential stimulation. Even more important, play provides memories of touch and sensation that give the infant feelings of happiness and playfulness that, if missed, can never be made up for by any amount of later physical pleasures.

We evolved to travel with our children. No other animal species posts signs warning that an establishment is for adults only; no other species holds parties for which the invitation states that children are not welcome. Infant primates are carried everywhere. In fact, the very first tool invented by humans was a carrying sling for infants, developed, of course, by women, as recent anthropological research has demonstrated. Unlike a pouch, a sling is not anatomically specific: It can be worn just as well by a man as by a woman. Men who carry babies in a sling find it to be an immensely satisfying experience: The physical closeness of the baby against your skin brings a wonderful sense of intimacy. For infants who are born with certain early health problems, a treatment used now around the world is "kangaroo care."[1] That is, the babies are to be held, as in a pouch, on a continuous basis. This has amazing healing properties, increasing children's growth hormone levels, their endorphin levels, keeping them warm, creating cardiac stability, and increasing oxygen in the blood cells. It is truly a miracle cure and it is completely natural. In every other species, once past immediate infancy, all children follow their parents to work. Only our children must stay behind. Fathers should go on strike: no more work, anywhere, unless our young children are there, in crèches, in nurseries, in play-schools, or play-camps. Think how much happier we would be if we could check in on our children every few hours. (There are companies in California that realize that people work better when they can take their dogs to work, and allow them to do so.) We did not evolve to have the family broken up for anything but a fraction of the day. Maternity *and* paternity leave should both be a minimum of two years throughout the world.

We evolved to be in the natural environment. We evolved in the African savanna, in an outdoor habitat (our first mistake was heading north, into temperate climates for which our bodies were not adapted). No wonder children get bored when they are confined indoors. They have an *innate* preference for the trees and hills and grasses of the savanna. Walking, wandering, and being outdoors most of every day is what children desire and need. We did not evolve to use automobiles; and the speed with which they move makes close observation of our surroundings impossible. Research has shown that babies are happiest when they are carried while the parents are walking at a speed of three to four miles per hour. Becoming familiar with our physical environment was crucial to survival and is an inborn need. The great ethologist Nikolas Tinbergen talked about exploratory learning, and how important it is that we raise our children in an environment where they can explore the natural world with minimal interference from adults except encouragement and stimulation.[2] Every animal has this opportunity from early on; our children deserve no less.

We are not the only species to have evolved this way. If we look around us we see a rich biological diversity of fatherhood. Humans are always looking for their uniqueness, some one thing that places them where they believe they belong, at the apex of creation. Every decade some new discovery pushes us decisively off our pedestal: We thought we were the only animal to use language, until the great apes showed that they could learn the essentials of human language in about the same time it takes our children to do so. Moreover, when it comes to communicating, other animals, even bees, have done so very efficiently for hundreds of millions of years. We thought we were the only animal to make tools until Jane Goodall showed that chimpanzees also make them, and we know that many other animals use tools as well, including birds. We thought we were the only animal to transmit information through culture, but now we learn that elephants do so, as do chimpanzees, some monkeys, and probably whales as well. Then we thought we were the only animal who was self-aware, until experiments with mirrors showed that chimpanzees and orangutans used them much the same way we do. Recently the evolutionary psychologist Robert Wright claimed that only humans could feel pain and pleasure, sorrow and gladness with such complexity and subtlety. When it comes to the emotions, however, as I have said before, I firmly believe that we rank lower than dogs and wolves, who are our superiors in this respect. Finally, we have believed for too long that there are no good animal dads, that good fathering is a human prerogative. We were wrong. You have just read about prodigious feats of fatherhood in penguins, in sea horses, in wolves, in marmosets, and in many other animals.

But there are some ways in which we may be unique as parents and caregivers. Does any other animal sing a lullaby to its infant? Since whales and elephants sing at sound levels too low for the human ear, maybe we have missed it. There are other ways in which we are certainly unique: Although we may not be the only species moved to tears by the birth (or death) of our infants, we are probably the only species moved to tears by the birth (or death) of the infant of another species. No other animal takes a completely different species into its home, providing food and shelter, just for the pleasure of its company. We do. Finally, and here we come to the core of this book, we appear to be the only species that can consciously choose how involved we want to be as fathers.

We can learn to be less like bears, lions, male elephants, and Hanuman langurs, and more like penguins and mallee fowl, wolves and foxes, beavers and sea horses, marmosets and tamarins, prairie dogs and tropical frogs. For these fathers (even for the mound builder, who spends the greater part of one year building the mound for the single egg), parenting is a profound, all-encompassing experience, something that involves his whole being, and not just a surrogate activity to replace "real" life (no animal father does his wife a "favor" and "baby-sits"). These animals demonstrate the fact that for some species there is nothing, after all, that could be more real than *being* a father. Fatherhood is not a state that one comes in and out of, as in "I *was* a father, but now I am a free man." We do not get through and then get over fatherhood. It is, on the contrary, the greatest joy and the greatest expression of love of which the human male is capable.

Some readers of my previous two books about animals have criticized me for being too hard on science and scientists, especially the science of evolution. I feel that I am only trying to make a plea for the greatest Darwinian of them all, Charles Darwin himself. In many ways he is my intellectual hero, and the hero of this book as well—not just for what he found, but for how he found it. He was never afraid of direct observation and if what he found did not correspond to current prejudices, so much the worse for the prejudices. (The French hypnotist Jean Martin Charcot used a phrase that became Freud's favorite science dictum: *La théorie c'est bon, mais cela n'empêche pas d'exister;* theory is fine, but it does not prevent the facts from being what they are.) Darwin was not willing to accommodate ideas he believed were simply untrue. In his posthumously published little essay on instinct he saw continuity with humans in both the emotional and mental life of animals. Nor did he confine his examples to the negative emotions, anger, fear, aggression. So in the footnotes he comments on an altruistic cross-species act:

Capt. Sulivan, R.N., informs me that he watched for more than half an hour, at the Falkland Islands, a Logger-headed Duck defending a wounded Upland Goose from the repeated attacks of a Carrion Hawk. The upland goose first took to the water, and the duck swam close alongside her, always defending her with its strong beak; when the goose crawled ashore, the duck followed, going round and round her, and when the goose again took to the sea the duck was still vigorously defending her; yet at other times this duck *never* associates with this goose, for their food and place of habitation are utterly different. I very much fear, from what we see of little birds chasing hawks, that it would be more philosophical to attribute this conduct in the duck to hatred of the carrion hawk rather than to benevolence for the goose.[3]

It seems only fitting that Darwin should temper his far-reaching observations with a recognition that the mystery of kindness lies before our eyes, unfathomable, yet real. It is a lesson for everybody, but particularly one for fathers. Too often a father feels it is his duty to let his child know that the world is a hard place, filled with falseness, cruelty, and injustice. Darwin believed, and I do, too, that while this may well describe the world we know, it is one of the chief functions of fathers to protect their children from those same cruelties and unkindnesses and instill in them the deeper lessons of compassion and care, and that they do this best by the example of their own lives, caring for their children and other helpless creatures with intense devotion and joy at the wonder of the world we have evolved to share with other creatures so like us, and yet so enchantingly different.

Endnotes

Introduction

1. See Michael S. Roth, "Dying of the past: medical studies of nostalgia in nineteenth-century France," *History and Memory* 3 (1991): 5-29. On nostalgia as a disease, see George Rosen, "Nostalgia: a 'forgotten' psychological disorder," *Clio Medica* 10, no. 1 (1975): 28-51, and Jean Starobinski, "Le concept de nostalgie," *Diogène* 54 (1966): 92-115.

Chapter One

2. A very lively account of this can be read in an essay by Nancy Mitford that begins, "Apsley Cherry-Garrard has said 'polar exploration is at once the cleanest and most isolated way of having a bad time that has yet been devised.' Nobody could deny that he and the twenty-four other members of Captain Scott's expedition to the South Pole had a bad time; in fact, all other bad times, embarked on by men of their own free will, pale before it." See her *A Talent to Annoy: Essays, Articles and Reviews 1929-1968,* edited by Charlotte Mosley (New York: Beaufort Books, 1986).

3. Actually, this myth originated in *The Worst Journey in the World,* vol. 2, by Apsley Cherry-Garrard (1922; reprint, Harmondsworth: Penguin Books 1937) p. 548: "They are really worried by a horrid suspicion that a sea-leopard is waiting to eat the first to dive. The really noble bird, according to our theories, would say, 'I will go first and if I am killed I shall at any rate have died unselfishly, sacrificing my life for my companions' and in time all the

most noble birds would be dead. What they really do is to try and persuade a companion of weaker mind to plunge: failing this, they hastily pass a conscription act and push him over. And then—bang, helter-skelter, in go all the rest."

4. Curiously, the fact that it is exclusively the male who broods the egg eluded all scholars until it was noticed by the French explorer J. Cendron, who published his findings in 1952. Wilson was under the mistaken impression that the birds (male and female) took turns brooding the eggs. In fact, it is always the father, unassisted by anyone else, who keeps his egg on his feet until the return of the mother.

5. Konrad Lorenz, *The Year of the Greylag Goose,* translated by Robert Martin (New York: Harcourt Brace Jovanovich, 1979).

6. Alexander Skutch, *The Minds of Birds* (College Station, Tex.: Texas A&M University Press, 1996).

7. Bernard Stonehouse, "The Emperor Penguin. 1: Breeding Behaviour and Development," Falkland Islands Dependencies Survey, *Scientific Reports* 6 (1953).

8. Esther Cullen, "Adaptations in the kittiwake to cliff-nesting," *the Ibis* 99, no. 2 (1957): 275-302.

9. Robert Cushman Murphy, *Oceanic Birds of South America,* vol. 2 (New York: American Museum of Natural History, 1936), p. 364.

10. George Gaylord Simpson, *Penguins Past and Present, Here and There* (New Haven: Yale University Press, 1976).

Chapter Two

1. I checked on this by consulting one of the world's foremost experts on wild canids, Marc Bekoff at the University of Colorado. He confirmed that to his knowledge there had never been an authenticated account of an attack on a human by a healthy wild wolf within the United States. European folklore is filled with such attacks, which gives us something to reflect upon about the limitations of the human imagination. Or could European wolves be so different?

2. Eric Zimen, an ethologist from Germany, compared the behavior of wolves and poodles and found that at feeding sites, wolves were extremely social;

young animals and nursing mothers have priority. Not so the poodles, who can be very aggressive at the feeding site, even when young puppies are present. When adult wolves are in a group of juveniles, he showed, they move with special care, while poodles show no such increase in orienting behavior. See the section on the behavior of domestic animals from *Grzimek's Encyclopedia of Ethology,* edited by Klaus Immelmann (New York: Van Nostrand Reinhold, 1977). Zimen's excellent book, in German, is *Wölfe und Königspudel: Vergleichende Verhaltensbeobachtungen* (Munich: Piper Verlag, 1974).

3. Why rabbits would live near their most fierce enemy is a puzzle. The red fox will often share its denning site with rabbits. Perhaps the rabbits warn the fox of the approach of its traditional enemies—for example, man. The rabbit in turn benefits from living near a powerful predator, for the fox keeps other predators away. The foxes, however, do not eat the rabbits, unlike the wolves. But perhaps the trade-off is still worthwhile for the rabbit.

4. This is not the opinion of Richard Fiennes. He says that wolves readily attack and eat dogs. On the other hand, wolves will not attack other wolves unless one is badly wounded, at which point it is killed and eaten. "Evidently, therefore, they detect some fundamental differences between themselves and dogs, even those that are most closely related to them. That they do not normally attack man would appear to indicate that they regard him as more akin to themselves than they do dogs. This is a very difficult feature of wolf behaviour to explain." See *The Order of Wolves* (New York: Bobbs-Merrill, 1976), p. 143. Note that the idea that a wolf will not kill another wolf has been shown to be wrong in more recent publications, such as *The Wolves of Denali,* edited by L. David Mech (Minneapolis: University of Minnesota Press, 1998).

5. Jim Brandenburg, *White Wolf: Living with an Arctic Legend* (Minocqua, Wisc.: NorthWord Press, 1990), p. 144.

Chapter Three

1. Actually, the discovery goes back to the Nobel prize–winner Karl von Frisch in 1938. Hara says that "he accidentally discovered that when an injured European minnow, *Phoximus phoximus,* was introduced into a shoal, they became frightened and dispersed." Evidently von Frisch saw a kingfisher swoop down and attack a school of minnows. As it was flying away it dropped the minnow and von Frisch noticed that the other minnows, which were still schooling, suddenly dispersed. Hara explains that when the skin of a fish is damaged, alarm substance cells are broken and release the alarm substance, which is then smelled

by nearby conspecifics. The article by Toshiaki J. Hara is "Role of olfaction in fish behaviour," in *Behaviour of Teleost Fishes,* 2nd ed., edited by Tony J. Pitcher (London: Chapman & Hall, 1993) pp. 171-200). The original article by Frisch is entitled "Zur Psychologie des Fisch-Schwarmes," in *Naturwissenschaften* 26 (1938): 601-606. Hara also cites a 1941 article by Frisch, which, judging from its title, seems more relevant: "Über einen Schreckstoff der Fischhaut und seine biologische Bedeutung" ("On the biological significance of warning chemicals on the fish skin"), in *Zeitschrift für vergleichende Physiologie* 29: 46-145. I don't know if Frisch used this as evidence of fish feeling pain, but Hara does not. The inference, with which I agree, is from Bateson.

2. From a scientific point of view, fish have been well studied. There is an enormous scholarly and scientific literature on every aspect of piscine parental behavior, most of it extremely technical.

3. These figures are often confusing. Mart R. Gross and R. Craig Sargent from the Department of Biological Sciences at Simon Fraser University in British Columbia, in their article "The volution of male and female parental care in fishes" *(American Zoologist* 25 [1985], pp. 807-822), write that "Bony fishes (Osteichthyes) are comprised of approximately 422 families (primarily teleosts) and represent over 95% of the living fishes. Parental care is presently known in at least 87 families representing 3,000-5,000 species." They go on to say that 61 percent of the families that have care have male care, and also that taxonomic pedigree analyses suggest an evolutionary progression in parental care from no care to male care to biparental care.

4. Konrad Lorenz, *King Solomon's Ring: New Light on Animal Ways* (New York: Time, Inc., 1952), pp. 42-43.

5. The description of the stickleback is from Nikolas Tinbergen, "The curious behavior of the stickleback," in *Twentieth-Century Bestiary* by the Editors of Scientific American (New York: Simon & Schuster, 1955).

6. Ernst Mayr's observation is found in "Sexual selection and natural selection," in *Sexual Selection and the Descent of Man,* edited by B. Campbell (Chicago: Aldine Press, 1972). See also his classic work, *Animal Species and Evolutuion* (Cambridge, Mass.: Harvard University Press, 1963).

7. Amanda C. J. Vincent, "A sea horse father makes a good mother," *Natural History* 12 (1990): 34-43.

8. Male lactation is one of those topics that has fascinated people for a long time, but information is very scarce. Darwin, in *The Descent of Man and Selection in Relation to Sex* (1871) claimed that "In man and some other male

mammals [the mammary glands] have been known occasionally to become so well developed as to yield a fair supply of milk."According to Martin Daly, this is merely a myth. See his outstanding article, "Why don't male mammals lactate?" in *Journal of Theoretical Biology* 78 (1979): 325-345. According to Stephen J. Gould, male nipples are merely a spin-off, a vestigial creation with no function. One wonders.

9. For the comment by Hulse, see Frederick S. Hulse, *The Human Species* (New York: Random House, 1963), p. 114.

10. David Badger, *Frogs* (Stillwater, Minn.: Voyageur Press, 1995).

11. Robert Trivers, in *Social Evolution* (Menlo Park, Ca.: The Benjamin/ Cummings Publishing Co., 1985), points out that female frogs test males by bumping them off eggs: "In four cases where the male bolted from the nest upon being bumped, the female quickly withdrew and did not return." She suspected, evidently, that he would not make a very attentive father. Did she *choose* to leave the male? Could this have been a decision at more than the automatic level?

12. See K. D. Wells, "The social behaviour of anuran amphibians," in *Animal Behaviour* 25 (1977): 666-693. "Prolonged amplexus also occurs in neotropical frogs in the genus *Atelopus*. In *A. oxyrynchus*, pairs may stay in amplexus for many months and males become extremely emaciated because of the restriction imposed on their food intake."

13. This story is found in a note by Klaus Busse, "Care of the young by male *Rhinoderma darwini*," published in *Copeia* 2 (1970): 395.

14. William Duellman, quoted in Badger, *Frogs*.

Chapter Four

1. Katy Payne, *Silent Thunder: In the Presence of Elephants* (New York: Simon & Schuster, 1998).

2. Needless to say, this is a personal opinion. Nobody has canvassed the elephants themselves. Cynthia Moss, on the other hand, disagrees with me: "An adult bull spends his days alone or with a few male companions, eating, drinking, bathing, dusting, wallowing, resting, and playing. In fact, within the parks and reserves, where elephants are protected from hunters (and usually from poachers), the adult bull's life appears very pleasant by human standards. Bulls do not have to worry about any of the nonhuman predators, and

they are not restricted in their day-to-day movements, as are cows, by the distance the small calves can travel." See her *Portraits in the Wild: Behavior Studies of East African Mammals,* 2nd ed. (Chicago: University of Chicago Press, 1982), p. 9.

3. "We were gathering the bones of Jezebel, my favorite female, and presenting them to her own family. The family approached her remains and then suddenly stopped and became silent. They neared the bones very slowly and then spent the next hour turning the skull, the jaw, and the long bones over and over. The elephants, who appeared to be in a sort of trance, neither interacted nor vocalized and seemed to focus only on the dead elephant. Jolene, Jezebel's daughter, appeared to be the most absorbed of the group. What was she thinking: This is my mother; she died in a lot of pain; life is not the same without my mother? Why would an elephant stand in silence over the bones of its relative for an hour if it were not having some thoughts, *conscious* thoughts, and perhaps memories?" Joyce Poole, *Coming of Age with Elephants: A Memoir* (New York: Hyperion, 1996), p. 161.

4. There are far less speculative reasons of a psychological nature that would explain the widespread phenomenon of philopatry, and they have been given in detail by Ernst Mayr in his classic *Animal Species and Evolution* (Cambridge, Mass.: Harvard University Press, 1963, pp. 565 ff., esp. p. 568). Mayr, who notes that philopatry is found among mice, lizards, turtles, snakes, fish, snails, and butterflies, quotes a fascinating 1940 study by G. Niethammer, who showed that in southwest Africa reddish larks are found only on red soil, and dark ones on dark soil. The birds, he says, are conscious of the color that corresponds to their own coloration and cannot be induced to pass over the color barrier even when chased.

5. Richard Alexander, *Darwinism and Human Affairs* (Seattle: University of Washington Press, 1979), p. 162. Also see Alexander's "How did humans evolve? Reflections on the uniquely unique species," *University of Michigan Special Publication No. 1,* Museum of Zoology, 1990, p.12.

6. I have talked of solitary males. Some bear researchers, however, report that unrelated bears will sometimes team up, traveling, foraging, and playing together for weeks or even years. "Very little is known about these relationships other than that they exist. When the partners are two females with cubs there are some obvious advantages in terms of baby-sitting availability and mutual defense, but when the friends are both adult males—a pattern that is seen fairly commonly among polar bears—nothing seems to be clear beyond the fact that the bears obviously like each other. Clearly the whole subject of bears as antag-

onistic loners needs a close critical look." William Ashworth, *Bears: Their Life and Behavior,* (New York: Crown Publishers, 1992), p. 164.

7. I spoke to Lynn Rogers by phone from Berkeley, California, on January 30, 1998.

8. To be fair to the opposition, however, I must admit to the cogency of the counterargument here. Hrdy and Hausfater, in the introduction to their symposium, *Infanticide* (1984) remind us that terrestrial and diurnal field workers rarely witness aerial or nocturnal predators actually kill a monkey, but we do not doubt that it happens often enough to convince all primatologists that predation has been an important factor in primate evolution. It strikes me as similar to overlooking incest because we can't see it. "Direct observation of predation on jungle fowl by various animals is exceedingly rare, even by persons with a lifetime of experience in the forest . . . Once during our stay in the Saharanpur Forest Division a leopard passed coughing and growling near the dak bungalow and fairly close to a jungle fowl roost. But the jungle cock in the vicinity of this roost continued his evening crowing, paying no apparent attention to the leopard." Nicholas E. Collias and Elsie C. Collias, "A field study of the red jungle fowl in North-Central India," *The Condor* 69, no. 4 (1967): 375.

9. See Anne Pusey and Craig Packer, "Infanticide in lions: consequences and counterstrategies," in Stefano Parmigiani and Frederick S. vom Saal, eds., *Infanticide and Parental Care* (Chur, Switzerland: Harwood Academic Publishers, 1994), pp. 277-299.

10. George B. Schaller, *The Serengeti Lion: A Study of Predator-Prey Relations* (Chicago: University of Chicago Press, 1972).

11. Once again I must cite evidence that speaks against my neat categories. L. David Mech, the world's leading wolf researcher, in his latest book about the wolves of Denali, believes that 60 percent of wolf mortality may be due to wolf-on-wolf attacks, a fact not previously suspected. See L. David Mech, ed., *The Wolves of Denali* (Minneapolis: University of Minnesota Press, 1998), p. 59: "The primary mortality cause of 57 wolves aged 9 months or older in Denali Park and Preserve during our study was death from other wolves, and that cause claimed about five times the rate of wolf deaths as any other known natural cause such as accidents or disease." See, too, p. 81: "Of 57 radio-collared wolves that died while in the study area, 39% were known to have been killed by neighboring wolf packs. Another 26% died of unknown natural causes, most of which were also probably wolf kills. Thus as much as 65% of the wolf mortality was probably due to other wolves. This is the highest rate reported by any study."

12. See Sarah Hrdy, *The Langurs of Abu* (Cambridge, Mass.: Harvard University Press, 1977), and *The Woman That Never Evolved* (Cambridge, Mass.: Harvard University Press, 1981).

13. See Paul W. Sherman, "Reproductive competition and infanticide in Belding's ground squirrels and other animals," in Richard D. Alexander and Donald W. Tinkle, *Natural Selection and Social Behavior: Recent Research and New Theory* (New York: Chiron Press, 1981), pp.311-331.

14. *Mensch und Tier im Zoo: Tiergarten-Biologie* (Zurich: Albert Mueller Verlag, 1965).

15. This comes from Robert O. Stephenson and Robert R. Ahgook, "The Eskimo Hunter's View of World Ecology and Behavior," in M. W. Fox, ed., *The Wild Canids: Their Systematics, Behavioral Ecology and Evolution* (New York: Van Nostrand Reinhold, 1975), pp. 286-291.

Chapter Five

1. The story of the sungrebe is from David Attenborough's *The Life of Birds* (Princeton: Princeton University Press, 1998), p. 257.

2. The Sheila Kitzinger survey is quoted in Elaine Morgan, *The Descent of the Child: Human Evolution from a New Perspective* (New York: Oxford University Press, 1995).

3. C. Lewis, "The role of the father in the human family," in W. Sluckin and Martin Herbert, *Parental Behavior* (Oxford: Basil Blackwell, 1986), pp. 228-258.

4. J. Adler, "Building a better dad," *Newsweek* (June 17, 1996), pp. 58-64.

5. The reference to marmosets and tamarins who assist in delivery at birth is found in Y. Spencer-Booth, "The relationship between mammalian young and conspecifics other than mothers and peers: a review," in Daniel S. Lehrman, Robert A. Hinde, and Evelyn Shaw, eds., *Advances in the Study of Behavior*, vol. 3 (New York: Academic Press, 1970), pp. 120–194. The 1981 study about circulating prolactin levels is cited in Michael Lamb, "A bisocial perspective on paternal behavior and involvement," in J. B. Lancaster, J. Altmann, A. S. Ross, and L. R. Sherrod, eds., *Parenting Across the Life Span* (New York: Aldine de Gruyter, 1987), pp. 111-142.

6. See his *Ecological Adaptations for Breeding in Birds* (London: Methuen, 1968).

7. Many other birds have a special sound they make when they wish to call

the attention of their young to a tasty morsel. Chicken fathers do this, but humans missed its significance until recently. It was assumed the cock was merely expressing his own pleasure in finding food.

8. W. H. Thorpe, *Animal Nature and Human Nature* (New York: Doubleday, 1974), p. 228, points out that as early as 1873, D. A. Spalding observed that a newly hatched duckling or gosling will follow practically any moving object it sees in the same way that it would follow its own parent. Konrad Lorenz's teacher, Oskar Heinroth, first gave it the name of *praegung* (imprinting) in 1910. Spalding wrote that "a chicken that has not heard the call of the mother until eight or ten days old then hears it as if it heard it not." See Eric Fabricius, "Crucial periods in the development of the following response in young nidifugous birds," *Zeitschrift für Tierpsychologie,* 21, no. 3 (1964): 326-337. Patrick Bateson, from the University of Cambridge, sent me many of his articles on this topic, which proved very useful to my understanding of the many subtleties involved. See his "How do sensitive periods arise and what are they for?" in *Animal Behaviour* 27 (1979): 470-486. Klaus Immelmann, in his article "Sexual and other long-term aspects of imprinting in birds and other species," *Advances in the Study of Behavior,* 4 (1972), p. 167, writes: "In species where only the female cares for the young (for example, ducks and fowl) there may be a strong selection pressure against female imprintability, since it would result in homosexual pairing among adult females." He refers to a paper by Patrick Bateson, "The characteristics and context of imprinting," *Biological Review* 41 (1966): 177-220.

9. *The Cambridge Encyclopedia of Ornithology,* edited by Michael Brooke and Tim Birkhead (New York: Cambridge University Press, 1991) p. 255, puts it like this: "Mate recognition processes must also allow for sexually dimorphic species in which only one sex looks after the brood. For example, drake Mallards imprint on their mothers but female preferences are largely independent of early experiences. In monomorphic species, on the other hand, both sexes imprint on the parent's appearance." The main experiments were pioneered by Schutz: "After experiments involving 232 birds from 10 different species he concluded that the females of dimorphic duck species 'are almost incapable of becoming imprinted as they react innately to the releasers of the male courtship dress.' In contrast about two-thirds of Mallard drakes reared by a foster mother or with a foster sibling of a different species later attempted to pair with an individual of that species. . . . Perhaps sympatric male dabbling ducks have to have such distinctive and different plumages simply because females have only a very basic innate model of the conspecific male which cannot be greatly improved by learning during the brood period." Diane M. Williams, "Mate choice in the

Mallard," in Patrick Bateson, ed., in *Mate Choice* (Cambridge: Cambridge University Press, 1983), p. 301.

10. Note what Michael Bright says in *The Private Life of Birds: A Worldwide Exploration of Bird Behaviour* (London: Bantam Books, 1993), p. 297, about an ostrich pair: "The ostrich produces an egg every two days. A normal clutch of twenty would take thirty-nine days to complete and the first to be laid would be cooking in the sun. By laying in other nests and accepting the eggs of others into her nest she ensures that the clutches are built up more quickly. The pair, however, don't just accept the regulation twenty; the two breeding birds might gather thirty or more. Twenty of them are selected, including the main female's own eggs—no mean task as they are seemingly identical—and they are placed centrally to gain maximum benefit from incubation. The rest are placed in a ring around the edge of the nest, an insurance against sneaky nest predators."

11. Kiwis, much smaller birds who make up the last member of the ratite family, are monogamous. But the chicks stay with the adults for a much shorter time, usually only three weeks. Nonetheless, adult brown kiwis have been known to accompany juveniles for as long as a year and even for as long as three years.

12. D. Lack, in *Ecological Adaptations for Breeding in Birds* (London: Methuen, 1968), p. 150, points out that in geese the male guards the sitting female, and in these and many other nidifugous birds, both parents escort and protect their young, though they do not feed them.

13. Personal communication from Professor Robert Trivers to the author, September 4, 1998.

14. Gerald Borgia, "Sexual selection in bowerbirds," in Douglas W. Mock, ed., *Behavior and Evolution of Birds* (New York: W. H. Freeman and Co., 1991). The original article was published in 1986. Jared Diamond asked: "Could it be that birds prefer blue *because* blue is rare, so that females can recognize a superior male by his ability to retain the rare blue objects in the face of theft attempts by other males?" He also points out that some bowerbirds take four to seven years to develop the bower style characteristics of adults. For years, young males of these species build rudimentary bowers with atypical structures and no or atypical decorations. See his valuable article "Bower-building and decoration by the bowerbird *Amblyonis inornatus,*" *Ethology* 74, no. 3 (1987): 177-204.

15. Ernst Mayr, in his brilliant article "Sexual selection and natural selection" (in Bernard G. Campbell, ed., *Sexual Selection and the Descent of Man*

1871-1971 [Chicago: Aldine Press, 1972], p. 90), writes that there "are numerous species of birds in which the males are brightly colored and adorned with special plumes, such as the birds of paradise or the peacocks. Such spectacular structures could never have evolved, says Darwin, unless females exercise a choice among various eligible males and, more than that, unless females have a sense for beauty." He then quotes Darwin: "Just as man can give beauty according to his standard of taste, to his male poultry, or more strictly can modify the beauty originally acquired by the parent species, so it appears that female birds in a state of nature, have by a long selection of the more attractive males added to their beauty or other attractive qualities. No doubt this implies powers of discrimination and taste on the part of the female which will at first appear extremely improbable; but by the facts to be adduced hereafter, I hope to be able to shew that the females actually have these powers."

16. E. Thomas Gilliard, *Birds of Paradise and Bower Birds* (London: Weidenfeld and Nicolson, 1969), p. 54-55.

17. "Females exert strong preference in mating, and only a small proportion of males achieve most of the matings. Males with high quality bowers—with symmetrical walls formed from thin, densely packed sticks—and many decorations on their courts mate most often." Gerald Borgia, "Why do bowerbirds build bowers?" *American Scientist* 83, no. 6 (1995): 542-547. He also points out in this article (p. 547) that male avenue-building great bowerbirds, who have lilac crests, place green objects beneath the spot where they display, because the decorations are a complementary color to the crest and increase the contrast of his display. The hutlike cover on some maypole-bower courts also orients a female to a male's display.

18. This quote is found in Gilliard, *Birds of Paradise,* p. 51, and draws on material from C. R. Stonor, *Courtship and Display Among Birds* (London: Country Life 1940).

19. But note the caution of Ernst Mayr, in his classic article "Sexual selection and natural selection" (p. 89): "There is a strong selection pressure for reduced size in the females of hole nesting species of ducks (only the females incubate!). Consequently, there is an increased size dimorphism in these species which, at least, initially, had nothing to do with sexual selection."

20. In the California sea lion, the Steller sea lion, and the northern fur seal, the adult males are three to six or more times heavier than the adult females. However, the noted ethologist George W. Barlow, from the University of California at Berkeley, has challenged the notion that no paternal behavior has

ever been seen in these species. He described the behavior of some territorial Galapagos Island sea lion bulls *(Zolophus californianus),* who definitely seemed to be protecting their pups by attacking sharks intruding into the rookery. The article drew an unexpectedly wide response, because it is the first published report of a paternal role in a pinniped. See "Galapagos sea lions are paternal," in *Evolution* 28, no. 3 (1974), 476-478, for a reply to his critics.

Chapter Six

1. Edward Westermarck, *The History of Human Marriage,* 3 vols., 5th ed. (New York: The Allerton Books Co., 1922).

2. Bronislaw Malinowski, *An Ethnographic Account of Courtship, Marriage and Family Life Among the Natives of the Trobriand Islands, British New Guinea* (New York: Halcyon House, 1929).

3. Jerram L. Brown, "Cooperative breeding and altruistic behavior in the Mexican jay, *Aphelocoma ultramarina,*" *Animal Behaviour* 18, no. 2 (1970): 366-378.

4. This quote by Exley is from Jonathan Yardley, *Misfit: The Strange Life of Frederick Exley* (New York: Random House, 1997), p. 119.

5. Junichiro Itani, "Paternal care in the wild Japanese monkey, *Macaca fuscata fuscata,*" *Primates* 2, no. 1 (1959): 61-93. Apparently he was the first author to "discover" paternal care in the Japanese monkey, in 1953 at Takasakiyama in Japan.

6. John Bowlby, *Child Care and the Growth of Love,* 2nd. ed. of the report *Maternal Care and Mental Health,* Margaret Fry, ed. (1953; reprint, New York: Penguin Books, 1990).

7. Benson Jaffee and David Fanshel, *How They Fared in Adoption: A Follow-up Study* (New York: Columbia University Press, 1970), pp. 317-318.

8. Hugo van Lawick, *Solo: The Story of an African Dog,* with an introduction by Jane Van Lawick Goodall (New York: Houghton Mifflin Co., 1974).

9. Itani, op. cit.

10. Margo Wilson and Martin Daly, "The psychology of parenting in evolutionary perspective and the case of human filicide," in Glenn Hausfater and Sarah Blaffer Hrdy, eds., *Infanticide: Comparative and Evolutionary Perspectives* (New York: Aldine Press, 1984), pp.73-103.

11. The incident was also reported in the BBC's *Wildlife Magazine,* May 1996, p. 98.

Chapter Seven

1. George Gaylord Simpson, *Penguins Past and Present, Here and There* (New Haven: Yale University Press, 1976).

2. Toshisada Nishida, "Alloparental behavior in wild chimpanzees of the Mahale mountains, Tanzania," *Folia Primatologica* 183, no. 41: 1-33.

3. John A. King, "Social behavior, social organization, and population dynamics in a black-tailed prairie dog town in the Black Hills of South Dakota," *Contributions from the Laboratory of Vertebrate Biology,* University of Michigan, 67 (April 1955): 1-120. A few years later, a popular version of his thesis was published in *Scientific American,* in the October 1959 issue, "The Social Behavior of the Prairie Dogs," and has been subsequently anthologized.

4. The world's leading expert on black-tailed prairie dogs, Dr. John Hoogland, claims that there is no such thing as an all-clear signal. I find this hard to believe. In his monograph, the Ph.D. thesis, John King wrote (p. 35), "When the eagle or hawk has passed by, prairie dogs respond vocally with a call, which on this occasion serves as an all-is-well signal." I wondered whether Dr. King agrees with Hoogland. I wrote to King, who is now seventy-seven, and he agrees with me: "What you offered about the prairie dog 'all is well' cry makes sense to me, though I did not think of it before you mentioned it. However, I remember it well, after hearing the dogs bark at an eagle flying overhead how they then give the 'yahoo' call when it flew out of range, which could suggest nothing other than "the threat is gone." (personal communication, November 10, 1998). In a later communication, he wrote to me that the "'all is well' signal is remarkable for the energy and the uniqueness of it. Perhaps it is comparable to the howl of a wolf or coyote, or the call of the grasshopper mouse, which calls almost like a wolf, but at a much higher pitch, of course."

5. This quotation from Barbara Smuts comes from a fascinating new book about the rights of animals by the eminent South African novelist J. M. Coetzee, *The Lives of Animals* (Princeton: Princeton University Press, 1999).

6. This quote from Buffon I found in a fine little book by Boria Sax, *The Frog King: On Legends, Fables, Fairy Tales and Anecdotes of Animals* (New York: Pace University Press, 1990).

7. Father Chrestien Le Clercq, *New Relation of Gaspesia,* translated by William F. Ganon (Toronto: Champlain Society, 1910), p. 421, quoted in Rosemary Rodd, *Biology, Ethics, and Animals* (Oxford: Oxford University Press, 1990), p. 243.

Chapter Eight

1. See Patrick J. Weatherhead, "Do savannah sparrows commit the Concorde fallacy?" *Behavioral Ecology and Sociobiology* 5 (1979): 373-381. He points out at the end of his article that birds must possess a sophisticated analytical ability with respect to weighing factors about an unpredictable future. This acute ability is said to be innate. But how can it be innate when the variables are constantly in flux? It is far more parsimonious to concede that the brains of birds may be infinitely more flexible and complex than we assumed. Donald Griffin has sought to convey this insight for many years in a series of outstanding books on the cognitive abilities of animals. See his *The Question of Animal Awareness: Evolutionary Continuity of Mental Experience,* 2nd. ed. (New York: Rockefeller University Press, 1981); *Animal Thinking* (Cambridge, Mass.: Harvard University Press, 1984); and *Animal Minds* (Chicago: University of Chicago Press, 1992).

2. This is not true of the crocodilians, however. Recent research shows elaborate parental care. In Mexico, male caimans have been observed gently picking up the young in their mouths in batches and carrying them in a throat pouch. American alligators carry their hatchlings to specially excavated pools. Nile crocodile mothers have nursery areas in quiet backwaters where they protect their young for three months, and American alligators may take care of their children for up to two years. See *The Encyclopedia of Reptiles and Amphibians,* edited by Tim Halliday and Kraig Adler (New York: Facts on File, 1986), p. 140.

3. The calculations about the amount of work involved by the male mallee fowl is from Wesley W. Weathers, et al., "Energetics of mound-tending behaviour in the mallee fowl, *Leipoa ocellata* (Megapodidae)," *Animal Behaviour* 45, no. 2 (1993): 333-341.

4. See George A. Clark, "Life histories and the evolution of megapodes," *The Living Bird* 3 (1964): 149-166. He suggests (p. 159) that "the repeated diggings of the adults to check and regulate mound temperature apparently also function in keeping the contents of the mound loose, thus aiding the escape of the young."

5. America's foremost ornithologist, Alexander Skutch, has recently written *The Minds of Birds* (College Station, Tex.: A&M University Press, 1996), speculating about matters that, now that he has reached the age of ninety-five, he feels entitled to speculate about. One of America's leading psychologists, Theodore Xenophon Barber, has also chimed in, with *The Human Nature of Birds: A Scientific Discovery with Startling Implications* (New York: St. Martin's Press, 1993). In his classic field study, "The courtship habits of the Great Crested Grebe" (written in 1914!), Julian Huxley wrote that "by comparing the actions of the birds with our own in circumstances as similar as possible, we can deduce the bird's emotions with much more probability of accuracy than we can possibly have about their nervous processes: that is to say, we can interpret the facts psychologically better than we can physiologically." (Proceedings of the Zoological Society of London 35: 491-562.) Note, too, that Huxley also wrote an article in 1923 entitled: "Ils n'ont que de l'âme: an essay on bird-mind," published in *Cornhill Magazine* 54 (1923): 415-427.

6. It is not clear why the Dall porpoise is different in this respect from other porpoises that clearly do sleep. See the article by Ray Meddis, "On the function of sleep," *Animal Behaviour* 23 (1975): 676-691, which contains a superb bibliography on animal sleep. In German, people say: *Ich schlaf wie ein Murmeltier* (I slept like a groundhog). The idea is that the marmot or groundhog hibernates ("I slept like a bear," is our equivalent).

Epilogue

1. Kangaroo care is explained in Susan M. Ludington-Hoe and Susan K. Golant, *Kangaroo Care: The Best You Can Do to Help Your Preterm Infant* (New York: Bantam Books, 1993).

2. Tinbergen's comments can be found in his 1972 address "Functional ethology and the human sciences," in *The Animal in Its World: Laboratory Experiments and General Papers* (Cambridge, Mass.: Harvard University Press, 1972).

3. Darwin is quoted in George Hohn Romanes, *Mental Evolution in Animals,* with a posthumous essay on instinct by Charles Darwin (New York: S. Appleton & Co., 1900).

Suggested Reading

Chapter One

It was really not until Jean Prévost visited Pointe Geologie, Terre Adélie, once in 1952 and again in 1956, and studied for an entire winter the 12,500 emperor penguins living there, many of them banded, that we were able to discover with certainty many facts about these fascinating birds. I am heavily indebted, in this chapter, to Prévost's wonderful book, yet to be translated into English, *Écologie du Manchot Empereur, Aptenodytes forsteri Gray* (Paris: Hermann, 1961). For information on the discovery of penguins, I have used Dietland Müller-Schwarze's *The Behavior of Penguins Adapted to Ice and Tropics* (Albany: State University of New York Press, 1984). Apsley Cherry-Garrard's book is *The Worst Journey in the World: The Story of Scott's Last Expedition to the South Pole*, 2 vols. (1922; reprint, Harmondsworth: Penguin Books 1937). Edward A. Wilson's book is *National Antarctic Expedition 1901-1904: Natural History*, vol. 2: *Zoology (Vertebrata: Mollusca: Crustacea)*, chapter 3 *(Vertebrata)*, Part II: Aves by Edward A. Wilson (London: British Museum, 1907), pp. 1-118. On the emperor penguin, see Bernard Stonehouse, "The Emperor Penguin. 1: Breeding Behaviour and Development," Falkland Islands Dependencies Survey, *Scientific Reports* 6 (1953), pp. 1-33. Also his book *Penguins* (New York: Golden Press, 1968). Further on penguins, see Diane Ackerman, *The Moon by Whale Light: And Other Adventures Among Bats, Penguins,*

Crocodilians, and Whales (New York: Random House, 1991); William Ashworth, *Penguins, Puffins, and Auks: Their Lives and Behavior* (New York: Crown Publishers, 1993); Lloyd S. Davis and John T. Darby, eds., *Penguin Biology* (San Diego: Academic Press, 1990); James Gorman, *The Total Penguin* (New York: Prentice-Hall, 1990); Roger Kirkwood and Graham Robertson, "The foraging ecology of female emperor penguins in winter," *Ecological Monographs* 67, no. 2 (1997): 155-176; Gerald L. Kooyman, et al., "Penguin dispersal after fledging," *Nature* 383 issue 6599, (October 3, 1996); 397. Also see G. L. Kooyman and T. G. Kooyman, "Diving behavior of emperor penguins nurturing chicks at Coulman Island, Antarctica," *The Condor* 97 (1995): 536-549; E. Kooyman, "Foraging behaviour of emperor penguins as a resource detector in winter and summer," *Nature* 360 issue 6402, (November 26, 1992): 336-339; John Love, *Penguins* (Stillwater, Minn.: Voyageur Press, 1997); Yvon Le Maho, "The emperor penguin: a strategy to live and breed in the cold," *American Scientist* 65, no. 6 (1974); Roger Tory Peterson, *Penguins* (Boston: Houghton Mifflin Co., 1979); L. E. Richdale, *Sexual Behavior in Penguins* (Lawrence, Kansas: University of Kansas Press, 1951); Jean Rivolier, *Emperor Penguins,* translated from the French by Peter Wiles (New York: Robert Speller & Sons, 1958); George Gaylord Simpson, *Penguins Past and Present, Here and There* (New Haven: Yale University Press, 1976); John Sparks and Tony Soper, *Penguins* (Newton, Mass.: David and Charles, 1967); Tony D. Williams, *The Penguins Speniscidae* (Oxford: Oxford University Press, 1995); Euan Young, *Skua and Penguin: Predator and Prey, Studies in Polar Research* (Cambridge: Cambridge University Press, 1994); Pierre Jouventin, et al., "Le chant du Manchot Empereur et sa signification adaptive," *Behaviour* 70, no. 3 (1979): 231-250; also "Comportement et structure sociale chez le Manchot Empereur," *La Terre et la Vie* 25, no. 4 (1971): 510-586; J. Cendron, "Une visite hivernale à une rookerie de Manchots Empereurs," *La Terre et la Vie* 6 (1952): 101-108. Birds who call from within the egg are discussed by Gilbert Gottlieb in *Development of Species Identification in Birds: An Inquiry into the Prenatal Determinants of Perception* (Chicago: University of Chicago Press, 1971). Edward Hoagland's *Tigers and Ice* is published by the Lyons Press (New York: 1999).

Chapter Two

On domestication in general, see Juliet Clutton-Brock in *The Cambridge Encyclopedia of Human Evolution* (Cambridge: Cambridge

University Press, 1997). See also her article "Man-made dogs," in *Science* 197 (1977): 1340-1342); F. E. Zeuner: *A History of Domesticated Animals* (London: Hutchinson & Co., 1963); Ernst Mayr, *Animal Species and Evolution* (Cambridge, Mass.: Harvard University Press, 1963). See also Stanley C. Ratner and Robert Boice, "Effects of domestication on behaviour," in E. S. E. Hafez, ed., *The Behaviour of Domestic Animals,* 3rd ed. (London: Bailliere Tindall, 1963), and also *Adaptation of Domestic Animals,* edited by E. S. E. Hafez (Philadelphia: Lea & Febiger, 1968). For the dog in particular, see Michael W. Fox, *The Dog: Its Domestication and Behavior* (Malabar, Fla.: Krieger Publishing Co., 1987). For wolves, the most authoritative book is by L. David Mech, *The Wolf: The Ecology and Behavior of an Endangered Species* (Minneapolis: University of Minnesota Press, 1970). I also used Michael W. Fox, *Behavior of Wolves, Dogs and Related Canids* (New York: Harper & Row, 1971); G. B. Rabb, B. E. Ginsburg, and Susan Andrews, "Comparative studies of canid behavior IV: mating behavior in relation to social structure in wolves," *American Zoologist* 2 (1962). On the dingo, see N. W. G. Macintosh, "The Origin of Dingo: An Enigma," in *The Wild Canids: Their Systematics, Behavioral Ecology and Evolution,* M. W. Fox, ed. (New York: Van Nostrand Reinhold Co., 1975), pp. 87-106. On male parental care in general, see Devra G. Kleiman and James R. Malcolm, "The evolution of male parental investment in mammals," in *Parental Care in Mammals,* D. J. Gubernick and P. H. Klopfer, eds. (New York: Plenum Press, 1981). On male parental care in the canids, see R. F. Ewer, *The Carnivores* (London: Weidenfeld & Nicolson, 1973), and D. G. Kleiman, "Some aspects of social behavior in the Canidae," *American Zoologist* 7 (1967): 365-372. On foxes, see R. Burrows, *Wild Fox* (Newton Abbot, England: David Charles, 1968). On the red fox, see G. Tembrock: "Das Verhalten des Rotfuchses," *Handbuch der Zoologie* 8 (1957): 1-20. Also see Leonard Lee Rue III, *The World of the Red Fox* (New York: J. B. Lippincott, 1969). The passage from David Macdonald is from his book *Running with the Fox* (London and Sydney: Unwin Hyman, 1987). The story from J. David Henry is from his excellent book *Red Fox: The Catlike Canine* (Washington: Smithsonian Institution Press, 1986). On helpers, see D. W. Macdonald, "Helpers in fox society," *Nature* 282 (1979): 69-71. By the same author, with P. D. Moehlman, see "Cooperation, altruism, and restraint in the repro-duction of carnivores," *Perspectives in Ethology* 5 (1982): 433-467. On the coyote, see J. van Wormer, *The World of the Coyote* (New York: J. B. Lippincott, 1964), and Hope Ryden, *God's Dog: The North American Coyote* (New York: Lyons & Burford, 1975). Also see Marc Bekoff and

M. C. Wells, "Behavioral ecology of coyotes: social organization, rearing patterns, space use, and resource defense," *Zeitschrift fur Tierpsychologie* 60 (1982): 281-305; and "Social behavior and ecology of coyotes," *Advances in the Study of Behavior* 16 (1986): 251-338. Also see Itsuko Yamamoto, "Male parental care in the raccoon dog *(Nycteseutes procyonoides)* during the early rearing period," in *Animal Societies: Theories and Facts,* Y. Ito, et al., eds. (Tokyo: Japan Scientist Society Press, 1982), pp.189-195. For feral dogs, I am grateful to conversations with Thomas Daniels and Luigi Boitani in April of 1998. On human preferences, see David M. Buss, "Sex differences in human mate preferences: evolutionary hypotheses tested in 37 cultures," *Behavioral and Brain Sciences* 12, no. 1 (1989): 1-49. Darwin's observation about ducks is in *The Descent of Man and Selection in Relation to Sex* (London: n.p., 1871), p. 873. I have talked about wolf children in an appendix to my book *The Wild Child: The Unsolved Mystery of Kaspar Hauser* (New York: The Free Press, 1996).

Chapter Three

On pain in fish, see Patrick Bateson's useful "Assessment of pain in animals," *Animal Behaviour* 42 (1991): 827-939. On fish as fathers, see Stephen S. Crawford and Eugene K. Balon, "Cause and effect of parental care in fishes: an epigenetic perspective," *Advances in the Study of Behavior* 25 (1996): 53-107; Lawrence S. Blumer, "Male parental care in the bony fishes," *Quarterly Review of Biology* 54, no. 2 (1979): 149-161; R. Oppenheimer, "Mouthbreeding in fishes," *Animal Behavior* 18, no. 3 (1970): 493-503; Jeffrey R. Baylis, "The evolution of parental care in fishes, with reference to Darwin's rule of male sexual selection," *Environmental Biology of Fishes* 6, no. 2 (1981): 223-251, in which the criticism is found on p. 228. On sea horses, see Amanda C. J. Vincent and Laila M. Sadler, "Faithful pair bonds in wild sea horse, *Hippocampus whitei,*" *Animal Behaviour* 50 (1995): 1557-1569. Also see Amanda Vincent, "A role for daily greetings in maintaining seahorse pair bonds," *Animal Behaviour* 49, no. 1 (1995): 258-260; "The improbable seahorse," *National Geographic* 186, no. 4 (1994): 126-140; "A sea horse father makes a good mother," *Natural History* 12 (1990): 34-43; and Vincent's article with Rose Woodroffe, "Mother's little helpers: patterns of male care in mammals," *Trends in Ecology and Evolution* 9, no. 8 (1994): 294-297. See the fine pictures of sea horses in John Sparks, *Battle of the Sexes: The Natural History of Sex* (London: BBC Books, 1999), p. 150. On cleaner fish and their hosts,

I used the influential article by Robert Trivers, "The evolution of reciprocal altruism," *The Quarterly Review of Biology* 46, no. 1 (1971): 35-57.
Trivers may have oversimplified the issue, and I have gone even further in
this direction. For the more nuanced and complicated version, see the
authoritative article by Dennis L. Gorlick, Paul D. Atkins, and George S.
Losey, "Cleaning stations as water holes, garbage dumps, and sites for the
evolution of reciprocal altruism," *The American Naturalist* 112, no. 984
(1978): 341-353. See also G. S. Losey, "Cleaning symbiosis," *Symbiosis* 4
(1987): 229-58, as well as his 1979 article "Fish cleaning symbiosis: prox-
imate causes of host behavior," *Animal Behaviour* 27: 669-685. If I am not
mistaken, the first reference to this fascinating phenomenon is by the
ethologist I. Eibl-Eibesfeldt in 1955: "Über Symbiosen, Parasitismus und
andere besondere zwischenartliche Beziehungen tropischer Meeresfische,"
Zeitschrift für Tierpsychologie 12: 203-219. On frogs, see the description and
wonderful pictures in John Sparks's *Battle of the Sexes: The Natural History
of Sex* (London: BBC Books, 1999); Michael J. Ryan, *The Tungara Frog: A
Study in Sexual Selection and Communication* (Chicago: University of Chicago
Press, 1985); K. D. Wells, "The social behaviour of anuran amphibians,"
Animal Behaviour 25 (1977): 666-693; S. Emlen, "Lek organization and
mating strategies in the bullfrog," *Behavioral Ecology and Sociobiology* 1
(1976): 283-313; W. E. Duellman, *Hylid Frogs of Middle America,*
(Lawrence, Kansas: University of Kansas Press, 1970); T. R. Halliday, "Do
frogs and toads choose their mates?" *Nature* 306 (1983): 226-27. On mate
choice, see Anthony Arak, "Male-male competition and mate choice in
anuran amphibians," in *Mate Choice,* Patrick Bateson, ed. (Cambridge:
Cambridge University Press, 1983); Daniel S. Townsend, et al., "Male
parental care and its adaptive significance in a neotropical frog," *Animal
Behaviour* 32, no. 2 (1984): 421-431; Rafael Marquez, "Female choice in
the midwife toads (*Alytes obstetricans* and *A. cisternasii*)," *Behaviour* 132 (1-
2) (1995), 151-161; Paul A. Verrell and Lauren E. Brown, "Competition
among females for mates in a species with male parental care, the midwife
toad *Alytes obstetricans,*" *Ethology* 93, no. 3 (1993): 247-257. The terrestrial
breeding frog is discussed in Martin P. Simon, "The ecology of parental
care in a terrestrial breeding frog from New Guinea," *Behavioral Ecology
and Sociobiology* 14, no. 1 (1983): 61-67. A popular and thoroughly enjoy-
able book with spectacular photographs is *Frogs* by David Badger
(Stillwater, Minn.: Voyageur Press, 1995), from which I took some of my
facts about frogs and toads. Midwife toads were the subject of a brilliant
but cranky book by Arthur Koestler, *The Case of the Midwife Toad* (New
York: Random House, 1971). A talented Austrian biologist, Paul
Kammerer, set out to prove that the toad could inherit Lamarckian traits,

and was unjustly (according to Koestler) accused of a hoax by English colleagues, primarily William Bateson (Gregory Bateson's father). He committed suicide. I have also used Tim Halliday's *The Encyclopedia of Reptiles and Amphibians* (New York: Facts on File, 1986). Susan Alport's excellent overview of parenting in the animal world is called *A Natural History of Parenting* (New York: Harmony Books, 1997). Edward Hoagland's new book is *Tigers and Ice: Reflections on Nature and Life* (New York: Lyons Press, 1999).

Chapter Four

ELEPHANTS

My information about elephants comes in part from: Cynthia Moss, *Portraits in the Wild: Behavior Studies of East African Mammals,* 2nd ed. (Chicago: University of Chicago Press, 1982). The most authoritative work on elephants is probably her book *Elephant Memories: Thirteen Years in the Life of an Elephant Family* (New York: William Morrow & Co., 1988). Two excellent books by leading researchers, both of whom worked with Moss, are Katy Payne, *Silent Thunder: In the Presence of Elephants* (New York: Simon & Schuster, 1998), and Joyce Poole, *Coming of Age with Elephants: A Memoir* (New York: Hyperion, 1996). Also see I. Douglas-Hamilton and O. Douglas-Hamilton, *Among the Elephants* (London: Collins Publishers, 1975), and R. M. Laws: *Elephants and Their Habitats: The Ecology of Elephants in North Bunyoro, Uganda* (Oxford: Clarendon Press, 1975). On musth, see Joyce Poole, "Rutting behaviour in African elephants: the phenomenon of musth," *Behaviour* 102 (1987): 283-316, and Joyce Poole, "Mate-guarding, reproductive success and female choice in African elephants," *Animal Behaviour* 37, no. 5 (1989): 842-849.

WHALES

On whales and dolphins, see the excellent book by Richard C. Connor and Dawn M. Peterson, *The Lives of Whales and Dolphins* (New York: Henry Holt & Co., 1994), pp. 165 and 177. See also Richard C. Connor, Janet Mann, Peter L. Tyack, and Hal Whitehead, "Social evolution in toothed whales," *Tree* 13, no. 6 (1998): 228-232. On philopatry, apart from the reference in the note, see Kay E. Holekamp and Paul W. Sherman, "Why male ground squirrels disperse," *American Scientist* 77 (1989): 232-239.

BEARS

My information about bears comes from the following sources: *Bears: Their Life and Behavior,* by William Ashworth (New York: Crown Publishers, 1992); Jeff Fair, with technical editing by Lynn Rogers, *The Great American Bear* (Minocqua, Wisc.: NorthWord Press, 1990); Frank C. Craighead, Jr., *Track of the Grizzly* (San Francisco: Sierra Club, 1979); John J. Craighead, Maurice G. Hornocker, and Frank C. Craighead, Jr. "Reproductive biology of young female grizzly bears," *Journal of Reproduction and Fertility,* supp. 6 (Feb. 1969): 447-475; Mike Cramond, *Of Bears and Man* (Norman, Okla.: University of Oklahoma Press, 1986); Ralph A. Nelson, "Winter sleep in the black bear: a physiologic and metabolic marvel," *Mayo Clinic Proceedings* 48, no. 9 (1973): 733-737; Ralph Nelson, et al., "Metabolism of bears before, during, and after winter sleep," *American Journal of Physiology* 224, no. 2 (1973): 491-496; David E. N. Tait, "Abandonment as a reproductive tactic— the example of grizzly bears," *The American Naturalist* 115, no. 6 (1980): 800-808; P. Schullery, *The Bears of Yellowstone* (Yellowstone Natl. Park, Wyo.: Yellowstone Library and Museum Assoc., 1980). See also John A. Mack, "Black bear dens in the Beartooth Face, south-central Montana," in *Bears—Their Biology and Management: A Selection of Papers from the Eighth International Conference on Bear Research and Management, Victoria, British Columbia, Canada, February 1989,* Laura M. Darling and W. Ralph Archibald, eds. (Eli, Minn.: International Association for Bear Research and Management, 1990), pp. 273-277; L. L. Rogers, "Effects of food supply, predation, cannibalism, parasites, and other health problems on black bear populations," in *Symposium on Natural Regulation of Wildlife Populations: Proceedings of the Northwest Section, the Wildlife Society, Vancouver, British Columbia, March 10, 1978,* Fred L. Bunnell, et al., eds. (Moscow, Idaho: Forest, Wildlife and Range Experiment Station, University of Idaho, 1983), p. 205.

LIONS

My information on lions comes from the following sources: George B. Schaller, *The Serengeti Lion: A Study of Predator-Prey Relations* (Chicago: University of Chicago Press, 1972); Brian Bertram, *Pride of Lions* (London: J. M. Dent & Sons, 1978); Jonathan Kingdon, *East African Mammals: An Atlas of Evolution in Africa,* vol. 3a: *Carnivores* (Chicago: University of Chicago Press, 1977); Anne E. Pusey and Craig Packer, "Infanticide in lions: consequences and counterstrategies," in S. Parmigiani and Frederick S. vom Saal, eds., *Infanticide and Parental*

Care (Chur, Switzerland: Harwood Academic Publishers, 1994), pp. 277-299; C. Packer and A. E. Pusey, "Infanticide in carnivores," in G. Hausfater and S. B. Hrdy, eds., *Infanticide: Comparative and Evolutionary Perspectives* (New York: Aldine Press, 1984), pp. 31-42.

LANGURS

Much information in this section was derived from the 1984 Hausfater and Hrdy book. Also see Sarah Hrdy's *The Langurs of Abu* (Cambridge, Mass.: Harvard University Press, 1977) and *The Woman That Never Evolved* (Cambridge, Mass.: Harvard University Press, 1981). Also see Christian Vogel and Hartmut Loch, "Reproductive parameters, adult-male replacements, and infanticide among free-ranging langurs at Jodhpur (Rajasthan), India," in Hausfater and Hrdy, *Infanticide,* pp. 237-255.

SQUIRRELS AND PRAIRIE DOGS

See Paul W. Sherman, "Reproductive competition and infanticide in Belding's ground squirrels and other animals," in Richard D. Alexander and Donald W. Tinkle, *Natural Selection and Social Behavior: Recent Research and New Theory* (New York: Chiron Press, 1981), pp. 311-331; John L. Hoogland: *The Black-Tailed Prairie Dog: Social Life of a Burrowing Mammal* (Chicago: University of Chicago Press, 1995).

Chapter Five

On the siamang, see John MacKinnon, *The Ape within Us* (London: Collins Publishers, 1978). Also see David John Chivers, *The Siamang in Malaya: A Field Study of a Primate in Tropical Rain Forest,* Contributions to Primatology, vol. 4 (Basel, Switzerland: S. Karger, 1974). On the owl monkey, see "Biparental care in *Aotus trvirgatus* and *Callicebus moloch,*" in Meredith F. Small, ed., *Female Primates: Studies by Women Primatologists* (New York: Alan R. Liss, 1984), pp. 59-75. The night, or owl, monkey, as this creature is called, lives either alone or in monogamous families with one offspring. Both parents care for the infant, but after he is nine days old he is carried by the adult male at all times except when nursing on the mother. See M. Moynihan, "Some behavior patterns of platyrrhine monkeys: the night monkey *(Aotus trvirgatus),*" *Smithsonian Miscellaneous Collections* 146, no. 5 (1964). See also Gary Mitchell and Edna M. Brandt, "Paternal behavior in primates," in Frank E. Poirier, ed., *Primate Socialization* (New

York: Random House, 1972), pp. 173-207. On the muriqui, see Karen B. Strier, *Faces in the Forest: The Endangered Muriqui Monkeys of Brazil* (Oxford: Oxford University Press, 1992). See also her article "Causes and consequences of nonaggression in the woolly spider monkey, or muriqui *(Brachyteles arachnoides),*" in James Silverberg and J. Patrick Gray, eds. *Aggression and Peacefulness in Humans and Other Primates* (New York: Oxford University Press, 1992), pp. 100-116. See also Richard Wrangham and Dale Peterson, *Demonic Males: Apes and the Origins of Human Violence* (Boston: Houghton Mifflin Company, 1996). On DNA fingerprinting, see T. Birkhead and A. Moller, *Sperm Competition in Birds: Evolutionary Causes and Consequences* (San Diego: Academic Press, 1992), and their article "Female control of paternity," in *Trends in Ecological Evolution* 8 (1993): 100-104. See also P. A. Gowaty and D. W. Mock, *Avian Monogamy,* American Ornithological Union, Ornithological Monograph 37 (Lawrence, Kansas: Allen Press, 1985), and the book edited by Jeffrey M. Black, *Partnerships in Birds: The Study of Monogamy* (New York: Oxford University Press, 1996). For more on K strategists and r-selected species, see Stephen Jay Gould, *Ontogeny and Phylogeny* (Cambridge, Mass.: Harvard University Press, 1977). On the petrel, see M. J. Imber, "Breeding biology of the grey-faced petrel *Pterodroma macroptera guouldi,*" *Ibis* 118 (1976): 51-64. Bernd Heinrich's new book is called *Mind of the Raven: Investigations and Adventures with Wolf-Birds* (New York: Cliff Street Books, 1999). The information on the wandering albatross comes from Michael Bright's *The Private Life of Birds* (London: Bantam Books, 1993). My information on ratites comes from the authoritative *Handbook of the Birds of the World, Vol. I, Ostrich to Ducks,* edited by Josep del Hoyo, Andrew Elliott, and Jordi Sargatal (Barcelona, Spain: Lynx Edicions, 1992). I also used a fine technical study by Brian C. R. Bertram, *The Ostrich Communal Nesting Systems* (Princeton: Princeton University Press, 1992). On the jacana, see Donald A. Jenni and G. Collier, "Polyandry in the American Jacana," *Auk* 89 (1972): 743-789. Some of the information in this chapter comes from Fred Hapgood, *Why Males Exist: An Inquiry into the Evolution of Sex* (New York: William Morrow, 1979). For general information on birds, I have used *The Cambridge Encyclopedia of Ornithology,* edited by Michael Brooke and Tim Birkhead (Cambridge: Cambridge University Press, 1991); *The Life of Birds* by Joel Carl Welty (New York: Alfred A. Knopf, 1968); and *A New Dictionary of Birds,* edited by A. Landsborough Thomson (New York: McGraw-Hill Book Co., 1964). See also Lester L. Short (the Lamont Curator of Birds at the American Museum of Natural

History), *The Lives of Birds: Birds of the World and Their Behavior* (New York: Henry Holt, 1993); S. Charles Kendeigh, *Parental Care and Its Evolution in Birds* (Urbana, Ill.: University of Illinois Press, 1952); Margaret Morse Nice, *Development of Behavior in Precocial Birds,* Transactions of the Linnaean Society of New York, vol. 8 (July 1962), pp. 1-212; S. K. Skutch, *Parent Birds and Their Young* (Austin, Tex.: University of Texas Press, 1976). On pigeons, see Alexander F. Skutch, *The Minds of Birds* (College Station, Tex.: Texas A&M University Press, 1996), and especially the marvelous book by A. W. Schorger, *The Passenger Pigeon: Its Natural History and Extinction* (Norman, Okla.: University of Oklahoma Press, 1955). On bowerbirds, see J. Diamond, "Bower-building and decoration by the bowerbird *Amblyonis inornatus,*" *Ethology* 74, no. 3 (1987): 177-204; Paul A. Johnsgaard, *Arena Birds: Sexual Selection and Behavior* (Washington, D.C.: Smithsonian Institution Press, 1994); E. Thomas Gilliard, "The evolution of bowerbirds," *Scientific American* 209, no. 2 (1963): 38-46. Gilliard's book *Birds of Paradise and Bower Birds* (Garden City, N.Y.: Natural History Press, 1969) is outstanding. On homosexual animals, see Bruce Bagemihl, *Biological Exuberance: Animal Homosexuality and Natural Diversity* (New York: St. Martin's Press, 1999).

Chapter Six

On kin selection in general, see Jeffrey A. Kurland, "Kin selection theory: a review and selective bibliography," *Ethology and Sociobiology* 1, no. 4 (1980): 255-274. Also see the volume edited by Peter G. Hepper, *Kin Recognition* (Cambridge: Cambridge University Press, 1991). On the stickleback, see P. H. Pressley, "Parental effort and the evolution of nest-guarding tactics in the threespine stickleback, *Gasterosteus aculeautus,*" *Evolution* 35 (1981): 282-295. Pressley says: "The results of the field experiment demonstrate an increase in the intensity of a male's defense for a larger number of older eggs in the nest." For avian examples, see two early articles, E. A. Armstrong, "Distraction display and the human predator," *Ibis* 98 (1956): 641-654; and the article by K. E. L. Simmons, "The nature of predator-reactions of waders towards humans," *Behaviour* 8 (1955): 130-173. See also D. P. Barash, "Evolutionary aspects of parental behavior: distraction behavior of the alpine accentor," *Wilson Bulletin* 87 (1975): 532-541. The information on baby geese comes from Erika K. Honore and Peter H. Klopfer, *A Concise Survey of Animal Behavior* (San Diego: Academic Press, 1990).

On swans and their young, see P. Bateson, W. Lotwick, and D. K. Scott, "Similarities between the faces of parents and offspring in Bewick's swan and the differences between mates," *Journal of Zoology* (London) 191 (1980): 61-74. Paul Sherman's work is beautifully presented in "Nepotism and the evolution of alarm calls," in John Maynard Smith, ed., *Evolution Now: A Century After Darwin* (San Francisco: W. H. Freeman and Co., 1982), pp. 183-203. The Tinbergen book is *The Study of Instinct* (Oxford: Oxford University Press, 1951). For the full story of African wild dogs (also called cape hunting dogs and painted dogs), see Hugo van Lawick, *Solo: The Story of an African Dog* (New York: Houghton Mifflin Co., 1974). See also John McNutt and Lesly Boggs, *Running Wild: Dispelling the Myths of the African Wild Dog* (Washington, D.C.: Smithsonian Institution Press, 1996), which has stunning photographs by Hélène Heldring and Dave Hamman. On adoption by animals, see L. D. Wolfe, "A case of male adoption in a troop of Japanese monkeys," in A. B. Chiarelli and R. S. Corruccini, eds., *Primate Behavior and Sociobiology* (Berlin: Springer Verlag, 1981), pp. 156-160. Also see B. K. Alexander, "Parental behavior of adult male Japanese monkeys," *Behaviour* 36 (1970): 270-285. On wild dogs, see George B. Schaller and Gordon R. Lowther, "The relevance of carnivore behavior to the study of early hominids," *Southwestern Journal of Anthropology* 25, no. 4 (1969): 307-341. On cheetahs, see T. M. Caro, *Cheetahs of the Serengeti Plain: Group Living in an Asocial Species* (Chicago: University of Chicago Press, 1994). In general, see M. L. Riedman, "The evolution of alloparental care and adoption in mammals and birds," *Quarterly Review of Biology* 57 (1982): 405-432. On adoption, see Joan B. Silk, "Human adoption in evolutionary perspective," *Human Nature* 1, no. 1 (1990): 25-52, and B. Tizard, *Adoption: A Second Chance* (London: Open Books, 1977). For a critique of attachment theory, see S. Chess and A. Thomas, "Infant bonding: mystique and reality," *American Journal of Orthopsychiatry* 52 (1982): 213-222. The literature on special children is vast. I recommend Beth Kephart, *A Slant of Sun: One Child's Courage* (New York: W. W. Norton, 1998); Margo Wilson and Martin Daly is for "The psychology of parenting in evolutionary perspective and the case of human filicide," in Glenn Hausfater and Sarah Blaffer Hrdy, eds., *Infanticide: Comparative and Evolutionary Perspectives* (New York: Aldine Press, 1984), pp. 73-103. See also Sarah Lenington, "Child abuse: the limits of sociobiology," and J. T. Weston, "The pathology of child abuse," in R. E. Helfer and C. H. Kempe, eds., *The Battered Child* (Chicago: University of Chicago Press, 1974), pp. 61-86. Daly and Wilson make no bones about it: "No other conclusion seems possible:

stepparenthood per se is a major risk factor for child maltreatment, as a Darwinian perspective on parental love would lead one to expect." See "The Darwinian psychology of discriminative parental solicitude," *Nebraska Symposium on Motivation* 35 (1987): 91-144, 123.

Chapter Seven

See John L. Hoogland, *The Black-Tailed Prairie Dog: Social Life of a Burrowing Mammal* (Chicago: University of Chicago Press, 1995). On the alarm calls of prairie dogs, see C. N. Slobodchikoff and J. Kiriazis's forthcoming "Alarm-calling patterns of Gunnison's prairie dogs: elements of a referential grammar." Also see C. N. Slobodchikoff, C. Fischer, and J. Shapiro, "Predator-specific alarm calls of prairie dogs," *American Zoologist* 26 (1986): 557; and Slobodchikoff, Kiriazis, Fischer, and E. Creef, "Semantic information distinguishing individual predators in the alarm calls of Gunnison's prairie dogs," *Animal Behaviour* 42 (1991): 713-719. Note that Paul W. Sherman, in "Alarm calls of Belding's ground squirrels to aerial predators: nepotism or self-preservation?" *(Behavioral Ecology and Sociobiology* 17 [1985]: 313-323), finds that these animals "do discriminate between dangerous and harmless animals, near and distant predators, and rapidly versus slowly moving predators." For a view of alarm calls as nepotism, see the valuable article by Paul W. Sherman, "Nepotism and the evolution of alarm calls," *Science* 197 (1977): 1246-1253. For beavers, the main work is the sublime book by Hope Ryden, *Lily Pond: Four Years with a Family of Beavers* (New York: William Morrow, 1989). I also used her earlier book *The Beaver* (New York: G. P. Putnam's Sons, 1986). A charming account of a woman who has befriended tame beavers who live in her house is found in Dorothy Richards (with Hope Sawyer Buyukmichi), *Beaversprite: My Years Building an Animal Sanctuary* (San Francisco: Chronicle Books, 1977). The classic work is Lewis H. Morgan, *The American Beaver and His Works* (Philadelphia: J. B. Lippincott & Co., 1868). It was reprinted by Dover in 1986. It tells a great deal about hunting the beaver, but almost nothing about its behavior. On universal fears of children, see N. Blurton-Jones, ed., *Ethological Studies of Child Behaviour* (Cambridge: Cambridge University Press, 1972), and Adah Maurer, "What children fear," *Journal of Genetic Psychology* 106 (1965): 265-277. On dwarf mongooses, see Anne Rasa's detailed book *Mongoose Watch: A Family Observed* (New York: Doubleday & Co., 1985).

Chapter Eight

On the megapodes, see Jared Diamond, "The reproductive biology of mound-building birds," *Nature* 301 (27 Jan. 1983): 288-289; K. Immelmann and R. Sossinka, "Parental behaviour in birds," in Wladyslaw Sluckin and Martin Herbert, eds., *Parental Behaviour* (Oxford: Basil Blackwell, 1986), pp. 8-33. See also G. A. Clark: "Life histories and the evolution of megapodes," *Living Bird* 3 (1964): 149-67; H. J. Frith, "Breeding habits in the family *Magapodiidae*," *Ibis* 98 (1959): 620-640; Tomasz Wesolowski, "On the origin of parental care and the early evolution of male and female parental roles in birds," *The American Naturalist* 143, no. 1 (1994): 39-58. The major work is by H. J. Frith, *The Mallee-Fowl* (Sydney: Angus and Robertson, 1962). On megapodes in general, see Frank B. Gill, *Ornithology* (New York: W. H. Freeman & Co., 1989), p. 358. On homosexual animals, see the new comprehensive and brilliant book by Bruce Bagemihl, *Biological Exuberance: Animal Homosexuality and Natural Diversity* (New York: St. Martin's Press, 1999).

Epilogue

On cosleeping, see *The Family Bed* by Tine Thevenin Wayne (New Jersey: Avery Publishing Group, 1987). Also see Deborah Jackson, *Three in a Bed: Why You Should Sleep with Your Baby* (London: Bloomsbury, 1989), especially James J. McKenna, et al., "Infant-parent co-sleeping in an evolutionary perspective," p. 279. As Melvin Konner points out, "Direct, continuous mother-infant contact during infant sleep is characteristic of all nonhuman higher primates." In other words, all our close relatives in the animal world sleep with their infants. See "Sudden infant death syndrome: an anthropological hypothesis," by Melvin J. Konner and Charles M. Super, in *The Role of Culture in Developmental Disorder,* edited by Charles Super and Sarah Harkness, (New York: The Academic Press, 1987), pp. 95-108. On the rabbit, see L. G. Ingles, "Natural history observations on the Audubon cottontail," *Journal of Mammalogy* 22 (1941): 227-250. On the tree shrew, see R. D. Martin, "Tree shrews: unique reproductive mechanism of systematic importance," *Science* 152 (1996): 1402-1404.

Index

fear of humans, 42–43
feeding of young, 38, 43, 51
and grown children, 195–96
individuality of, 103
kinship with humans, 11, 12, 55
mating behavior of, 40, 52, 53
mourning behavior of, 161
prejudice against, 38–39
similarity to dogs, 49, 50
status of children, 44
and tameness, 49–50, 52
and wolf–children claims, 12,
    39–40, 55
Wolves of Denali, The (Mech), 196
Woman That Never Evolved, The
    (Hrdy), 98

Worst Journey in the World, The
    (Bowers and Cherry-Garrard),
    15, 16–17
Wrangham, Richard, 102, 109, 111
Wright, Patricia, 110
Wright, Robert, 208

Y
Year of the Greylag Goose, The
    (Lorenz), 26

Z
Zoomorphism, 2